Weapons of Mass Destruction

Also by Edward M. Spiers

ARMY AND SOCIETY, 1815–1914

CHEMICAL WARFARE

CHEMICAL AND BIOLOGICAL WEAPONS: A Study of Proliferation

CHEMICAL WEAPONRY: A Continuing Challenge

HALDANE: An Army Reformer

RADICAL GENERAL: Sir George de Lacy Evans

SUDAN: The Reconquest Reappraised (*editor*)

THE LATE VICTORIAN ARMY, 1868–1914

Weapons of
Mass Destruction

Prospects for Proliferation

Edward M. Spiers

First published in Great Britain 2000 by
MACMILLAN PRESS LTD
Houndmills, Basingstoke, Hampshire RG21 6XS and London
Companies and representatives throughout the world

A catalogue record for this book is available from the British Library.

ISBN 0–333–73938–8

First published in the United States of America 2000 by
ST. MARTIN'S PRESS, INC.,
Scholarly and Reference Division,
175 Fifth Avenue, New York, N.Y. 10010

ISBN 0–312–22852–X

Library of Congress Cataloging-in-Publication Data
Spiers, Edward M.
Weapons of mass destruction : prospects for proliferation / Edward M. Spiers.
p.   cm.
Includes bibliographical references and index.
ISBN 0–312–22852–X (cloth)
1. Weapons of mass destruction.   2. World politics — 1989–   I. Title.

U793 .S65   1999
327.1'74 — dc21
                                                                99–042136

This book is printed on paper suitable for recycling and made from fully managed and sustained forest sources.

10   9   8   7   6   5   4   3   2   1
09   08   07   06   05   04   03   02   01   00

Printed and bound in Great Britain by
Antony Rowe Ltd, Chippenham, Wiltshire

Contents

Preface

In writing about weapons of mass destruction (WMD) as a collective description of nuclear, biological and chemical weapons, I am aware that the term is far from exact. These weapons have different properties, relative lethalities, and areas of coverage; they can even be used in ways that might not be construed as massively destructive. As security issues, though, they remain all too prominent in the post-Cold War era, reflecting the continuing political and security concerns of particular states and the widespread diffusion of scientific and technological expertise. This proliferation has raised legitimate anxieties about their usage in regional conflicts, as instruments of terror, and as countervailing factors to the overwhelming conventional weapons superiority of the United States, its allies, and any US-led coalitions. Although there are novel aspects to the contemporary phenomenon, as confirmed by the revelations about the capabilities of Iraq, the former Soviet Union and Aum Shinrikyo, I shall argue that proliferation has its roots in the Cold War, and that these weapons have a continuing political and military utility. I shall also claim that the challenge posed by these weapons is becoming more diverse and daunting as the technology, particularly of biological weapons, steadily evolves and as these weapons are generally much less conspicuous than the military power deployed by the Soviets during the Cold War.

In examining how these weapons may be countered, I shall argue that neither diplomacy nor military strikes will suffice in and of themselves, and that there are no panaceas available. Strengthening international norms, arms control, and to a lesser extent export controls may help, especially if supported by the requisite political determination and an array of offensive and defensive military assets. The combination may bolster deterrence and persuade some states to abandon their WMD capabilities. I shall assert, though, that events in the 1990s have demonstrated the limitations of intrusive on-site inspections against a determined proliferator; the shortcomings of 'precision' aerial bombardments; and the controversies aroused by attempts to resolve WMD crises by diplomatic endeavour and economic inducements. I shall argue that any effective response will depend upon consistent American leadership, with a broad measure of international support in matters of intelligence, diplomatic activity, and, if necessary, military effort.

I should like to acknowledge my indebtedness to the many individuals and institutions who have assisted me in my research. I am particularly grateful to Dr Graham Pearson, Dr John Walker (Foreign and Commonwealth Office), Professor Adam Roberts, Professor Malcolm Dando, Professor John Gooch, Dr Rachel Utley, Dr Richard Latter and Donato Kiniger-Passigli (head of Media and Public Affairs Branch, External Affairs Division, Organisation for the Prohibition of Chemical Weapons). I am also obliged to the staffs of the Australian High Commission, Resource Center (US Embassy London), the United Nations Information Centre, the Royal Institute of International Affairs, the Arms Control and Disarmament Agency, the German Embassy, the Henry L. Stimson Center, the British Library Colindale, the Library of the *Washington Times*, and the inter-library loan staff of the University of Leeds. Like many other scholars, I am especially grateful to the website maintained by Ms Melinda Havers-Lamont (Chem-Bio Terror News of the Center for Nonproliferation Studies at the Washington DC office of the Monterey Institute of International Studies).

As ever, I received enormous assistance and many useful briefings in the United States. I am indebted to Steve Bowman (Congressional Research Service), Dr Brad Roberts (Institute for Defense Analyses), Mr William W. Cawood (General Accounting Office), Dr Zachary S. Davis (US Arms Control and Disarmament Agency), Dr Randy J. Rydell (Professional Staff, Senate Committee on Governmental Affairs), General Walter L. Busbee (Deputy Assistant to the Secretary of Defense for Counterproliferation and Chemical/Biological Defense), Michael Moodie (Chemical and Biological Arms Control Institute), and Dr Ted Prociv (Chemical Demilitarisation).

I am particularly grateful to Mrs Margaret Walkington and Mrs Christine Cascarino for their secretarial assistance in the preparation of this work. I remain indebted to Fiona, my wife, and Robert and Amanda for all their support and tolerance in the preparation of this manuscript.

27 April 1999   Edward M. Spiers

Abbreviations

AAAS	American Association for the Advancement of Science
ACDA	Arms Control and Disarmament Agency
BIDS	Biological Integrated Detection System
BTWC	Biological and Toxin Weapons Convention
BW	biological warfare
CAM	Chemical Agent Monitor
CBIRF	Chemical/Biological Incident Response Force
CBM	confidence-building measure
CBW	chemical and biological warfare
CBWCB	*The CBW Conventions Bulletin*
CCD	camouflage, concealment or deception
CEN	*Chemical & Engineering News*
CIA	Central Intelligence Agency
CIS	Commonwealth of Independent States
COCOM	Coordinating Committee for Multilateral Export Controls
CPRC	Counterproliferation Review Committee
CTBT	Comprehensive Test Ban Treaty
CW	chemical warfare
CWC	Chemical Weapons Convention
DARPA	Defense Advanced Research Projects Agency
DCI	Defense Counterproliferation Initiative
DGP	Senior Defence Group on Proliferation
DHHS	Department of Health and Human Services
DIA	Defense Intelligence Agency
DoD	Department of Defense
DoE	Department of Energy
EMIS	Electro-Magnetic Isotope Separation
EPA	Environmental Protection Agency
EPCI	Enhanced Proliferation Control Initiative
FBI	Federal Bureau of Investigation
FBIS	Foreign Broadcast Information Service
FCO	Foreign and Commonwealth Office
FEMA	Federal Emergency Management Agency
GAO	General Accounting Office
GPS	Global Positioning System

HEU	highly enriched uranium
HUMINT	human intelligence
IAEA	International Atomic Energy Agency
IDR	*International Defense Review*
IISS	International Institute for Strategic Studies
JAMA	*Journal of the American Medical Association*
JDW	*Jane's Defense Weekly*
JIR	*Jane's Intelligence Review*
JSLIST	Joint Service Lightweight Integrated Suit Technology
KT	kiloton
KTO	Kuwaiti Theatre of Operations
LR-BSDS	Long Range Biological Standoff Detection System
LWR	light-water reactor
MEADS	Medium Extended Air Defense System
MoD	Ministry of Defence
MOPP	Mission-Oriented Protective Posture
MoU	Memorandum of Understanding
MT	megaton
MTCR	Missile Technology Control Regime
Mw	megawatt
NAIAD	Nerve Agent Immobilized Enzyme Alarm
NBC	nuclear, biological and chemical
NDPO	National Defense Preparedness Office
NEST	Nuclear Emergency Search Team
NIS	newly independent states
NPT	Non-Proliferation Treaty
NSG	Nuclear Suppliers' Group
OMV	Ongoing Monitoring and Verification
OPCW	Organization for the Prohibition of Chemical Weapons
OSI	on-site inspection
OTA	Office of Technology Assessment
PAL	Permissive Action Link
RAID	Rapid Assessment and Initial Detection
RPV	Remotely Piloted Vehicle
RSCAAL	Remote Sensing Chemical Agent Alarm
RUSI	Royal United Services Institute for Defence Studies
SIPRI	Stockholm International Peace Research Institute
SIR	Status of Implementation Report
START	Strategic Arms Reduction Treaty
THAAD	Theater High Altitude Area Defense
TMD	theatre missile defence

UAV	unmanned air vehicles
UNSCOM	United Nations Special Commission
USIS	United States Information Service
VEE	Venezuelan equine encephalitis
VIR	Verification Implementation Report
WMD	weapons of mass destruction

1
Weapons of Mass Destruction: The Cold War Context

Nuclear, biological and chemical (NBC) weapons have been elevated as a major issue of international concern in the post-Cold War era. As early as 9 February 1989, President George Bush claimed that the spread and 'even use of sophisticated weaponry threatens global security as never before. Chemical weapons must be banned from the face of the earth, never to be used again. ... And, the spread of nuclear weapons must be stopped.'[1] US Intelligence and Pentagon officials amplified these concerns in their Congressional testimony; Judge William Webster, then Director of the Central Intelligence Agency (CIA), warned that 'the odds on use [of nuclear weapons and ballistic missiles] are growing as more countries develop the technologies to settle old scores'.[2] These anxieties were compounded by the Gulf War (1991), the belated admission by President Boris Yeltsin of the covert biological warfare programme of the former Soviet Union (February 1992), and the subsequent revelations about the extent of the Iraqi NBC programmes.[3] The Clinton administration sustained this concern. It described nonproliferation as 'one of our nation's highest priorities',[4] and a succession of CIA directors – Robert Gates, R. James Woolsey and Dr John Deutch – testified to 'a steady and worrisome growth in the proliferation of advanced weapons'; to the 'recent' emergence of the proliferation issue with its 'serious and far-reaching implications for global and regional security'; and to 'the proliferation of weapons of mass destruction and advanced conventional weapon systems' as posing 'the gravest threat to national security and to world stability'.[5]

Although the implications of these claims will be examined in subsequent chapters, the terminology, characteristics, and evolution of the weaponry merit initial explanation. The collective description of NBC weapons as weapons of mass destruction (WMD) is far from precise.

The juxtaposition reflects an attempt to distinguish them from conventional weapons by virtue of their ability to 'compress the time and the effort needed to kill'[6] (injure or incapacitate). Their effectiveness in this respect reflects their capacity to inflict death, injury, (and physical destruction in the case of nuclear weapons) over considerable areas, with the related possibility of causing extensive collateral damage (that is, by injuring a large number of people indiscriminately). Yet this categorisation is hardly absolute. Just as the distinction between these weapons and conventional weaponry is no longer so clear with the development of powerful conventional weapons, such as fuel air explosives, so the juxtaposition blurs the many differences between NBC weapons themselves. These differences will become more apparent by examining the characteristics of these weapons and then by assessing how their proliferation evolved during the Cold War. Although the proliferation of these weapons may have assumed a fresh significance following the disintegration of the former Soviet Union, the revelations about the Iraqi NBC programmes, and the terrorist activities of the Aum Shinrikyo cult,[7] many of the weapon programmes currently causing concern had their origins during the Cold War.

All NBC weapons have been extensively studied and their characteristics, properties and potential effects examined by the United Nations, national governments, including reports by the Office of Technology Assessment (OTA),[8] independent research institutes, and individual scholars. Unlike chemical or biological weapons, nuclear weapons have been used strategically at Hiroshima and Nagasaki (6 and 9 August 1945), thereby yielding actual as well as experimental data on their devastating effects. Nuclear weapons derive their force from the energy released at unprecedented speeds (in about one millionth of a second) by the splitting of uranium or plutonium nuclei into lighter fragments (fission products) or by fusing together the nuclei of heavy hydrogen isotopes – deuterium and tritium – at very high temperatures, triggered through the fission process.[9] The fission process produces far less energy per unit weight in the atomic bomb than the fusion process produces in a thermonuclear bomb. The explosive force is known as the yield and is measured in numbers of tons of TNT which would have been necessary to produce an equivalent explosion. A nuclear explosion with a yield equivalent to that of 1,000 tons of TNT is known as a one kiloton (KT) explosion and one with a yield equivalent to 1,000,000 tons of TNT is known as a one megaton (MT) explosion. Fission yields rarely exceed 500 KT (as the reaction depends upon the production of a critical mass of fissionable material and large amounts of such material would explode spontaneously) but the yields of fusion weapons are not limited (hence the megaton-size weapons in the arsenals of the great powers).

To sustain the chain reaction in a fission explosion requires a critical mass of fissionable material. In making a nuclear fission explosive device, uranium-235 (U-235) and plutonium-239 (Pu-239) are both suitable materials. The rare isotope, U-235, constitutes only 0.7% of natural uranium (the rest being U-238) and the fraction of U-235 has to be increased in an isotope enrichment facility (by various expensive techniques, using sophisticated engineering, such as gaseous diffusion, gas centrifuge, Electro-Magnetic Isotope Separation, aerodynamic separation, laser enrichment or chemical separation). The five Iraqi enrichment programmes, involving 20,000 personnel, 7,000 of whom were scientists, cost an estimated $8 to $10 billion over a decade. The production of plutonium – a natural by-product of nuclear plants producing electrical power – is much cheaper. Once produced in a nuclear reactor, Pu-239 can be separated from the spent fuel elements in a chemical separation plant – a reprocessing process that is much less expensive to construct and operate (and much less conspicuous) than gaseous diffusion. Estimates of the critical mass required for a nuclear explosive device vary considerably, depending upon the design and sophistication of the weapon and the quality of the materials involved, but a UN report has stated that the 'mass can range from 15 to 25 kg for uranium-235 and from 4 to 8 kg for plutonium-239'.[10]

A nuclear weapon causes damage by its powerful blast, intense thermal radiation, electromagnetic pulse, nuclear radiation from the fireball, and residual radiation or 'fallout'. The impact would vary with the method of detonation (whether air burst or ground burst or conceivably sub-surface at sea), local topographical and demographic factors (which largely explained why a yield of 22 kilotons inflicted far fewer casualties upon Nagasaki than the smaller yield of 13 kilotons upon Hiroshima), and local meteorological conditions (for example, the high incidence of burn injuries at Hiroshima reflected the timing of the attack – in the morning – on a bright, clear day when many people were out of doors). Only warning of an attack and access to fallout shelters or specially-hardened facilities could protect against the effects of blast and immediate radiation.[11]

Apart from India and possibly Israel, the new nuclear proliferants may only possess or be able to develop first generation, fission weapons. The yields of these weapons may compare with those of the original US nuclear weapons, although they could be more compact and lighter (possibly 500 kg).[12] Such weapons had a devastating impact when air-bursted over the cities of Hiroshima and Nagasaki. The OTA has calculated that a similar weapon (12.5 KT), launched on a SCUD-like ballistic missile, could, if air-bursted on an overcast day or night over a city in which 3,000 to 10,000 unprotected people were living in each square kilometre (km^2), cause destruction over a circular area of 7.8 km^2, killing some 23,000 to 80,000 people. A similar missile, loaded with 300 kg of the nerve agent, sarin, could kill between 60 and 200 people in an area of 0.22 km^2 or, if loaded with 30 kg of anthrax spores, kill 30,000 to 100,000 people in a cigar-shaped area of 10 km^2. If the population density and weather conditions were more propitious, chemical or biological weapons could kill more people than this estimate; under worse conditions, they could kill far fewer.[13]

Unlike nuclear weapons, neither chemical nor biological weapons can damage the physical infrastructure. If detected, they can both be defended against by the use of respirators, protective clothing, collective shelters, medical countermeasures, and decontamination procedures (albeit at a price of degrading the military effectiveness of the troops forced to wear this protective kit in battle over a sustained period of time). Chemical warfare (CW) agents, whether the classical gases used in the First World War (including chlorine, phosgene, hydrogen cyanide and mustard) or the more toxic nerve agents (both the G-agents like tabun, sarin and soman and the V-agents such as VX) are 'chemical substances, whether gaseous, liquid, or solid, which might be employed because of their direct toxic effects on man, animals and plants'.[14] These agents vary enormously in their properties, in their physiological effects, and in the persistence of those effects. Some may cause their victims a degree of sensory irritation, others may incapacitate, and some may incapacitate or kill. While some CW agents are relatively transient in their effects, others may contaminate areas over a period of hours, days or even many weeks (depending upon the properties of the agent, primarily its volatility and stability; the manner of its release, whether as a liquid, aerosol or vapour; and the local meteorological and environmental factors). Although the classical war gases of the First World War could be used in Third World conflicts, particularly mustard gas which was used in the Iran–Iraq War (1980–88),[15] only the more toxic, rapid-acting, odourless and colourless nerve agents could be classed as weapons of mass destruction. As shown in Tables 1 and 2, based on studies completed by the Secretary-General of the United Nations in 1969 and Steve Fetter of the University of Maryland in 1991,[16] chemical weapons have significantly

Table 1 Comparative estimates of the effects of hypothetical attacks upon unprotected populations using nuclear, biological or chemical weapons

Criteria for estimate	Type of weapon		
	Nuclear (1 megaton)	Chemical (15 tons)	Biological (10 tons)
Area affected	Up to 300 km^2	Up to 60 km^2	Up to 100,000 km^2
Time delay before onset of effect	Seconds	Minutes	Days
Damage to structures	Destruction over an area of 100 km^2	None	None
Normal use after attack	3–6 months after attack	Limited during period of contamination	After end of incubation period or subsidence of epidemic

Note: The selected tonnages were reckoned to be those that could be carried by a single strategic bomber in 1969.

Source: *Report of the Secretary-General on Chemical and Bacteriological (Biological) Weapons and the Effects of Their Possible Use*, United Nations General Assembly, A/7575, 1 July 1969, p. 57.

Table 2 Conventional/chemical/biological/nuclear warhead comparisons

Warhead type	Dead	Injured
Conventional (1 ton of HE)	5	13
Chemical (300 kg of sarin)	200–3,000	200–3,000
Biological (30 kg of anthrax spores)	20,000–80,000	
Nuclear (20-kiloton yield)	40,000	40,000

Note: Warhead delivered by a missile with a 1 tonne warhead against a city with an average population density of 30 unprotected people per hectacre.

Source: S. Fetter, 'Ballistic Missiles and Weapons of Mass Destruction: What is the Threat? What Should Be Done?' *International Security*, vol. 16, no. 1 (1991), p. 27.

greater effects than conventional weapons, if not nuclear or biological weapons.

Within the spectrum from chemical to biological warfare agents, as defined by the Chemical and Biological Defence Establishment (Porton Down), there are many potential 'mid-spectrum' agents. They include highly toxic industrial, pharmaceutical and agricultural chemicals; agents of biological origin such as peptides (chains of amino acids that could be genetically manipulated to affect the mental process or regulatory factors of mood, consciousness, temperature control, sleep or emotions); toxins – the non-living products of micro-organisms, plants or living animals that can also be chemically synthesised; and genetically manipulated bacteria or viruses or combinations of substances (designed to mask detection, or create organisms of greater virulence, antibiotic resistance and environmental stability).[17] Biological warfare (BW) agents (bacteria, viruses and rickettsia) 'are living organisms, whatever their nature, or infective material derived from them, which are intended to cause disease or death in man, animals, or plants, and which depend for their effects on their ability to multiply in the person, animal or plant attacked'.[18] The range of potential BW agents includes 'over 30 known viruses, microorganisms and toxins suitable for use as weapons':[19] namely bacteria that produce diseases such as anthrax, plague, and tularemia; viruses such as Venezuelan equine encephalitis; rickettsia, notably the organism that produces Q-fever; fungi producing diseases like coccidiomycosis; and toxins such as botulinum toxin, ricin, and saxitoxin.

Like CW agents, BW agents can be dispersed in the atmosphere and travel with the wind with a view to incapacitating or killing their victims. However, these are not absolute distinctions; some individuals may survive an attack with a lethal agent, whereas others – for example, infants, the elderly, or those weakened by disease or malnutrition – may succumb fatally to an incapacitating agent. The time to take effect is in the order of 12 hours or more for toxins and a few days or more for microbial agents (as the micro-organism has to replicate within the host and cause the corresponding disease). The delayed onset of symptoms is one of the principal differences between nerve agents and BW agents, although some CW agents, notably mustard and phosgene, take several hours to produce symptoms.[20]

BW agents have several specific attractions as military weapons. Their extreme potency means that only small quantities are necessary to take effect, and that they can injure or kill over far greater distances than CW agents. Their long-time effect may mean that they leave only a minimal "signature", especially if a naturally occurring disease is selected. They may be produced in a clandestine manner, using dual-use facilities, more cheaply than either nuclear or chemical weapons. They may also be deployed with little risk to one's own forces if a non-transmissible agent is selected. On the other hand, they have not been used extensively in war and their utility has only been demonstrated 'by all means short of their actual use in war'.[21] As living organisms, BW agents are also more susceptible than CW agents to sunlight, temperature and other environmental factors. Once disseminated, a BW agent can retain its viability (ability to live and multiply) while losing its virulence (ability to produce disease and injury). Although such variables have given BW agents the reputation of being unpredictable and indiscriminate weapons,[22] the use of modern meteorological forecasting, coupled with the choice of appropriate agents and means of delivery, could make these weapons highly effective. Anthrax spores, for example, are remarkably stable (remaining alive in soil or water for many years), produce a disease that is not infectious (in the sense that someone who caught the disease could pass it onto another person), and so they could be used with some discrimination. The estimates of the mean lethal dose of anthrax range from 8,000 to 20,000 spores, but even the larger number weighs only about one hundred-millionth of a gram. In its pulmonary form it could prove fatal in 95% of cases within seven days (vaccines are available but ought to be given before exposure and their effects following high infective doses of the organism are uncertain – antibiotics would have to be administered before the signs of the disease became apparent).[23] As the OTA calculated, a single aeroplane could attack a city of the size and population density of Washington, DC, by dispersing 100 kg of anthrax spores in a line to its windward side. On a clear sunny day with a light breeze, 46 km^2 would be affected and 130,000 to 460,000 people could die; on an overcast day or night, with a moderate wind, 140 km^2 would be affected and 420,000 to 1,400,000 could die; and on a clear, calm night, 300 km^2 would be affected and between one and three million could die.[24] Judge Webster perceptively observed that

> Biological warfare agents, including toxins, are more potent than the most deadly chemical warfare agents, and provide the broadest area coverage per pound of payload of any weapons system.[25]

NBC weapons not only have differing characteristics, but they could also be used for a wide array of military purposes, some of which fall far short of "mass destruction". A low yield nuclear weapon could be used in a demonstration explosion against "solitary" targets – ships at sea, remote air or naval bases and isolated military or commercial installations. Chemical weapons have been used tactically on the battlefield for offensive and defensive purposes, as "force multipliers", compounding and complementing the effects of conventional ordnance, and in counter-insurgency campaigns against enemies in remote and relatively inaccessible areas or staunchly supported by local populations. Biological weapons could also be employed in diverse ways, either covertly in advance of hostilities or in tactical strikes on isolated targets or in more localised and specifically targeted actions (for example, the assassination of Georgi Markov with ricin in September 1978). Furthermore, chemical and biological weapons could be employed as incapacitants, conceivably with the aim of causing extensive casualties, overloading medical services, and possibly disrupting the movements and co-ordination of mobilised forces prior to the outbreak of hostilities. NBC strikes, if controlled and limited, could complicate the military responses of the victims and their allies, particularly if the latter had declaratory policies that retained the option of (or at least did not preclude) a nuclear response to an NBC attack.[26]

Yet the development and acquisition of NBC weapons gives the option of employing them in strategic roles (especially if tonnages of nerve agents were involved in a chemical strike), with the aim of causing large numbers of deaths and casualties, widespread terror, and, in the case of nuclear strikes, extensive physical damage. Even if the distinction between strategic and tactical strikes could be blurred in some cases, the devastating potential of such strikes would merit the term "mass destruction". Any indications that a state was seeking such capabilities would pose a major challenge to its neighbours or to great powers with interests in the region. Even if the capability began as a relatively modest CW option, it could be refined and expanded to encompass the development of nerve agents or serve as a basis for moving on from chemical to the less expensive (and more easily concealed) BW option.[27] As a consequence, regional asymmetries could develop whereby the possession of one form of WMD was perceived as a counter, however imperfect in scope and potential, to the possession of another form of WMD by a neighbouring state. This could affect not only the security calculations of the states concerned but also their attitudes towards arms control (hence the reluctance of some Arab states to support a comprehensive chemical weapons ban as long as Israel retains its nuclear option).[28] So the interrelationship between such states and their differing WMD capabilities has to be considered.

The proliferation of these weapons and of their delivery systems began during the Cold War, and, in some states, the programmes were well under way before the Cold War reached its unexpected dénouement. Although the proliferation of the 1990s may have new and different aspects, it was not new in itself and so claims that 'During the Cold War, regional powers did not have NBC weapons. Now more than 20 nations are known to possess them'[29] are utterly erroneous. Proliferation as a term entered the lexicon of strategic studies in the late 1950s and early 1960s, referring primarily to the spread of nuclear weapons or of the capabilities to produce such weapons. In the early 1960s, it was recognised that many more states had the technological capacity to manufacture nuclear weapons than had actually done so, but there were still widespread fears of an imminent and burgeoning proliferation. As the late Leonard Beaton wrote in 1966, 'There is no question of a dozen or two dozen nuclear nuclear weapon programmes in the next few years.'[30] The superpowers were keen to curb or at least control "horizontal" nuclear proliferation: that is, proliferation among other states, including allies (hence the American sponsorship of ill-fated Multilateral Nuclear Force for NATO in the early 1960s). Both superpowers significantly inhibited the spread of nuclear weapons by the provision of security guarantees to their allies and satellites, and would continue to do so throughout the Cold War. Many states also concluded that the possession of nuclear weapons would not serve their political, strategic and military purposes, sometimes setting aside the advice of their nuclear scientists and military élites or resolving to promote nuclear disarmament as an international issue.[31]

The goal of stifling the spread of nuclear weapons produced both the first multilateral arms control measures and the first export control arrangements. The negotiation of the Non-Proliferation Treaty (NPT) in 1968 and its entry into force in 1970 established an international norm against the wider dissemination of nuclear weapons. As a compact between nuclear-weapon states (defined as those who had manufac-tured and exploded a nuclear weapon or other nuclear device before 1 January 1967) and non-nuclear-weapon states, the former pledged not to transfer nuclear weapons or other explosive nuclear devices to non-nuclear countries. The non-nuclear parties pledged not to receive or manufacture nuclear weapons or explosive nuclear devices and to place all their peaceful nuclear activities, including the receipt of '(a) source or special fissionable material, or (b) equipment or material designed or prepared for the processing, use or production of special fissionable material,' (Article III. 2) under safeguard arrangements. The latter were negotiated with, and monitored by, the International Atomic Energy Agency (IAEA). Under Article VI all parties were com-mitted to pursue negotiations 'in good faith' towards the cessation of the nuclear arms race 'at an early date' and towards the goal of nuclear disarmament. This treaty was supposedly bolstered by the tripartite Security Assurances Resolution, adopted by the UN Security Council on 19 June 1968, whereby Britain, the Soviet Union and the United States pledged to seek immediate Security Council action if a non-nuclear party to the NPT was threatened or attacked with nuclear weapons.[32]

Although the NPT was quickly ratified by a large number of states (83 did so by 1 December 1974, with another 23 signatories in the process of doing so), most of those states never had any nuclear ambitions anyway.[33] Two nuclear states (France and China) would not adhere to the treaty during the Cold War and several near-nuclear states would not do so either. This lack of appeal was hardly surprising; the NPT was criticised as a 'grossly' discriminatory treaty, with a lack of balance in its benefits and obligations, and one that was not really tailored towards the needs of the nations that it had to convince. The treaty, argued Alva Myrdal, failed to ensure preferential treatment for non-nuclear parties in the provision of information and material in the nuclear field, failed to arrest the nuclear arms race between the superpowers, and lacked the support of negative security guarantees (i.e. pledges by nuclear-weapon states not to attack non-nuclear weapon states with nuclear weapons). She concluded that 'it falls short of all reasonable expectations as a disarmament measure'.[34]

To underpin the treaty and agree an interpretation of Article III. 2, supply-side controls were agreed by the major nuclear suppliers. In 1974 the Zangger Committee produced, and thereafter kept up-to-date, a list of material and equipment 'especially designed or prepared' for nuclear use (i.e. not dual-use equipment). It also defined the technology, major critical components, and other items that could trigger safeguards. Following India's so-called 'peaceful nuclear explosion' on 18 May 1974, the major nuclear suppliers, including France, met in secret over several years to devise additional controls. Eventually agreed as the 'London Club' guidelines of the Nuclear Suppliers' Group on 21 September 1977, these additional controls sought to ensure that exports from these 15 countries with nuclear exporting industries could not be used to make a nuclear explosive of any kind. They required adequate physical protection of all exports, and the exercise of restraint in the export of sensitive technologies (for the purposes of enrichment, reprocessing, and heavy water production). These terms were less restrictive than those favoured by the United States, particularly the requirement of its own Nuclear Non-Proliferation Act (1977) that any consumer state, seeking nuclear supplies from the US, should implement "full scope" safeguards upon 'all nuclear materials and equipment regardless of whether these have been supplied by the United States'.[35] However gaps in the guidelines, especially over some sensitive and dual-use items, the limited membership of the supplier groups, deficiencies in the safeguards procedures, and the ineffective enforcement of the internationally agreed controls would all contribute to the continuing proliferation. Even worse, argued Paul Leventhal, a decade or more of secrecy and political machinations undermined the enforcement of the nuclear export controls: 'current US practice', he argued in 1992, 'is to abstain from enforcing nuclear export controls whenever competing interests are deemed to take precedence, which is almost always'.[36]

Nevertheless, the NPT steadily gathered more adherents through the 1970s and 1980s (acquiring 139 by 1989 of whom only 80 had completed their requisite safeguards agreements).[37] There were neither any additions to the 'nuclear club' of the United States, the Soviet Union, Britain, France and China, nor even any state willing to emulate the 'peaceful' nuclear explosion of India. Although many states could test their weapon designs under the Partial Test Ban Treaty (1963), the use of testing as a criteria for nuclear weapon status under the NPT probably inhibited prospective proliferants. In the absence of testing, proliferants could not assure themselves about the viability of weapon designs, so probably limiting their weapon development in some cases to the production of low-yield fission weapons.[38] Accordingly, several commentators were quite optimistic by the mid to late 1980s. 'The NPT', argued Boris Mayorsky, 'has convincingly proved its importance. There is every reason to say that its conclusion was a major step in curbing the nuclear arms race.'[39] Josef Goldblat was equally sanguine that 'there appears to be no danger of an open expansion of the nuclear club...the *status quo* will probably be maintained for some time'.[40] Yet nuclear proliferation was hardly under control. If the scale was less than once anticipated, and much of it unacknowledged or "opaque" as sometimes described,[41] it was nonetheless significant for the states concerned, their immediate neighbours, and the great powers with interests in their regions. Even before the Iraqi revelations, Judge Webster candidly admitted that 'we have found that nuclear technology is acquired illicitly and clandestinely through front companies, false export documents, and multiple transshipment points'.[42] In various parts of the developing world, states had either developed and produced nuclear weapons (South Africa and probably Israel), or could assemble such weapons in a matter of days or weeks (India and Pakistan), or were seeking a nuclear weapons capability (Iraq, probably North Korea and Iran, and possibly others).[43]

The proliferation of chemical weapons was more extensively chronicled, at least by US officials. Their concern pre-dated the confirmation of chemical attacks during the Iran–Iraq War, and derived initially from anxiety about the growing size and sophistication of the Soviet CW arsenal in the 1970s and 1980s. This capability – the largest in the world at 40,000 tons by the Soviets' own admission[44] – was fully integrated into Soviet military doctrine, training, and organization.[45] Quite apart from the allegations of chemical warfare, involving Soviet forces in Afghanistan or by Laotian and Vietnamese forces under Soviet supervision in Laos or using Soviet-made chemical agents and munitions in Kampuchea,[46] reports based on US intelligence claimed that several states had developed their CW programmes with Soviet assistance. Egyptian forces were allegedly the first to have received such assistance in the early 1960s, followed by Iraqi and later Ethiopian and Libyan soldiers. Syria had also relied upon Soviet support, and, by September 1983, had 'probably the most advanced chemical warfare capability in the Arab world', reportedly including CW agents and delivery systems supplied by the former Soviet Union and Czechoslovakia.[47]

This proliferation was depicted as growing in scale and significance. On 26 April 1984 Dominic Gasbarri of the US Defense Intelligence Agency (DIA) began the process of public disclosure by informing a subcommittee of the Senate Armed Services Committee that US intelligence, having hitherto concentrated upon the Soviet chemical threat, now had evidence that 'other countries want chemical weapons.'[48] As Dr Thomas Welch, then Deputy Assistant to the US Secretary of Defence, later explained, the number of states possessing offensive CW programmes had nearly doubled from seven in the 1960s to 'about 13' in the 1970s and had since grown to 'about 16' in the period 1980–84.[49] By the end of the 1980s US officials, including President Bush, were maintaining that proliferation was still growing, and that some 20 states either possessed chemical weapons or had the capability to do so.[50] Judge Webster linked this proliferation, and the spread of nuclear and biological weapons, with the proliferation of ballistic missiles, dubbing the combination as an 'alarming prospect' that could raise the significance and urgency of some 'regional problems' for the United States.[51]

These reports would arouse scepticism that their publication might reflect some ulterior motive, possibly boosting support for the expanding market in chemical protective equipment or for the binary chemical armament programme, then being sought by the Reagan administration.[52] They were also criticised as cursory in content (possibly giving the conclusions of various reports but not their complete analyses with likely nuances and qualifications),[53] lacking in precise definitions, and bereft of clear distinctions between a research and development programme and a capacity to produce such weapons, or between a production capacity and the possession of a stockpile of chemical weapons, or between a militarily useful CW capability and the obsolete remnants from the past history of the state in question.[54] Despite the insistence of Kenneth Adelman, as Director of the Arms Control and Disarmament Agency (ACDA), that officials were 'not talking about experimental possession, research possession', and that the stockpiles concerned were sufficiently large to prove militarily useful for the possessing country,[55] scepticism persisted, fed by the stream of imprecise and sometimes contradictory briefings. On 1 March 1988 Rear Admiral William O. Studeman, Director of Naval Intelligence, claimed that 'Worldwide, some ten countries possess a chemical warfare capability', and that 'as many are known or thought to be actively seeking it;' while eight days later, Dr Welsh asserted that 'at least 16 countries have an offensive chemical warfare capability'.[56] In January 1989 Major-General William F. Burns, a former Director of ACDA, appeared to concede part of the sceptics' case by admitting that although some twenty countries were capable of building poison gas weapons, 'no more than a handful, five or six, besides the Soviet Union and the United States' actually possessed stockpiles of such weapons.[57]

The ambiguities may have derived from several factors, not least a reluctance to be too specific about highly sensitive intelligence lest it compromise the sources concerned.[58] The information, too, may have been open to interpretation, whether involving suspicious-looking facilities and activities, or stockpiles of munitions without outward characteristics to distinguish chemical from conventional high explosive payloads, or allegations of chemical attacks in remote and inaccessible areas that could be erroneous, fabricated, or impossible to verify after lengthy delays between the alleged attack and an investigation.[59] In highlighting these ambiguities, sceptics did not deny that some proliferation was under way. The Iraqi use of chemical weapons in the Iran–Iraq War was 'unquestionable evidence of proliferation' and the Iraqi production of such weapons indicated that more was involved than the transfer of arms from state to state.[60]

This was doubly ironic as fifteen western industrialised governments had responded to the chemical attacks in the Iran–Iraq War by forming the Australia (Suppliers) Group in 1985 to impose export controls on certain chemicals, particularly those precursors that could be used to manufacture chemical weapons. As an informal body, it sought by regular, biannual meetings in the Australian embassy in Paris to coordinate the differing export policies of various national governments and the European Community, to share information on proliferation, and to devise increasingly comprehensive lists of chemicals for the purposes of export control (by May 1989, it had 50 chemicals on its 'core' and 'warning' lists). However, multilateral export controls imposed by different governments, in different ways (even with differing definitions of 'worldwide'),[61] were bound to have limited effects, especially as there were alternative sources of supply beyond the Group (including the option of indigenous production). The Group lacked any sanctions over its members, and bilateral action in the form of diplomatic démarches, and public exposure was still necessary to compel a member of the Group, West Germany, to take action over industrialists involved in the construction and equipping of the Rabta plant in Libya.[62] The Group, as a US diplomat argued, probably made 'the acquisition of these chemicals a bit more difficult and a bit more expensive'[63] but it neither curbed the Iraqi (and later the Iranian) CW effort nor stemmed the growing number of states reported as possessing or as seeking to possess chemical weapons.

Data about the proliferation of BW programmes only appeared towards the end of the 1980s, possibly reflecting the inherent difficulty of determining the intent of covert programmes. On 3 May 1988 Welch provided a joint congressional committee with a confidential list of 'about 10 countries with biological warfare capabilities'.[64] In 1988 and 1989 US intelligence spokesmen claimed that China, Taiwan and North Korea had BW programmes, as well as several Middle Eastern states, including Iraq, Syria, Egypt, Iran and Libya. On 9 February 1989 Judge Webster stated that 'at least 10 countries are working to produce both previously known and futuristic biological weapons.' Several other officials agreed that the number of countries with BW programmes had grown from four in 1972, when the Biological and Toxin Weapons Convention (BTWC) was signed, to ten in 1989.[65] Although these reports replicated many of the ambiguities of the reports on the proliferation of chemical weapons, they should not have caused much surprise. The BTWC, which banned the development, production and stockpiling of these weapons, could only be regarded as a 'disarmament success story'[66] by those who were reluctant to believe the oft-repeated allegations that the Soviet Union had persistently violated the treaty.

Since the mid- to late 1970s, US officials had been aware of, and in the 1980s had increasingly criticised, the 'scope and nature' of the Soviet biological and toxin weapons programme; the suspicious outbreak of anthrax in Sverdlovsk (April 1979); and the reports of Soviet investment in biotechnology and its possible military applications.[67] The Reagan administration sought additional funding for biological (and chemical) defensive research, planned to modernise its testing

facilities at Dugway Proving Ground, Utah, by building a P4 containment facility to test aerosols, and received encouragement from the
Chemical Warfare Review Commission in June 1985 to upgrade its
intelligence on chemical and biological warfare and conduct 'active
research on how biological science advances might be turned to military ends'.[68] Many sceptics questioned the justification, content and
implications of the revived defensive programme. They cast doubt on
the claims of Soviet violations, in one case arguing that US policy was
'driven less by sound evidence than by ideology'; feared lest defensive
research would become the first step towards the development of an
offensive BW capability; and dreaded that an 'arms race' in the development of 'uncontrollable' biological weapons would ensue. They
advocated the demilitarising of basic research and the enhancing of the
legal and moral barriers to biological warfare by strengthening the
Biological and Toxin Weapons Convention.[69]

These legal and moral barriers, though, had already been eroded by
the covert BW programmes of the Soviet Union, Iraq and possibly several other states. The vulnerability of many Western armed forces had
also grown as investment in BW defence had plummeted in the 1970s,
following the unilateral termination of the US BW programme in 1969,
the signing of the BTWC in 1972, and the desire to allocate scarce
resources to other defence programmes. Funding declined precipitously
on both sides of the Atlantic, and the British Labour government civil-
ianised the Microbiological Research Establishment at Porton Down.[70]
In making the case for renewed defensive research programmes, US
officials argued that biological weapons were 'effective' weapons, and
that toxins could be used tactically as well as strategically. They stressed,
too, that when the United States unilaterally renounced its BW capability in 1969, it had not done so because of doubts about the value of
biological weapons. As Professor Matthew Meselson later explained, an
interagency review in 1969 had concluded that biological weapons
posed a potential threat to populations that could be 'as great...as
nuclear weapons' without any reliable defence; that these weapons
could prove 'much simpler and less expensive' to produce than nuclear
weapons; and that if the US persisted with this 'easily duplicated technology', others would follow suit.[71] Although he could not confirm the
claims of BW proliferation in the 1980s,[72] several officials testified that
US forces were facing 'a very real, growing threat', and 'a more surreptitious' threat than that from chemical weapons. They justified a biological defence programme for US forces (not the civil population) as
a means of bolstering the deterrent against BW attacks, blunting the

effectiveness of such attacks should they occur (and thereby boosting service morale), and reducing the vulnerability of the United States to 'biological warfare coercion'.[73]

The proliferation of sophisticated delivery systems compounded concerns about the spread of these weapon programmes. If the transfer of ballistic missile technology attracted most attention in the 1980s, the acquisition of advanced strike aircraft by developing states was just as important. Aircraft such as the F-16 C/D and F-15 E, the SU-24 and MiG-29, the Mirage 2000 and the Tornado IDS, possessed heavier payloads and could operate at longer ranges, delivering warheads more accurately than the ballistic missiles generally available to developing states. As an estimated 2,500 aircraft were transferred to developing countries between 1980 and 1987, these familiar, versatile, reusable and recallable delivery systems had continuing attractions as delivery systems.[74] Nevertheless, the proliferation of ballistic missiles, which had been under way since the early 1960s, aroused acute anxiety during the 'War of the Cities' between Iran and Iraq. Although the 570 conventionally armed ballistic missiles launched during this conflict did not determine the outcome, they had a disproportionate political and psychological impact. The Iraqi missiles, despite causing relatively few casualties, sapped the will of many war-weary Iranians who fled Teheran towards the end of the war, and reportedly stimulated 'the demand for ballistic missiles … among Third World governments'.[75] By the end of the decade, the International Institute for Strategic Studies estimated that 'more than twenty developing countries have ballistic missile programmes, more than a dozen possess operational ballistic missile forces …'.[76]

Indigenous research, development and production of missile systems was perceived as less of a problem than their transfer between states (with the former Soviet Union being a major supplier of short-range missile systems). The considerable costs[77] and technological difficulties involved in the production of guidance systems, high-powered rocket motors and warheads had limited the extent of indigenous development (although there were several programmes under way, including the Israeli *Jericho* 1 and 2, the Indian *Prithivi* and *Agni*, and the Pakistani *Haft* 1 and 2). The transfer of missiles, sometimes under the cover of space launch programmes, posed more problems as once missiles were acquired, they could be modified (like the Iraqi *al-Hussein* and *al-Abbas* missiles), copied, and new designs produced in the quest for export markets to defray the costs involved.[78] As Jim E. Hinds, then Deputy Assistant Secretary of Defense, argued in May 1989, these relatively inaccurate missiles were ideally suited as 'terror weapons right now'. They could also could carry nuclear, biological or chemical payloads, and, on account of their inaccuracy, these area weapons could prove a 'militarily effective' option[79] (albeit with appropriate dispersal mechanisms to deliver chemical or biological agents effectively).

Efforts had already been made to curb the proliferation of nuclear-capable missiles. On 16 April 1987 seven Western states – Britain, Canada, France, Italy, Japan, the United States and West Germany – announced separate, but identical, national control policies. Known as the Missile Technology Control Regime (MTCR), these controls applied to any missile system, subsystem or technology capable of assembling missiles that could carry a 500 kilogram payload over a distance of 300 kilometres. Although a significant, if belated, achievement after several years of secret negotiations, and one that may have slowed the pace of missile proliferation, this 'consensual supplier cartel'[80] had several obvious limitations. As a voluntary, non-binding agreement, it lacked any enforcement mechanisms, or even an international agency to monitor compliance; it allowed sales of dual-use equipment in support of national space programmes; and it did not involve all potential suppliers (as graphically demonstrated in 1988 by the Chinese sale of CSS-2 intermediate-range ballistic missiles to Saudi Arabia). Although the US made frequent démarches over this issue in Beijing, and even elicited assurances from Prime Minister Li Peng, in March 1989, that China would desist from selling ballistic missiles abroad, China would not, at this time, embrace the guidelines of the MTCR. Nor would several other countries that either sold missiles or assisted states with their missile programmes abide by the MTCR guidelines.[81]

Like other export control regimes, the MTCR only focused on suppliers and did little to dampen the demand for ballistic or cruise missile technology (indeed, it possibly intensified a sense of resentment in some developing countries that they were being denied access to technology that the supplier states were utilising for their own civilian and military purposes).[82] The demand for ballistic missiles, like the demand for NBC weapons, was all too apparent before the end of the Cold War. These weapons and delivery systems were sought for a mix of political, military and economic motives, depending on the geo-strategic circumstances of the states concerned, internal pressures from their scientific and military élites, and the aspirations of political leaders at particular times. As Colonel Mu'ammar Qaddafi stated in Tripoli on 18 April 1990, 'When the world is playing around with rockets and bombs, we must be capable of playing the game. ... We want to create a deterrent force such as has been created by the world's tyrants.'[83] However, weapons sought for some purposes might come to serve others. If intended to match or offset the military capacities of regional rivals, they could compensate for gaps in military capabilities and ultimately serve as a new deterrent or weapon of last resort. They might meet the requirements of cost-effectiveness, provide economic spin-offs (space programmes, meteorological programmes, etc.), or boost national prestige. Missile technology, as Mark Heller argues, 'like most other military technology, is sought because countries want the best weaponry they can acquire'.[84] In short, proliferation was well under way before the Cold War ended: the demands fuelled in that era have served as a backdrop to the proliferation problems of the 1990s.

2
WMD Crises and Revelations in the 1990s

In January 1988 the US Commission On Integrated Long-Term Strategy produced a remarkably prescient report, 'Discriminate Deterrence', that summarised many of the concerns aroused by proliferation in the 1990s. The commission drew attention to the worldwide diffusion of advanced weapons and its implications for US strategy and diplomacy. It anticipated that the relationship between major and minor powers would change in the early 21st century, and that many of the latter will acquire 'sizeable arsenals', often including chemical weapons and short-range or even medium-range ballistic missiles. It also envisaged that atomic bombs would be produced in 'many countries not now possessing them' because of the spread of nuclear reactors and the technology associated with nuclear energy, and concluded that

> The arsenals of the lesser powers will make it riskier and more difficult for the superpowers to intervene in regional wars. The U.S. ability to support its allies around the world will increasingly be called into question. Where American intervention seems necessary, it will generally require far more co operation with Third World countries than has been required in the past.[1]

Although the commissioners could not have anticipated the events reviewed in this chapter – the Gulf War, the collapse of the Soviet Union, the North Korean nuclear programme, and the revelations of the United Nations Special Commission (UNSCOM) – they had anticipated many of the concerns expressed by US officials in the 1990s. Successive Directors of the CIA, Robert Gates and James Woolsey, among others argued that WMD proliferation is altogether more serious and significant than ever before. They claimed that proliferants by evading export controls, assisting each other, and exploiting both dual-use technologies and their own increasingly sophisticated scientific and industrial capacities, have sought 'state-of-the-art weapons that will give them prestige as well as first-class capabilities'.[2] If this trend continues, they maintained that it could stimulate or exacerbate regional rivalries, erode inhibitions on use, and enhance the military capabilities of the proliferants relative to those of the United States, which were being limited by 'budget reductions and arms control agreements', thereby possibly securing 'a compelling psychological deterrent'.[3] The Pentagon's *Quadrennial Defense Review* of May 1997 was even more emphatic:

> Between now and 2015, it is reasonable to assume that more than one aspiring regional power will have both the desire and the means to challenge U.S. interests militarily....
>
> Of particular concern is the spread of nuclear, biological, and chemical (NBC) weapons and their means of delivery....
>
> U.S. dominance in the conventional military arena may encourage adversaries to use such asymmetric means to attack our forces and interests overseas and Americans at home. That is, they are likely to seek advantage over the United States by using unconventional approaches to *circumvent* or *undermine* our strengths, while *exploiting* our vulnerabilities.[4]

Potentially, the main threat was not necessarily a direct challenge to the United States and its interests overseas. Although CIA Directors warned that 'hostile' nations could, after the turn of the century, develop ballistic missiles indigenously with a range to threaten the United States,[5] an indirect challenge was considered much more likely. State-sponsored terrorism, NBC threats, and environmental sabotage were all regarded as possible options, but, if a direct challenge could not be avoided, an asymmetric capability could be used to delay or deny American access to critical facilities, to deter allies or potential coalition partners, and threaten to inflict higher than expected American casualties.[6] At the very least this would transform the status of those medium-sized states, which were hostile to the existing international order and were often dubbed by US politicians as "rogue" regimes. Once these regimes acquired a usable arsenal of NBC weapons, this would in Senator Joseph Lieberman's words, 'add an entirely new dimension to world politics'.[7] In line with official policy under both the Bush and Clinton administrations, several US government agencies, including the CIA, elevated the task of curtailing weapons proliferation to one of their highest priorities.

Organizational and doctrinal changes followed: new co-ordination centres were established in the Pentagon and the intelligence community;
counterproliferation began to emerge as an operational concept, with
new initiatives and technological programmes; and, under the Clinton
administration, a new post was established as Assistant Secretary for
Nuclear Security and Counterproliferation. Ashton B. Carter, as the nom-
inated official, acknowledged that 'Proliferation is assuming a higher
profile as a future military threat to the United States, its forces, and
allies, and special operation forces will be a vital tool in countering the
threat.'[8]

The Gulf War (1991) had focused attention, as rarely before, on the
challenges posed by an adversary armed with chemical and biological
weapons and ballistic missiles, as well as programmes to build nuclear
weapons. Iraqi chemical weapons and ballistic missiles attracted the
most comment prior to hostilities; they had both been used extensively during the Iran–Iraq War, and Iraqi forces had unrivalled combat
experience in employing a diverse stock of chemical agents, including
mustard and nerve agents, both defensively and later offensively in the
recapture of the Fao peninsula in April 1988.[9] Whether Iraq would use
these weapons against a US-led coalition, either strategically in attacks
upon Israel and Saudi Arabia or tactically on the battlefield was extensively debated.[10] Colonel Trevor Dupuy doubted that Saddam Hussein
would dare to launch chemical attacks against an enemy able to retaliate-in-kind, or with something worse.[11] Julian Perry Robinson, Matthew
Meselson and Seth Carus argued that even if Iraq tried to mount chemical attacks, their impact was likely to be blunted by climatic conditions, the probable destruction of Iraq's air force (its most potent
means of delivery), the effectiveness of the coalition's protective kit,
and the inaccuracy of Iraq's SCUD missiles.[12]

The coalition military commanders made extensive preparations to
degrade, counter, and limit the potential damage from Iraqi chemical
and biological attacks. Aerial operations – in the course of a 38-day aerial campaign – were intended to neutralise key elements of Iraq's command, control and communications, destroy NBC production facilities,
disrupt logistic supplies, suppress aerial delivery capabilities and bom-
bard Iraqi artillery in the Kuwaiti Theatre of Operations (KTO). The
coalition forces also planned to counter any residual chemical strikes
by protecting air bases with surface-to-air missiles and by conducting
highly mobile ground operations. Service personnel, particularly those
of the principal belligerents, were protected against the effects of
chemical and biological attacks. Many units, too, had the opportunity

of training extensively in their full Mission-Oriented Protective Posture (MOPP) in Saudi conditions. Although Dr Billy Richardson, Deputy Assistant to the Secretary of Defense for Chemical Matters, would assert that US forces at 'the start of Operation Desert Storm...were the best equipped and trained in history to fight and survive on a CB [chemical/biological] battlefield',[13] the Pentagon subsequently acknowledged that 'CW/BW defensive readiness at the outset of the crisis was quite low'. The British, who maintained that their NBC kit was generally superior to the US equivalents, sold extra items of S-10 masks, M4 suits and Chemical Agent Monitors (CAMs) to coalition allies, and, unlike the Americans, had the support of nine prototype biological detection systems.[14] The Pentagon reported criticisms of its 30-year old M-17 masks, the weight of US protective clothing, the lack of collective protection for the medical facilities at the outset of Operation Desert Shield, and the many problems associated with the water-based decontamination systems.[15] In these circumstances, General H. Norman Schwarzkopf had prudently planned for 10,000 to 20,000 casualties: 'The possibility of mass casualties from chemical weapons', he wrote, 'was the main reason we had sixty-three hospitals, two hospital ships, and eighteen thousand beds ready in the war zone.'[16]

In the event the coalition forces, and the citizens of Israel and other neighbouring Arab countries, were spared any attacks with chemical and biological weapons. Iraq was almost certainly deterred by the threat of US retaliation. Although the Bush administration had resolved not to retaliate with nuclear and chemical weapons if coalition forces were attacked with chemical weapons, it sought to maximise Iraqi uncertainty by issuing unspecific threats of 'overwhelming' and 'devastating' retaliatory strikes. In his meeting with Iraq's Foreign Minister, Tariq Aziz, on 9 January 1991, US Secretary of State, James Baker, deliberately 'left the impression that the use of chemical or biological agents by Iraq could invite tactical nuclear retaliation'. He has argued subsequently that 'the calculated ambiguity regarding how we might respond has to be part of the reason' for the non-use of chemical weapons by Iraq.[17]

Tariq Aziz broadly agreed. While he recalled that Baker was not specific about the form of any response, he told Ambassador Rolf Ekéus that 'the Iraqi side took it for granted that it meant the use of maybe nuclear weapons against Baghdad, or something like that. And that threat was decisive for them not use the [chemical and biological] weapons.'[18] Ekéus also revealed that the Iraqi weapons, according to their own documentation, were intended as weapons of last resort – 'a thunderbolt' to be used in a surprise attack, and that local commanders had been given authority to use them during the Gulf War in response to an attack on Baghdad with weapons of mass destruction. Ekéus remained sceptical about the reasoning of Aziz, arguing that chemical weapons would have been 'practically useless' against a protected force.[19] The protection, though, was far from perfect. The Patriot missile defence system (PAC-2) performed less effectively than the wartime propaganda claimed. When deployed in Israel, it doubtless provided psychological reassurance, so serving the political purposes of the Israeli and American governments, but it had a very limited area of coverage and had difficulty in discriminating between incoming warheads and disintegrating pieces of missile. Patriot's computer software eventually succumbed in the defence of Dhahran air base, allowing an incoming SCUD to explode in an American barracks.[20]

Chemical weapons would certainly have proved difficult to use effectively against protected coalition forces, especially in the adverse climatic conditions often involving heavy rain and capricious winds.[21] Schwarzkopf, however, never accepted that protective kit, even of the quality used by the coalition, would blunt all the effects of chemical attacks. He admitted that:

> one of my biggest concerns from the outset was the psychological impact of the initial use of chemical weapons on the troops. If they fight through it, then it is no longer ever going to be a problem. But if it stops them dead in their tracks and scares them to death, that it a continuing problem. And that was one of the concerns we had all along.[22]

Similarly, he was deeply concerned about the political and psychological impact of the SCUD attacks. 'We were not concerned about the accuracy', he recalled, 'The biggest concern was a chemical warhead threat…each time they launched…the question was, is this going to be a chemical missile. That was what you were concerned about.'[23] General Colin Powell, if reasonably sanguine about the ability of protected forces to operate in chemically-contaminated conditions, later admitted that 'The one thing that scares me to death, perhaps even more than tactical nuclear weapons, and the one we have less capability against is biological weapons. This was my greatest concern during Operation Desert Storm, knowing that the Iraqis had been working on such a capability.'[24]

These concerns might have had less substance had the strategic air bombardment of Iraq's NBC facilities and SCUD missile production and launch capabilities been anything like as effective as claimed during and immediately after the war. In his post-war address to Congress on 6 March 1991, President Bush claimed that 'Tonight in Iraq Saddam Hussein walks amidst ruin. ... His war machine is crushed. His ability to threaten mass destruction is itself destroyed.'[25] Although this claim was doubtless based on evidence from battle damage reports, it was wildly optimistic.[26] Known production facilities were targeted and in most cases, heavily damaged, as were some mistaken facilities such as the baby milk factory, of which Powell had said 'It was a biological weapons facility. Of that we are sure, and we have taken it out.'[27] The failures and oversights derived more from gaps in intelligence than errors in bombing, although the *Gulf War Air Power Survey* failed to confirm the wartime claims of precision strikes against mobile SCUD launchers. While it accepted that a few mobile launchers may have been destroyed by aircraft or special forces, it could not confirm the destruction of a single mobile SCUD launcher by an aircraft operating independently.[28] Although the bombing caused far less damage than implied in various press briefings and speeches, it may have disrupted production programmes and forced the Iraqis to disperse and conceal equipment, materials and munitions. Undoubtedly it inhibited some planned operations and reduced their launch rates (particularly the firing of SCUD missiles in salvos as they had done during the Iran–Iraq War).

In essence, this operation and the subsequent UNSCOM revelations confirmed several key requirements for any counterproliferation operations. In the first place, intelligence collection and accurate analysis is a prerequisite (and in this case US intelligence detected WMD programmes and an extensive ballistic missile capability but seriously underestimated their scope and diversity). At the outset of Operation Desert Storm, only six nuclear sites were known and three were initially targeted, but after the war another 19 were discovered by the IAEA inspectors.[29] In the first summer of inspections UNSCOM uncovered 50 fixed SCUD launch pads, previously unknown SCUD missiles and mobile launchers, 23,000 additional chemical munitions, vast quantities of precursor chemicals, and two sites associated with the BW programme.[30] Admittedly, the coalition air forces could hardly be expected to bomb every bunker that might or might not contain chemical or biological weapons, and the bombing certainly inflicted heavy damage upon the chemical production, processing, and munition-filling facilities at Al Muthana and Habbaniyah, while disrupting Iraq's ability to move, load and fire such weapons.[31] Nevertheless, the shortcomings of the coalition's intelligence/aerial bombardment effort confirmed the difficulty of identifying and destroying all sites that could be involved in WMD programmes, especially BW programmes.

Secondly, if a counterproliferation action requires, as it did in the Gulf War, a lengthy period of preparatory diplomacy (to mobilise support nationally and internationally), this will only ensure that the adversary has extra time to dismantle, move, conceal and relocate vital pieces of equipment, materials and munitions. In these circumstances, extravagant claims about the damage likely to be caused by 'precision' aerial bombardments are unwise, and, in assessing the net value of the subsequent bombing, allowance has be made for the information inadvertently given to the proliferant, especially if key facilities are overlooked. The bombing may also have a longer term significance if the proliferant regime remains in office, retaining the wherewithal in concealed materials, equipment and munitions (as well as surviving scientists and technicians) to reconstitute, or at least recommence, the programmes concerned.

Less convincing as a lesson from the Gulf War is the claim that the non-use of chemical weapons by the Iraqis exposed the limited utility of these weapons. In the aftermath of the war, both Ronald F. Lehman, Director of ACDA, and Ambassador Stephen J. Ledogar asserted that the conflict had debunked the theory that chemical weapons constituted a 'poor man's atomic bomb'. Lehman insisted that Iraq had not only failed to deter the coalition but also that the potential effectiveness of its chemical stockpile had been countered by attacks on its command and control facilities with conventional weapons, by conducting highly mobile operations, and by equipping the coalition forces with anti-chemical defensive capabilities. He confidently asserted that

> a lot of nations looked at the gulf war and have come to the conclusion they don't want to go down the chemical weapons path – the risks are too great – and they want to make sure nobody else does, either. It is this attitude that has given us a boost for the Chemical Weapons Convention.[32]

Unfortunately these assertions appear to have been less than prescient. Reports of the proliferation of chemical (as well as nuclear and biological) weapons persisted after the Gulf War. Successive Directors of the CIA testified to the continuing phenomenon; on 22 February 1996, five years after the Gulf War was supposed to have inhibited CW proliferation, Dr John M. Deutch reported that 'At least 20 countries have or may be developing nuclear, chemical, biological and ballistic missile systems .... Chemical weapons programs are active in 18 countries .... Biological Weapons, often called the poor man's atomic bombs, are also on the rise.'[33] Pentagon spokesmen, NATO's Director of Nuclear Planning, the Russian Foreign Intelligence Service, and even ACDA[34] confirmed that these trends, including chemical proliferation, were continuing, even if they differed about the precise extent of the phenomenon.

This was none too surprising. The Gulf War was hardly a convincing precedent in matters of proliferation and counterproliferation. Operations Desert Shield and Desert Storm were triggered by Iraq's seizure of a neighbouring state and not by the proliferation programmes of Saddam Hussein. Prior to 2 August 1990, Iraq had not incurred any political penalty on account of its WMD programmes: indeed, Western states had maintained diplomatic and commercial relations with Iraq, despite periodic démarches over the latter's use of chemical weapons during the Iran–Iraq War and subsequent Iraqi threats towards neighbouring states, particularly Israel.[35] Once the Gulf War erupted, Saddam's supine strategy and feckless tactics revealed little or nothing about the combat effectiveness of any of the weapons at his disposal (conventional or unconventional). The war did not prove anything about a war in which the United States was not involved, either a war between developing states or a civil war and, in both contexts, chemical weapons could still prove useful as "force multipliers" on the battlefield or as weapons of terror against guerrilla forces and civilian communities. Few developing states, facing a chemical (or biological) threat in such circumstances, could emulate the conventional response of the United States and they might find themselves fighting over more difficult terrain or against a more resourceful enemy. Perceptions, in short, could vary: as Kathleen Bailey aptly remarked, 'Just because our own leaders do not view chemical weapons as usable or necessary does not mean that the leaders of other countries view them similarly.'[36]

If the legacy bequeathed by the Gulf War was not completely reassuring, the CBW capabilities of the former Soviet Union and later Russia continued to arouse controversy. The belated admission that the Soviet Union possessed a chemical weapons stockpile in 1987, and the claim that it amounted to 'no more than 50,000 tons' of agent (later reduced, without any visible means of destruction, to 40,000 tons), never silenced Western sceptics. Concerns were expressed about the Soviet methods of accounting as the claim was at the low end of Western estimates and very much lower than some claims of 300,000 tons.[37] The Bush administration sought clarification through the Memorandum of Understanding (MoU) signed by Secretary of State Baker and the Soviet Foreign Minister Eduard Shevardnadze at Jackson Hole, Wyoming (22–3 September 1989). Under the terms of the MoU, the two sides agreed to exchange more data and arrange confidence-building visits and on-site inspections. These failed to allay American doubts which were buttressed by the revelations of several former Soviet scientists – Vladimir Pasechnik, who defected to Britain in 1989, Vil Mirzayanov, who was imprisoned in 1992 and 1993 for revealing state secrets, and Dr Alexei Yablokov, a former member of Yeltsin's National Security Council. Pasechnik confirmed Western suspicions of the vast, illicit Soviet biological and toxin weapons programme – a programme not formally acknowledged until February 1992, when President Yeltsin promised to close it.[38] Mirzayanov (and Dr Lev Fedorov) claimed that the Soviet CW programme was still active in the early 1990s, and that it involved the development of binary weapons and a new toxicant, even more potent than the most toxic of the V-agents.[39] By the mid-1990s, Dr Yablokov was quoted as asserting that Russia's stockpile of chemical weapons was much larger than the declared 40,000 tons and had to be closer to 100,000 tons.[40]

Both British and American officials expressed scepticism about whether the Russians had provided a full disclosure of the former Soviet/Russian CW and BW programmes. They questioned whether these programmes had ceased and the capabilities been abandoned. After reviewing the phase 2 data supplied under the terms of the Wyoming MoU, James Woolsey declared that 'we have serious concerns over apparent incompleteness, inconsistency, and contradictory aspects of the data. Russia did not declare any binary weapons programs either in development or production.'[41] Although Woolsey emphasised that the United States would exercise its right under the terms of the MoU to raise questions about the data submitted, and hoped that the Russian data, even if incomplete and inconsistent, would still afford a basis for dialogue and discussion, American reservations persisted. The DIA flatly contradicted Yeltsin and maintained that 'there are compelling reasons to believe that the [BW] program continues, albeit on a reduced scale'.[42]

Ultimately despite the signing of a Trilateral Agreement in 1992, Russia, Britain and the United States failed to resolve their differences over the Russian BW programme, particularly over activities at some Russian military installations. Although the State Department claimed that the political will was present at the highest levels in Russia, it affirmed that intransigence, resistance and mismanagement persisted at lower levels. The Pentagon reiterated that it had 'a number of questions and concerns' about the CW programme reportedly consolidated by Russia at seven sites.[43] Even Russia's ratification of the Chemical Weapons Convention (CWC) on 5 November 1997 was far from reassuring as Russia had still not built any permanent destruction facilities, and had not indicated how it would find the equivalent of $5 billion to complete the destruction process. The former Soviet/Russian BW programme aroused even more concern as it was not only the world's largest offensive BW programme, with BW agents developed and weaponised as early as the 1950s, but the Pentagon claimed that

> Key components of the former Soviet program remain largely intact and may support a possible future mobilization capability for the production of biological agents and delivery systems. Moreover, work outside the scope of legitimate biological defense activity may be occurring now at selected facilities within Russia.[44]

The disintegration of the Soviet Union precipitated a host of new and unprecedented proliferation problems. The abortive coup of 19 August 1991 aroused acute American anxieties. On 27 September President Bush announced the unilateral elimination of the entire US arsenal of short-range nuclear missile warheads and artillery shells, as well as the withdrawal of all tactical warheads from ships and attack submarines, hoping to secure a similar commitment from Mikhail Gorbachev (which duly appeared on 3 October). Of even more importance in the longer term was the bi-partisan Congressional initiative of Senators Sam Nunn and Richard Lugar, allocating $400 million in discretionary funds from the US defence vote in November 1991, to facilitate the withdrawal, storage, and destruction of Soviet nuclear weapons. When the Soviet Union actually disintegrated in December 1991, the US had to confront the prospect that some 3,000 strategic and 6,500 tactical nuclear weapons would be located in republics outside Russia.

The Bush administration wanted to ensure that all former Soviet nuclear weapons, particularly the smaller, easily transported and widely dispersed tactical nuclear weapons, remained under single unified secure control, and that four independent nuclear states (Russia, the Ukraine, Kazakhstan and Belarus) did not emerge from the dissolution of the Soviet Union.[45] While James Baker briefly sounded the tocsin about a 'Yugoslavia with nukes', Robert Gates explained why the current situation could be 'dangerously unstable', referring to fears that the new regimes were not bound by the arms agreements of the former Soviet Union, and that safeguards might not be maintained during the process of reducing and dismantling the vast nuclear arsenal. He was particularly concerned lest equipment, materials and expertise should be sold in the international marketplace by the thousands of scientists, engineers and technicians formerly employed in well-paid, prestigious WMD and missile programmes.[46]

Compounding this range of problems was the sheer scale of the former Soviet WMD programmes. In 1992, the CIA estimated that these programmes involved 'about 30,000 nuclear weapons' and nearly one million people, of whom 1,000 or 2,000 possessed the skills needed to design and produce nuclear weapons (with a few thousand more able to develop and produce biological weapons).[47] However, the Bush administration acted promptly, pressing its concerns by diplomatic démarches, the widely reported speech of Baker at Princeton University on 12 December, and formal visits by Baker to the four republics at a time when all of them were seeking US recognition and economic aid. Assisted by Congressional allocations, Baker and his staff were able to offer technical advice and assistance on the disabling, transfer and secure storage of nuclear weapons as well as legal advice on the terms of the Strategic Arms Reduction Treaty (START 1, July 1991). The United States also delayed recognition until it was more confident that the three republics outside Russia would honour their assurances (at Alma Ata, 21 December 1991) to preserve a unified command and control under the Joint Military High Command of the Commonwealth of Independent States (CIS), based in Moscow. In January 1992, the administration sent another senior delegation to Moscow, Kiev, Minsk and Alma Ata to amplify US concerns and expectations. As Steven Miller has observed, 'US pressure, coming at a time when the republics were especially sensitive to Western concerns, may have been quite effective in affecting the calculations of leaders in the republics.'[48]

In many respects these nuclear proliferation problems were anomalous. The nuclear weapons had been inherited by newly independent states (NIS) at a time when they were highly susceptible to external pressure and economic inducement. Russia's President, Boris Yeltsin had every incentive to sustain the improvement in relations with the Bush and Clinton administrations. He knew that the nuclear weapons of the former Soviet Union were a prime American concern, and indicated a willingness to honour the nuclear reductions agreed under the START 1 treaty (July 1991), not least by signing the START 2 agreement (3 January 1993).[49] He appreciated that Russia's interests would be served by removing all tactical nuclear weapons from the other republics (which would be completed between January and 6 May 1992); by the other NIS honouring the terms of START 1 (as they would pledge to do under the Lisbon Protocol of 23 May 1992); and by the removal of strategic nuclear weapons from neighbouring territories (especially some 1,900 nuclear warheads in the Ukraine). As he declared in his State of the Union Address (February 1994), Russia sought to strengthen 'the arrangements governing the nonproliferation of mass destruction weapons and sophisticated technologies ...'.[50]

Of the other NIS, only the Ukraine had a perceived external security threat (and a fairly general, not specific, one from Russia) for which a nuclear deterrent might seem appropriate. Neither Belarus nor Kazakhstan had similar concerns (other than conceivably a Chinese threat in the latter's case), and both looked to Russia for security guarantees, so reducing the need for an independent nuclear arsenal. Any thoughts about the possible gains of international status to be derived from retaining nuclear weapons had to be balanced by the risks (including the possible loss of economic aid and the suspension of political ties) and the costs of doing so (notably the economic and technical demands of maintaining the inherited weapons).[51] A fervent nationalism in the Ukraine carried anti-Russian overtones, and the *Rada* (parliament) initially attached conditions to its ratification of START 1, seeking recognition of the Ukraine's 'administrative control' of the nuclear weapons on its territory.

Operational control, though, remained with Russia's Strategic Rocket Forces, even after the dissolution of the CIS's Joint Military High Command in June 1993. President Leonid Kravchuk and his senior policy-makers also realised that the Ukraine, as a newly independent and isolated state with a parlous economy, could not afford the political and economic costs of retaining an overt nuclear weapons programme. It sought both economic compensation and strategic reassurances from Russia and the United States, eventually signing a tripartite pact in Moscow (14 January 1994) whereby the Ukraine agreed to transfer all nuclear warheads on its territory to Russia for dismantling, in exchange for fuel rods from Russia for its nuclear plants, economic aid (including forgiveness of its multi-billion dollar oil and gas debt to Russia), and security assurances from Russia and the United States. The United States had vastly increased its financial inducements, both indirectly through Russia (offering to purchase 500 tons of highly enriched uranium (HEU) for 'approximately $12 billion' and increasing the Nunn Lugar (or the Cooperative Threat Reduction) funds to $1.2 billion), and directly to the Ukraine (pledging at the Washington summit of March 1994, some $350 million to assist in the nuclear dismantlement and a similar amount in direct economic aid).[52] Following the offer of further aid from 14 European states (another $234 million) and more specific security assurances from Russia, the United States and Britain (November 1994), the Ukraine agreed to join the NPT as a non-nuclear weapon state. Adhering to an international norm doubtless helped to rationalise the purchase of Ukrainian weapons by foreign governments.[53]

By June 1996 the Ukraine had removed some 1900 strategic nuclear weapons from its territory and deactivated all of its 176 Intercontinental Ballistic Missile (ICBM) silos. Kazakhstan, having ratified START 1 and the Lisbon Protocol in 1992, acceded to the NPT as a non-nuclear weapon state in 1993 and let the United States purchase and plan the removal of a vulnerable cache of 600 kg of HEU for safe storage in the US Department of Energy's facility at Oak Ridge, Tennessee. Kazakhstan removed all nuclear warheads to Russia by April 1995 and eliminated all 104 of its deployed SS-18 silos by the autumn of 1996. Under a series of bilateral accords between Moscow and Alma Ata, Russia and Kazakhstan pledged to retain close military ties, including Moscow's twenty-year lease of Baikonur Cosmodrome (Tyuratain Space Missile Test Centre) and various missile test ranges. Belarus also honoured its commitments to denuclearization, ratifying START 1 and the Lisbon Protocol in February 1993, acceding to the NPT as a non-nuclear weapon state, and removing all strategic warheads to Russia by December 1996.[54]

American officials accepted that the Russian Ministry of Defence could keep the nuclear weapons under its control secure from theft or unauthorised use, and welcomed the reduction of the number of nuclear storage sites from over 500 in the former Soviet Union and Eastern Europe to less than 100 in 1996, mainly in Russia itself.[55] However Deutch, like previous Directors of the CIA, continued to evince concern about the tons of weapon-usable materials that had been distributed over the previous 40 years to non-military organizations, institutes, and centres for nuclear projects. He worried about the accountability of the weapon-usable material recovered from the reduction of nuclear warheads and the possible behaviour of a 'large disaffected population' of scientists, engineers and technicians who had formerly held prestigious and well-paid posts in the Soviet nuclear complex. Despite joint endeavours to construct a secure storage facility at the Mayark Production Association near Ozersk, and the cooperation between nuclear-weapon laboratories (Los Alamos and Arzamas), as well as the creation of International Science and Technology Centres in Moscow and Kiev to find alternative work for nuclear engineers and weapon designers, reports of fissile-smuggling persisted. Although the vast majority of these reports proved to be hoaxes, fraudulent or erroneous, three cases involving minuscule amounts of fissile material were confirmed in 1992 and 1993, and two more alarming incidents occurred in 1994. In May, 5.6 g of weapons-grade plutonium (99.75% Pu-239), mixed with 50 g of metallic alloy, was seized in Tengen, Germany and, on 14 December, 2.72 kg of HEU at 87.7% was intercepted in Prague. These incidents confirmed both the feasibility of illegal movements, especially as 1 kg of plutonium is only the size of a golf ball, and the seriousness of the risks (as, hypothetically, significant quantities of fissile materials could be 'as few as four kilograms'). The movements did not need to involve fissile materials, as non-fissile (but radioactive) materials, such as cesium-137, strontium-90 and cobalt-60, might be desired by terrorist groups.[56] So monitoring nuclear developments in the former Soviet Union remained a high priority for the United States.

The perceived 'nuclearization' of North Korea proved the next major WMD crisis. It was described by Charles Krauthammer as the 'single most dangerous problem in the world'[57] on account of the geo-strategic significance of the Korean peninsula, its legacy of conflict and inter-state rivalry, the nature of the North Korean regime that was both politically-isolated and heavily-armed (with missiles able to hit Japan), and the dangers of triggering a regional arms race. Although the origins, evolution and outcome of the crisis have been extensively examined,[58] some key points are relevant for this study, not least the slow evolution of the crisis. By adhering to the NPT in 1985, North Korea had substantially allayed fears about its nuclear ambitions, and placed its gas-cooled, graphite 5-megawatt (Mw) reactor (and smaller research reactor at Yongbyon) within the remit of the international inspection process. In 1989 alarms were raised when US satellite photography revealed that a plutonium-reprocessing plant was under construction at Yongbyon,[59] and these were later compounded by confirmation that two new reactors – a 50 Mw and a 200 Mw – were also being built. Despite Seoul and Pyongyang signing a Joint Declaration on Denuclearization in December 1991, and the North finally signing a nuclear safeguards agreement with the IAEA in early 1992 (thereby making its declared nuclear facilities belatedly subject to regular IAEA inspections), Robert Gates questioned the sincerity of Pyongyang's actions. He described North Korea as 'one of the world's major proliferation threats'.[60]

The actual crisis was precipitated by the IAEA's findings that there were discrepancies between the amounts of plutonium produced and declared by North Korea. The Agency then requested, on 9 February 1993, that sites not declared by North Korea (suspected waste disposal sites) should be subjected to 'special inspections' – the first such request in the IAEA's history. On 12 March 1993 North Korea responded by exercising its legal right to announce its withdrawal from the NPT, giving the requisite three month's notice. After extensive negotiation and brinkmanship, North Korea agreed on 11 June – the eve of its deadline – to 'suspend' withdrawal from the NPT. In the ensuing diplomacy involving North Korea, the IAEA and the United States, the Clinton administration initially adopted an absolutist stance: North Korea, stated the President in November 1993, 'must not be allowed to develop a nuclear bomb'.[61] Nevertheless, US officials recognised that North Korea probably had sufficient material to make 'one or perhaps two bombs', and that by its actions in May and June 1994, when it removed some 8,000 fuel rods to place them in pond storage, the North might be able to separate sufficient plutonium for another four or five nuclear weapons.[62]

American options were hardly attractive. A pre-emptive military strike, as advocated by several commentators, could have destroyed the North's nuclear facilities and by late June 1994, when the 5 Mw reactor and the reprocessing facilities were empty, might not have posed too great a risk of radioactive fallout. However an aerial strike, as General Merrill McPeak, the US Air Force Chief of Staff, admitted, could not guarantee the destruction of all the hidden caches of plutonium and it risked provoking an invasion of the South.[63] Economic sanctions also seemed problematic: they would have been slow to take effect as North Korea was already 'one of the world's most isolated nations', Chinese support was not guaranteed, and North Korea's reaction could have been highly belligerent.[64] In any event ex-President Jimmy Carter pre-empted this option by visiting Pyongyang in June 1994 and securing the offer of a freeze of the North's nuclear programme in exchange for direct bilateral talks with the United States.[65]

The eventual accord, signed on 21 October 1994, required North Korea to freeze construction of its new 50 Mw and 200 Mw reactors, seal its reprocessing facility (described as a radiochemical laboratory), shut down its 5 Mw reactor and place its 8,000 fuel rods in special cans for long-term storage. In exchange the US promised not to use nuclear weapons against the North, to begin lifting barriers to political and economic contacts between the two countries, to compensate for any lost energy by making regular supplies of oil (at a cost of some $50 million for some 500,000 metric tons annually), and to arrange for the future

supply of two modern light-water reactor (LWR) systems capable of producing 2000 Mw of energy, costing some $4 billion, by a target date of
2003. In a phased process, possibly after the year 2000, as the first LWR
approached completion, North Korea was supposed to allow the IAEA
special inspections and then dismantle all its graphite reactors and the
reprocessing facility prior to completion of the second LWR.[66]

The agreement proved immensely controversial. Critics condemned
the litany of American concessions and inducements as 'front-loaded' in
favour of North Korea, as a 'tendered bribe to North Korea in exchange
for a limit on its nuclear weapons program', and as a capitulation to
blackmail (effectively treating North Korea as a special case, paying it
to honour the non-nuclear obligations that it had once accepted and
then violated). Moreover, by seeking to freeze the future nuclear programme, the accord left North Korea with any bombs it had already
made (or could make before the special inspections occurred) and set a
bleak precedent for countering proliferation. 'The message to other
countries is clear', wrote Dr Gary Milhollin (Director of the Wisconsin
Project on Nuclear Arms Control), 'If you join the Nonproliferation
Treaty and break it by secretly making bombs, you will receive billions
of dollars worth of free nuclear- and fossil-fuel energy.'[67] Clinton officials accepted that the accord was far from ideal, but claimed that it
was 'better than war'. They asserted that North Korea's future nuclear
programme posed a far greater threat than its past one, that flexibility
had only been shown on the matter of timing, and that the ultimate
aims of US policy were still intact, namely halting the existing programme, removing the spent fuel rods, resolving issues about North
Korea's nuclear past, and dismantling all existing nuclear facilities. As
Defense Secretary William Perry added, if Pyongyang reneged on the
agreement in the future, 'we would be no worse off at that point than
we were at the beginning of the agreement'. He argued, too, that the
accord did not constitute a dangerous precedent, and that the 'circumstances and dynamics of each region and country in which proliferation occurs are usually unique and do not lend themselves to
comparisons'.[68] More fundamentally, the administration argued that
once the North Korean officials became enmeshed in implementing
the deal, and received outside technical assistance to construct and
operate the LWR systems, so the process would 'accelerate a series of
political changes there that are already underway'. Critics promptly
countered that the provision of vast amounts of oil could simply bolster the struggling economy of North Korea and prolong the longevity
of its political regime.[69]

Arguably this controversy might have been less intense had the Clinton administration either desisted from its absolutist rhetoric or accepted the consequences of trying to uphold it. Bob Galluci, Assistant Secretary for Politico-Military Affairs, State Department, set high expectations: 'if the North Korean situation is not dealt with properly', he declared, 'there will be a weakening of the barriers against the proliferation of nuclear weapons.'[70] As spokesmen diluted this rhetoric, with Perry arguing in April 1994 that US policy only sought 'to try to keep North Korea from getting a significant nuclear-weapon capability',[71] so critics claimed that the costs of pursuing the absolutist objective, not merely for the United States but also for its regional allies, had proved too high. Ultimately the accord constituted a pragmatic response to this dilemma, effectively postponing a resolution of the crisis[72] while not letting it deteriorate further, and avoiding the less palatable options of sanctions or war. Nevertheless, a price was paid beyond the economic inducements paid to Pyongyang. If proliferants did not know about the photographic capacities of US LACROSSE satellites with their radar-imaging sensors able to see through clouds, the precision of isotopic analysis in detecting levels of americium present in samples of plutonium, and the difficulty of concealing nuclear waste, they do now.[73] The exclusive focus upon the nuclear programme not only accorded it unprecedented diplomatic leverage but also left North Korea free to continue developing other aspects of its WMD capabilities (including a diverse stockpile of CW agents, possibly in the region of 1,000 to 5,000 tons, and an active BW programme) as well as a burgeoning arsenal of ballistic missiles.[74] Nor were US suspicions eased by North Korea honouring the accord in its early years, as the North retained the expertise and key nuclear technology to restart the programme, should it decide to do so. In March 1994, the DIA anticipated these lingering doubts: 'Based on North Korean actions to date, the DIA assesses that Pyongyang will continue its nuclear weapon program despite any agreements it signs to the contrary.'[75]

Meanwhile the UNSCOM inspectors revealed ever more about the scale and diversity of the Iraqi WMD and ballistic missile capabilities. Constituted under the terms of UN Security Council Resolution 687, and originally headed by the Swedish diplomat, Ambassador Ekéus, UNSCOM evolved into a 200 strong body with a headquarters in New York, a permanent Monitoring and Verification Centre in Baghdad, and a field office in Bahrain. It was accorded unprecedented rights of entry and exit, access to any site or facility, rights to request, receive, examine and copy any record, the right to designate any site for inspection, the right to install monitoring equipment, take and analyse samples, and the right to destroy or render harmless any items specified under the terms of Resolution 687. These items included all chemical and biological weapons, stocks of agents, related subsystems and components, research, development, support and manufacturing facilities; all ballistic missiles with a range in excess of 150 kilometres; and nuclear weapon facilities. UNSCOM was also required to monitor Iraq's compliance with its undertaking 'not to use, develop, construct or acquire any of the items specified'. To support its activities, UNSCOM drew initially upon frozen Iraqi assets under Resolution 778 and enjoyed lavish aerial support (two C-160 Transall aircraft for purposes of transportation in and out of Iraq; three CH-53 helicopters to facilitate rapid transportation of expert teams, vehicles and equipment within Iraq, and the lease of an American U-2 aircraft for aerial surveillance). Above all, UNSCOM was a subsidiary organ of the Security Council, and initially benefited from the political support of the Council, especially the United States and the United Kingdom (see Chapter 6 on the subsequent erosion of political unity within the Council).[76]

By February 1998, UNSCOM had destroyed or supervised the destruction of 38,537 CW munitions (some 28,000 filled and the rest empty); 480,000 litres of CW agents; 3,000 tonnes of CW precursors; the 'supergun' as well as its components and propellant; the Al Hakam BW production facility; and 48 operational SCUD-type missiles, 28 operational fixed launch pads (and another 32 under construction), six mobile launchers, and 30 chemical and 18 conventional warheads (while verifying the Iraqi destruction of 83 SCUD-type missiles and nine mobile launchers).[77] UNSCOM and IAEA inspectors discovered that Iraq's nuclear weapon activities were larger than expected (involving some 20,000 employees at 25 major sites), better funded (some $8 to $10 billion over a decade), and more advanced (including a crash programme launched after the invasion of Kuwait to build an implosion-type atomic bomb). On the basis of the evidence uncovered, estimates of how close Iraq was to producing a bomb vary considerably (ranging from 12 to 18 months from the end of the Gulf War to five years), but the effort was more diverse than anticipated, involving five programmes to 1990, with two main ones – a gas centrifuge enrichment process and a slower, less efficient Electro-Magnetic Isotopic Separation (EMIS). The CIA only knew of the former. The IAEA inspectors discovered the calutrons acquired for the EMIS at a facility near Baghdad.[78]

Iraqi WMD programmes differed in many respects from similar programmes that had been developed in the West. Conspicuous containment facilities, traditionally associated with offensive BW programmes, were missing, and much less attention was paid to the safety of workers in the production plants or to the local environment.[79] Iraq had not accumulated vast stocks of filled munitions, with agents chosen for their long-term stability in storage. Its CW programme was designed to fill and distribute such weapons for immediate use on the battlefield: as Brad Roberts observed, 'it was a classical surge capability, held in reserve by a state intending to use weapons not to deter but to fight and win'.[80] Iraq had experimented, too, with different agents and combinations of agents, notably GF, a semi-persistent nerve agent, to be used in a binary warhead,[81] Agent 15, a mental incapacitant (according to British reports),[82] and aflatoxin, noted for its induction of liver cancers.[83] Iraq had a much more advanced CW programme than many expected, having developed prototypes of binary weapons, flight-tested long-range missiles with chemical warheads, and developed a capacity to produce VX on 'an industrial scale'. Although Iraq claimed that the VX programme had failed, and that only 3.9 tonnes of VX could be produced between 1988 and 1990 without any VX weaponization, UNSCOM reported that Iraq had built a production capacity, imported 750 tonnes of VX precursors, and produced a further 55 tonnes indigenously, probably producing VX 'in quantity'. In 1998, too, there was evidence that Iraq may have loaded VX into some missile warheads (at least from the samples analysed in a US laboratory).[84] Finally, far from relying upon the importation of 818 SCUDs from the Soviet Union, Iraq had also undertaken the indigenous production of SCUD-type missiles, so complicating any assessment of its overall capability.[85] All these revelations testified to the capacity of an oil-rich state to amass a wide-ranging WMD programme and do so in a highly distinctive manner.

In uncovering this evidence, UNSCOM benefited from an unprecedented level of sharing of national intelligence information and techniques (and particularly from Israel, by July 1995, when the inspectors were seeking to penetrate the Iraqi concealment efforts). From the first inspection, UNSCOM inspectors had data from national technical means, the support of data-collection techniques and analytical capabilities, and later clues about Iraqi arms programmes passed on from human intelligence sources. Under Resolution 707 (August 1991), they gained evidence from aerial surveillance, notably from the leased U-2 aircraft, equipped with sensors, flying missions over Iraq.[86] Despite all these assets and seven years of investigations, UNSCOM (and a team of BW experts) remained unsatisfied with the purportedly 'full, final and complete' disclosures of Iraq.[87]

In particular UNSCOM struggled to uncover Iraq's BW programme, initially reporting a lack of any conclusive evidence of weaponization on 25 October 1991 – a finding immediately challenged by US government sources.[88] UNSCOM inspectors visited numerous sites over the period from 1991 to 1994, becoming increasingly suspicious of the facilities at Al Hakam, especially its location, layout of buildings, and the continued association of Dr Rahib Taha, who had formerly worked at Al Muthana (the central location of Iraq's CW programme and the original base for the BW programme). Interviews with Iraqi personnel associated with the BW activities (then designated as 'defensive') gave leads to overseas suppliers, and information from the suppliers revealed vast imports of so-called growth media (39 tonnes in 1988 alone, far in excess of Iraq's medical requirements), all of which had reportedly been lost in areas overrun by rioting after the Gulf War. Eventually on 1 July 1995 Iraq conceded that it had an offensive BW programme, that large quantities of bulk agent had been produced, and that Al Hakam was intended as a BW production facility. UNSCOM, though, had to rely on the fortuitous defection of Saddam's son-in-law, Lieutenant-General Hussein Kamel Hassan, a former Minister of Defence and Director of the Military Industrial Commission, before Iraq conceded that it had embarked on a far larger BW programme at Al Muthana in 1985, including weaponization, and that it had a crash nuclear programme during the Gulf War. To pre-empt Kamel, Iraqi authorities took Ekéus to a chicken farm where they gave him 140 cartons, containing some 680,000 pages of documents, computer disks, videotapes and other materials which they had 'just discovered'.[89]

While some commentators claim that this record vindicated the determination of the inspectors and the value of on-site inspections,[90] others emphasised that UNSCOM inspectors, despite all their advantages, only found circumstantial evidence and relied upon luck to secure their breakthrough.[91] Dr Robert Kadlec, a Pentagon official, and his associates understandably claim that 'The UNSCOM experience with Iraq raises questions about the effectiveness of various measures, no matter how intrusive, to conclusively detect or verify the existence of prohibited activities.'[92] In June 1996 Stephen Black, UNSCOM's historian, admitted that the biological investigators 'have, even after the admissions by Iraq and despite more than 35 inspections, never seen a filled BW weapon or bulk agent'.[93] If inspection successes derived from various factors, including information from Iraqi sources,[94] the key requirement, as both Ekéus and Hans Blix, director of the IAEA, conceded, was intelligence: 'knowledge of *where to inspect*', wrote Blix, was 'the fundamental condition for launching a successful surprise inspection'.[95] Similarly, Ekéus admitted that without knowledge of where to sample, the sampling domain could not be narrowed, and so the costs of sampling in monetary and political terms, even under the UNSCOM remit, would have become 'prohibitive'.[96]

More specifically, the process revealed the determination of the Iraqi regime to preserve as much as possible of its WMD capabilities. Those US officials, who claimed that the combination of a tight economic embargo and virtual political isolation would compel Iraqi compliance,[97] reckoned without Saddam's longevity and determination, especially when he realised that the price of obstruction would only involve the resumption of air strikes (as launched in January 1993 and in Operation Desert Fox, 17–19 December 1998). Meanwhile Iraq supplied documentation replete with gaps and inconsistencies, harassed and delayed teams of inspectors, removed or destroyed documentation at various sites, challenged the rights of access in a series of 'cheat and retreat' manoeuvres, and reportedly developed facilities for moving equipment and components from site to site. Iraqi obstruction, if far from completely systematic, was coupled with assistance in some areas and with numerous 'full, final and complete' reports, doubtless intended to give the appearance of co-operation. The whole exercise sought to sap the will of the inspectors, frustrate the monitoring process, split the wartime coalition, and secure the removal of sanctions.[98]

Saddam's behaviour testified to how much his regime valued its WMD capabilities, including a willingness to forego estimated earnings from oil exports of some $15 billion a year (if sanctions had been lifted). If given the opportunity, Iraq would probably resume its WMD programmes; it retains the technical expertise to do so, including the requisite corps of scientists, engineers and technicians, and, despite its massive debts, has the world's third largest reserves of oil. UNSCOM had sought to curb Saddam's ambitions by imposing long-term monitoring upon designated sites (the Ongoing Monitoring and Verification plan).[99] Whether this plan, or some variant of it, survives Operation Desert Fox and the subsequent bombing of Iraq, or the great powers rely primarily upon sanctions and the threat of further aerial strikes will depend upon the political leadership of the United States and the support of resolute allies.

3
Political Leadership and Nonproliferation

Whatever the response to proliferation, political leadership is of the essence. In rather different ways both the Bush and the Clinton administrations sought to provide this leadership. By speeches, briefings to Congress, the press and allies, diplomatic démarches, bilateral and multilateral diplomacy, they endeavoured to raise awareness about the dimensions and dangers of proliferation, and the need to take collective action to arrest its development. Other than in crises (and sometimes even during crises) both experienced difficulties, domestically and internationally, in focusing attention, mustering support, and securing common agreement upon the salience of the specific issues and the mode of response. Although the United States retained an ability to project and use overwhelming conventional military power around the globe, proliferation persisted and posed difficulties for successive administrations. These difficulties derived partly from the political and economic circumstances of the United States after the Cold War, partly from the changing nature of inter-state relations, and partly from perceptions about the significance of proliferation and the possibilities of conflict in the post-Cold War era. While these issues would be earnestly debated throughout the early years of the Clinton administration, the practical impact and political challenges of proliferation would be revealed all too clearly by the nuclear testing of India and Pakistan in May 1998.

Under the Bush administration US foreign policy was based upon a prudent, pragmatic, and non-ideological approach, aimed at preserving the *status quo* where appropriate to do so, and responding to a series of crises in Europe, the Middle East and the former Soviet Union with skilled and careful management. As Maureen Dowd and Thomas Friedman argued, Bush and his Secretary of State, Baker, relied on their instincts to do the 'correct thing', without preparing any overarching justification or sense of direction for the policy process.[1] Only during Operation Desert Shield did Bush promote the concept of a 'new world order', envisaging nations moving towards an 'historic period of coop- eration' to support the rule of law and 'stand up to aggression', with 'America and the world' defending 'common vital interests'. As he informed Congress on 11 September 1990, 'Our role is to help our friends in their own self-defense, and, something else, to curb the pro- liferation of chemical, biological, ballistic, and, above all, nuclear tech- nologies.'[2] On 1 October 1990, in addressing the UN General Assembly, he described a similar vision of 'a new partnership of nations that tran- scends the Cold War', one based on 'consultation, cooperation and col- lective action', an equitable sharing of costs and commitment, and one that had a 'real possibility of using the United Nations as it was designed – as a center for international collective security'. The goals were to increase democracy, prosperity and peace, and at the same time reduce arms, particularly chemical weapons. He wanted to 'banish these terrible weapons from the face of the Earth' and advocated a redoubling of 'our efforts to stem the spread of nuclear weapons, bio- logical weapons, and the ballistic missiles that can rain destruction upon distant peoples'.[3] As Bush and other spokesmen continued to amplify these themes after the diplomatic and military triumphs of the Gulf War,[4] Charles Krauthammer advanced the thesis that America's 'unipolar moment' had arrived. The United States, he argued, had proved itself as 'the unchallenged superpower' whose role had been utterly decisive in the Gulf War. US 'military, diplomatic, political and economic assets', he added, 'enabled it to be a decisive player in any conflict in whatever part of the world it chooses to involve itself'. US leadership, though burdensome economically, was a necessity as the great challenge of the post-Cold War world was 'the emergence of a new strategic environment marked by the proliferation of weapons of mass destruction'. In his view, this constituted the 'greatest single threat to world security', one which made 'a new international order not an imperial dream or a Wilsonian fantasy but a matter of sheerest prudence'.[5]

Within the year, such assertions sounded distinctly jaded. As David Gergen observed, few outside the White House even alluded to a 'new world order', 'unless in jest'. American opinion, obsessed with the eco- nomic recession, had turned increasingly pessimistic, inward, and nationalistic by the end of 1991.[6] Critics now depicted the Gulf War as a 'hollow victory' since Saddam, whom Bush had denounced as 'a dictator worse than Hitler', remained in office, able to suppress internal dissent (prompting relief efforts on behalf of the Kurds), obstruct UN inspectors, and remain as a potential menace to his neighbours. While the administration appeared reluctant to act over the deteriorating situation in the former Yugoslavia, it seemed embroiled in the Gulf, signing a ten-year bilateral security accord with Kuwait in September 1991 and enforcing 'no-fly zones' over parts of Iraqi air space. Although American military pre-eminence was unquestioned, the world did not seem more orderly as the Soviet Union disintegrated and regional or intra-state conflicts persisted, reflecting a resurgence of ethnic and nationalistic tensions. Gergen described the Bush administration, then preoccupied with minimising the risk of nuclear proliferation spreading from the former Soviet Union, as 'far more adept at cleaning up the debris of an old world than building the framework of the new'.[7]

The 'new world order' had had some resonance when facing the challenge of overt aggression in an oil-rich region of the world, but James Baker would later admit that the administration had failed to project 'a single coherent, consistent rationale' for US policy:

> Our public pronouncements had ranged from the principled to the esoteric. At times we talked of standing up to aggression and creating a new world order. At others we called Saddam a new Hitler and cited the threat to global stability from rising oil prices.[8]

In mustering a broad base of international support, the administration had proffered a wide range of inducements (or ensured that others did so). It had muted its criticisms of particular states, especially China, with its power of veto on the Security Council, and Syria as a radical member of the anti-Iraq coalition (not to mention turning a blind eye to the human-rights abuses and lack of democracy in Kuwait and Saudi Arabia). Several known proliferants, such as Pakistan and Syria, joined the coalition out of their own interests and evinced little support for the more sweeping political aims of US rhetoric. Just as the widely publicised and feared use of weapons of mass destruction never occurred during the war, so the hopes for a radical solution to the region's problems, as embodied in the 'Damascus Declaration' of 6 March 1991, failed to materialise. All the hopes of the Bush administration that Arab states would assume responsibility for local security, that they would promote the control of weapons of mass destruction within the Middle East, that they would create a regional development bank for the benefit of the poorer areas within the region, and that they would make renewed endeavours to resolve the Arab–Israeli dispute on the basis of UN Security Council Resolutions 242 and 338 proved still-born.[9]

More substantively the Bush administration failed to think through the implications of the 'new world order' and adapt them to the changing nature of international relations. As Joseph Nye observed, the concept had not taken account of the more diverse sources of international conflict in the post-Cold War era, the impact of transnational developments in communications and transportation (so enhancing the rapidity with which human-rights violations and mass suffering could be reported on television), and the loss of Soviet technological controls and influence over its client states. In an era which was neither bipolar nor unipolar (other than in the US military supremacy) nor multipolar (in the sense of the power arrangements before the Second World War), the world order was, as Nye remarked, *sui generis*. Moreover it was still evolving, both institutionally and regionally, but seemed to presume a growing degree of 'multilevel interdependence' in the interaction and use of political, economic and military power.[10] Notwithstanding these changes, Brent Scowcroft, Bush's national security adviser, argued that the United States had to lead. He maintained that no other power or organization could emulate its capacity for political, economic and military intervention across the globe, and that the international community had to remain vigilant lest any 'early failures' set unfortunate precedents and encourage the flouting of 'world order'. Setting precedents, though, required common understandings of how recent international events had been resolved; "followers" who were willing to act in support of the "leading" state (which would prove far from clear during much of the Bosnian crisis or the Gulf crisis of February 1998); and a willingness to act in circumstances other than a clear-cut case of aggression across international borders.[11] Any major initiatives in US foreign policy would also require domestic support, and this was patently lacking as Bush stumbled towards electoral disaster in 1992. Less dramatic achievements, such as the consummation of a Chemical Weapons Convention in September 1992, which had been strongly supported by the president himself,[12] did little, if anything, to arrest his sliding popularity.

Understandably, the incoming Clinton administration sought to respond to the prevailing national mood and accord a higher priority to the domestic agenda (until the Democrats lost control of the Congress in the elections of November 1994). Foreign policy remained a largely secondary concern, although it was linked to domestic priorities by an emphasis on 'commercial diplomacy' – a strategy of helping American companies to open foreign markets, thereby spreading prosperity at home and American ideas and values abroad. When Clinton alluded to nonproliferation as 'one of our nation's highest priorities' in his address to the UN General Assembly on 27 September 1993, he claimed that it would be woven into relationships with all other states and institutions. He indicated that new initiatives would be pursued in attempts to control (or even ban) the production of materials for nuclear weapons and seek a comprehensive nuclear test ban. He also advocated the ratification of the Chemical Weapons Convention; the strengthening of the Biological and Toxin Weapons Convention by opening all biological activities to 'international scrutiny'; and the strengthening of the Missile Technology Control Regime by transforming it from an agreement of 23 nations to 'a set of rules that can command universal adherence'.[13]

This was neither a complete list of aims (the indefinite extension of the NPT in 1995 would be added to it) nor merely a declaratory policy. The US governmental machine would be organised to support the policy, with the National Security Council acting as the 'hub' of nonproliferation policy. While the State Department, acting in conjunction with ACDA and the Energy Department, represented US nonproliferation interests to other states, the Pentagon seized the opportunity to create a counterproliferation policy – encompassing a reduction of the former Soviet threat, force modernisation, improved defences, and operational planning. It vested responsibility in an Assistant Secretary of Defense for Nuclear Security and Counterproliferation (a title that later reverted to its original name, Assistant Secretary of Defense for International Security Policy), and later devised a Counterproliferation Concept Plan, tasking regional commanders-in-chief to develop operational plans for counterproliferation, and established a Counterproliferation Council to monitor the training, exercising and equipping of US forces for this mission (see Chapter 7). The Department of Energy provided expertise on nuclear issues, assisted in administering Nunn-Lugar-type programmes (as did the Pentagon), utilised its Nonproliferation Research Development programme to develop critical technologies for detecting nuclear production and monitoring nuclear agreements, and held responsibility for the Nuclear Emergency Search Team (NEST). The Department of Commerce monitored the licensing of dual-use exports, while the Department of the Treasury enforced export controls through the US Customs Service and monitored US embargoes through its Office of Foreign Assets Control. The CIA expanded the Nonproliferation Center established by Gates to coordinate the intelligence aspects of nonproliferation, facilitate more integrated support for the Pentagon's counterproliferation policy, and support the activities of the law enforcement agencies. The CIA also launched several programmes to enhance its technical capacity to 'detect WMD activities at significantly longer ranges...'. ACDA retained responsibility for nonproliferation diplomacy, including the extension of the NPT and the negotiating of other agreements. Several interagency working groups were to coordinate the various responsibilities for nonproliferation policy.[14]

To pursue its policies, the Clinton administration sought to exploit the international opportunities of the post-Cold War world. It had little desire to assume the mantle of the "world's policeman" and any inclinations in this direction were swiftly doused by the disastrous intervention in Somalia. However salutary in its own terms, this enterprise also lowered expectations about the peace-enforcement capacities of the UN.[15] More realistically, the Clinton administration sought to engage the support of friends, allies (notably in NATO) and major powers (the G-7 and Russia, later known as the G-8) to correlate policies with like-minded states, promote issues of immediate concern and seek support for US initiatives. Successive Defense Secretaries recognised that whether the US was involved in preventing threats from arising, or in deterring (and, if necessary, defeating) those threats that did arise, close cooperation with American friends and allies was a prerequisite for US policy. In trying to curb the proliferation of NBC weapons, argued William Cohen, 'the United States must garner the cooperation of other nations that have access to NBC technology and materials'.[16]

The circumstances seemed increasingly propitious for these bilateral and multilateral endeavours: as communist and totalitarian regimes collapsed, so the US found that it could promote its nonproliferation agenda among an increasing number of democracies – regimes thought to be more reliable than other forms of government as partners in trade and diplomacy, and less likely to threaten the peace. Strobe Talbott, Deputy Secretary of State, recalled that when Bill Clinton was campaigning for the presidency in 1992 he had spoken of the beneficial effect that democracy had upon international life, and that after his election the promotion of democracy became a key principle in the conduct of US foreign policy. Despite criticisms from "realists" in the international relations fraternity, Talbott insisted that the approach remained valid: democracies, he claimed, 'are demonstrably more likely to maintain their international commitments, less likely to engage in terrorism or wreak environmental damage, and less likely to make war on each other'.[17]

After four years of endeavour Clinton officials would maintain that this new approach had proved immensely productive. Apart from the achievements in Russia, the NIS and North Korea, Lynn E. Davis, Undersecretary of State for Arms Control and International Security Affairs, would maintain that the US had a litany of 'important accomplishments'. These included the indefinite extension of the NPT in 1995 without conditions, sustained support for UNSCOM, agreement at the Moscow summit (April 1996) to support international efforts to strengthen the IAEA safeguards, and the launching of a multilateral programme to combat nuclear smuggling involving the G-7 countries, Russia and the Ukraine. She also implied that the US deserved credit for the acceptance by 'Russia, Brazil, Argentina, South Africa, South Korea, and Ukraine' of 'international guidelines preventing the spread of missiles and missile technologies'.[18] Membership of the export control regimes had expanded dramatically: by March 1997, there were 34 members in the Nuclear Suppliers' Group, 28 in the MTCR and 30 in the Australia Group.[19] US influence may be difficult to evaluate, but there were many gains for nonproliferation in the early 1990s – both before and during the Clinton administration. South African officials, though, claimed that US pressure was counterproductive in the process of abandoning its nuclear weapons programme, and that the newly elected government of F.W. de Klerk sought to normalise South Africa's external relations (in November 1989) after the collapse of Communism and the withdrawal of Cuban forces from Angola. Domestic political, economic and regional considerations were also critical in the decisions of Argentina and Brazil to adhere to the NPT.[20]

Yet reports of proliferation persisted. Generalised hopes that the spread of democracy and economic interdependence would increasingly inculcate the notion that military conflict was becoming outmoded and unacceptable had less resonance in the developing world, where most of the wars since 1945 have occurred. Many of the factors that contributed to previous wars remained – disputes over unsettled boundaries, economic inequalities, ethnic and communal divisions, repressive policies, and the widespread availability of arms. As Robert L. Rothstein noted, the evidence about the impact of democracy upon a propensity for conflict is debatable, and even assumptions about the relative lack of conflict between democracies cannot easily be applied to the weaker and unstable democracies of the developing world.[21] Some of the more established democracies in the developing world, notably India and Israel, are among the leading proliferants. Indian voters not only voted in huge numbers for the Hindu fundamentalist party, Bharatiya Janata Party (BJP), in 1998 but also strongly supported the coalition government of Atal Behari Vajpayee when it detonated nuclear explosions on 11 and 13 May 1998 (in a survey of six Indian cities, including Delhi and Bombay, 82% of the respondents supported India having nuclear weapons).[22]

If democratic credentials, or the lack of them, are an imperfect means of providing a focus for nonproliferation policy, the concept of a "rogue" state gained favour during the Clinton administration. ' "Rogue" regimes', argued Congressman Doug Bereuter, 'are those that have no commitment to the existing international order. "Rogue Regimes" play by their own rules. Their behaviour is difficult to predict and hard to deter.'[23] Although there was never a definitive list of such regimes, Iran, Iraq, Libya, North Korea, Cuba, Syria, Serbia, the Sudan, and perhaps Burma have all been described as "rogue" states. Iran and Iraq had already been targeted under Congressional legislation in the Iran–Iraq Arms Nonproliferation Act of 1992, which declared the opposition of the United States to any arms transfer that would assist Iran or Iraq to acquire nuclear, chemical, biological or advanced conventional weapons. It also required the President to impose sanctions on any person or foreign government engaged in such transfers (later amended by the 104th Congress to encompass all transfers contributing to the development of weapons of mass destruction). "Rogue" states were described as on the periphery of the international system, either unwilling to abide by international norms or with a record of sponsoring terrorism or, in the case of Iran, Iraq, Libya and North Korea, actively seeking a WMD capability.[24]

These descriptions, though, were hardly all encompassing. However provocative, repressive or unpredictable, the leaders of these states could act in a rational, if not error-free, manner. They could calculate their policies or initiatives in accordance with known facts, interests and external constraints, and some have assisted or traded with other proliferants.[25] The categorisation was entirely subjective – an American "rogue" could be a valuable customer or a strategic ally to another state – and the American response to 'roguish' behaviour was hardly a model of consistency. Although the Clinton administration repeatedly protested over Russian nuclear and missile co-operation with certain states, primarily Iran (and particularly over the construction of a thousand megawatt reactor at the Bushehr complex), it opposed the imposition of sanctions on Russia. Whereas Russia maintained that such a sale is perfectly legitimate as the reactor would be placed under IAEA safeguards, US officials claimed that the sale would enhance the training and expertise of Iranian technicians, moving them up the 'nuclear learning curve'.[26] Spokesmen for the Clinton administration justified the maintenance of diplomatic contacts with Russia as a means of constraining the scope of the Bushehr reactor, assisting Russia in the construction of an export control system, and facilitating Russian adherence to various nonproliferation regimes (joining the MTCR in 1995 and both the Wassenaar Arrangement and the Comprehensive Test Ban Treaty (CTBT) in 1996). Despite these developments and several pledges on nonproliferation by Russian leaders, the Clinton administration had to cope with embarrassing revelations of continuing sales of Russian missile components, missile-testing technology and further nuclear assistance to Iran, as well as the sale of two nuclear reactors to India in the wake of the Indian nuclear tests.[27]

The "rogue" concept may also be too restrictive and self-serving (inasmuch as it excludes regimes with which the US government wished to maintain a policy of constructive engagement). As Gary Milhollin argues, the "rogue" listing ignores several known proliferators, including China, whose exporting policy has assisted the WMD programmes of several states. During the 1990s China sold 34 M-11 ballistic missiles to Pakistan, and nuclear and missile technology, precursors and equipment usable in the production of chemical and biological weapons and advanced conventional weapons (notably the C-802 anti-ship cruise missile) to Iran.[28] The United States briefly imposed sanctions on China for its missile-related exports to Pakistan in 1991 and 1993, but then lifted them in October 1994 when China stated that it would abide by the guidelines and parameters of the MTCR. Thereafter the Clinton administration sought a 'constructive, stable, and mutually beneficial' relationship with China, preferring to raise concerns about proliferation in private démarches. When China sold some 5,000 custom-built ring magnets to Pakistan for $70,000 in 1995, which Pakistan then installed in centrifuges at an uninspected facility designed to enrich uranium for nuclear weapons, the Clinton administration claimed that 'there was an insufficient basis to determine that central Chinese governmental authorities knew in advance of the transfer or approved it'.[29] By refining the definition of "roguish" behaviour, the State Department avoided recommending the imposition of sanctions, as required under various acts of Congress. Milhollin understandably observed that 'you should not make a rogue stronger while he is still a rogue and you do not stop a rogue from being a rogue by treating him like a non-rogue'.[30]

All this depends on the priority accorded to the curbing of proliferation, and its relative importance compared with other goals in foreign policy. If other goals take precedence, and if the pursuit of these goals fails to inhibit proliferation, then the order of priorities will be criticised by those who regard nonproliferation as the prime consideration. It is also clear that the State Department drew distinctions between the intentions and actions of various "rogue" states. It questioned whether some states, irrespective of their professed intentions, could exercise sufficient control over the export of sensitive goods and technologies from their countries. It also justified the US policy of offering some states (not only North Korea but also Russia) large financial inducements to refrain from breaking their international commitments.[31] By this approach, it hardly enhanced the prospects of securing a clear, coordinated and consistent support for US policy.

The repercussions were abundantly clear at the G-8 summit which met in Birmingham within days of India's nuclear tests of 11 and 13 May 1998. American calls for collective sanctions foundered, and the communiqué merely condemned India's nuclear tests, urged restraint on India's neighbours, and called on India and Pakistan to adhere unconditionally to the NPT and the CTBT. This was described by Robin Cook, Britain's Foreign Secretary, as a point of 'maximum unity', but it was more aptly regarded by Shamshad Ahmad, secretary of Pakistan's foreign ministry, as 'a very weak response'.[32] Ironically, only a month after joining in the condemnation of India for nuclear testing, Russia initialled an agreement in New Delhi (20 June 1998) to provide India with two 1,000-megawatt nuclear reactors. Although the deal, worth $2.6 billion, involved only commercial plant, it was another embarrassment for the Clinton administration, especially as the president chose to veto a Congressional bill on 23 June 1998 to impose sanctions on Russia for selling missile technology to Iran. In dealing with Russia on matters of trade and proliferation, the Clinton administration clearly preferred to rely on diplomatic endeavours.[33]

Irrespective of the way in which proliferant regimes are characterised, they are likely to be relatively small nations (apart from India and China): Judge Webster once described proliferation as 'a small nation's response'.[34] If this judgment applied during the Cold War, it was even more applicable after the Gulf War in which the United States had projected its formidable power to a distant part of the globe, organised an international coalition, dominated the conflict with its conventional military might, and did so in the absence of any viable alternative power (with the then Soviet Union in decline, and neither Germany nor Japan possessing the full range of power resources to emulate or compete with the United States). Admittedly the Gulf War was undertaken with an unrepeatable use of Cold War resources: by 1999, US defence forces were about one third smaller than they were in 1988, and in real terms the US defence budget was about 40% less than it was in 1988. In 1995 General John M. Shalikashvili, as Chairman of the Joint Chiefs of Staff, maintained that the US global strategy was now focused on regional threats, and that US forces were repositioned, with equipment and war stocks being aligned to support a new global power projection strategy. US forces were being prepared for joint oper-ations, and they would continue to exploit the doctrinal and techno-logical innovations displayed in the Gulf. He claimed that the US retained the ability 'to fight and win two, nearly simultaneous, major regional conflicts':

> Our improving capabilities to fight at night and in poor weather, and our dominance in space that ensures that our commanders have extraordinary situational awareness, are giving our forces the ability to drive the tempo and depth of battle beyond the endurance and capability of any potential enemy.[35]

If few disputed the pertinence of this assessment for the mid-1990s, some longer term trends were worrying. As a result of diminishing threat perceptions, Lieutenant-General James R. Clapper (Director, DIA) forecast that there would be a further decline in levels of defence readiness and the size of military forces. If this trend applied to most major military powers (other than China), so possibly reducing the likelihood of an imminent challenge to the US from a well-trained and well-equipped major regional aggressor, it did not preclude a recur-rence of ethnic, religious and sectarian violence both within countries and across borders. He feared that 'we could see a reversal in many of the gains of the last several years'.[36] Less apocalyptic, but possibly even more serious would be the long-term erosion of confidence in US secu-rity guarantees – the same guarantees that have inhibited many of the technologically-capable friends and allies of the United States from developing their own WMD capabilities.[37]

In the near term, though, the imbalance of conventional forces remains tilted heavily in favour of the United States, so underpinning its super power status. The collapse of the Soviet Union has removed not only a major potential adversary, with numerous clients in the developing world, but also a principal supplier of arms, expertise and military training. As arms transfers from Russia to the developing world have plummeted by 1997 to a tenth of what they were a decade ago, armies that were heavily dependent on the former Soviet Union have seen much of their equipment become increasingly obsolescent. While India has responded to this predicament by embarking on a long-term drive for military self-sufficiency,[38] other states face more profound dilemmas, notably North Korea with its lack of hard currency and Iraq with the continuing burden of international sanctions. As conventional arms become increasingly expensive, so weapons of mass destruction may seem increasingly attractive. They will not necessarily become a means of "equalising" or defeating a powerful regional enemy, still less a US-led intervention force, but could possibly serve as a deterrent, raising the costs and risks of conflict and complicating the task of forming and maintaining hostile coalitions against the state concerned. General Krishnaswami Sundarji, India's former Chief of Army Staff, envisaged the use of a nuclear preparedness as a bulwark against 'any ill-conceived US plan of pressurising or bullying India or the region'.[39] By seeking such capabilities, smaller countries would hope to exert political leverage and complicate the ability of US and allied forces to operate in particular regions.[40]

Moving down this path, however, is neither a cost- nor risk-free option for smaller states. Financial costs could prove considerable not merely in the research and development stages (and Iraq's nuclear programme proved extremely expensive) but also in moving beyond a minimal capability to create a significant arsenal of weapons, an effective means of delivering them, a survivable base of operations, and a command and control system. These costs are likely to be compounded by indirect costs (if involved a clandestine programme), political and economic costs (if a programme was detected and sanctions incurred), and military costs (if the programme stimulated a regional arms race or tempted a neighbour into launching a pre-emptive strike). Even if a developing state wished to persevere along the path of proliferation, it might have to consider whether its military could absorb, assimilate and integrate the new technology (a task which was not beyond Iraq at least in its development of a chemical weapons capability). Finally, it would certainly have to consider whether it would be prudent to concentrate a significant proportion of its defence resources on the accretion of military capabilities whose potential value might prove questionable.[41] Obviously such calculations will vary from state to state, or from government to government within the same state, but much will depend upon the proliferant's view of the international system.

If smaller states shared the belief of Tariq Aziz that American predominance was merely a passing phenomenon, then they would be tempted to avoid an immediate challenge to the existing international order (unless they felt that they had no option, as Pakistan apparently did following the Indian nuclear tests) and await evidence of the American decline. Tariq Aziz was convinced that this decline would occur. He was convinced that the US budget and trade deficits of the early 1990s

> constitute the gravest internal threat to American military power and superior political posture. The world has never seen an empire capable of maintaining military and political hegemony without a firm and stable financial base.[42]

If uncannily reminiscent of the debates about the purported decline of American power in the 1980s, and hardly apposite by the late 1990s when the US budget had moved into surplus, these arguments almost certainly reflected a perception of the United States during Gulf War. The lobbying of friends and allies for financial support, multilateral backing (to provide domestic and international legitimacy), regional bases, overflight rights, and logistical support hardly demonstrated an unbridled degree of self-confidence and self-sufficiency. It indicated that future interventions, at least outside central America, were likely to be conducted on an international or at least bilateral basis (other than in limited punitive strikes).[43]

However, forecasters of US decline have rarely indicated that it was a short-term probability (and they have doubtless adjusted their forecasts to take account of the US economic recovery of the mid-1990s and the economic difficulties of some states in East Asia). Meanwhile small states, if bent upon acquiring a covert WMD capability, cannot afford any precipitate clash with the United States. They have had to reassure external powers and avoid actions that might provoke international action, especially one including US military involvement. Determining the precise threshold which might trigger such intervention was, as Patrick Garrity argues, a major problem for smaller regional powers, inducing an understandable caution in the wake of the Gulf War and only limited probes to determine where the 'red lines' exist.[44] States had not merely to eschew deliberate acts of provocation and international isolation but they also had to avoid a hostile international response to any revelations about their covert activities.

Interventions, though, are neither cost-free undertakings nor guaranteed to prove successful. Even if the intervening states possess a substantial military superiority, they might have difficulty in employing it successfully or in sustaining domestic or international support for their activities. Quite apart from the topographical differences from one war to another, the differing leaderships and resilience of opposing forces, and the relative degrees of national or vital interests involved, the outcomes may hinge on other forms of proliferation. As Henry Sokolski, a former Pentagon official, argued, the proliferation of conventional technologies – 'nonapocalyptic proliferation' in his terminology – could have a profound bearing upon the feasibility of some interventions. He emphasised the potential of conventional submarines operating in confined waters, unmanned air vehicles (UAVs) with their target accuracy greatly enhanced by satellite imagery services, and more robust command, control, communications and intelligence capabilities (including systems provided by civilian satellites). The prospect of slow, low-flying UAVs (carrying conventional or nonconventional ordnance) that could be precisely-targeted against fixed military assets, and operated in conjunction with more accurate ballistic missiles, could challenge to the 'already stressed US air defense systems'. All these capabilities raised questions about how the US and its allies might undertake military interventions in the future and added to the risks involved.[45]

Political leaders would doubtless take military advice in such circumstances, but even considering a military response over an issue involving proliferation *per se* might seem fanciful after the flaccid international response to the nuclear detonations of India and Pakistan. As the world's largest democracy, India could not be subjected to the sort of pressures that might be brought to bear on a smaller "rogue" state. Moreover, neither India nor Pakistan had broken any international agreements in conducting their explosions, but they had punctured the international norms that the Clinton administration had tried to erect through the CTBT. Only adopted in September 1996 after France and China had completed their nuclear-testing,[46] the treaty was not due to come into force until all 44-capable nuclear powers had ratified it. India voted against it in the United Nations General Assembly, and conducted its tests, so fulfilling the BJP's election pledge to 'exercise the option to induct nuclear weapons'. This testing of 'a fissile device, a low-yield device and a thermonuclear device' at the Pokhran range on 11 May 1998 occurred only a month after Pakistan had flight-tested its *Ghauri* missile with a range of 1,490 kilometers. The Indian test completely escaped the vigilance of the US intelligence agencies, prompting Senator Richard Shelby, chairman of the Senate Intelligence Committee, to describe it as the 'biggest failure of intelligence for a decade'.[47] Clinton's threat to impose sanctions, as required under American law, and his exhortations that India should desist from further tests and should sign the CTBT immediately and without conditions,[48] were promptly followed by another two tests by India on 13 May.

The fact that only a few states followed the American lead and imposed sanctions, with Japan, India's largest aid donor, only suspending its grants-in-aid, was not lost on New Delhi or Islamabad. Britain, France and Russia specifically refused to follow suit, relying in Britain's case upon diplomatic démarches and expressions of 'shock and dismay'.[49] Diplomatic attention switched to Pakistan whose prime minister, Nawaz Sharif, had informed the G-8 countries prior to their Birmingham summit that India's tests posed 'an immediate threat to our security'. Although Clinton secured only scant support from the other G-8 states, he mounted a major diplomatic offensive to prevent Pakistan from retaliating-in-kind. He despatched a high-level delegation, headed by Strobe Talbott, to Islamabad, urged China to use its influence, spoke repeatedly to Nawaz Sharif by telephone, and proffered a whole range of inducements (including the promised delivery of 28 F-16 aircraft that Pakistan had paid for but never received, an offer to try to remove the US constraints on economic and military aid, and an undertaking to seek the establishment of a new security relationship). After listening to Clinton Sharif reportedly replied, 'You have said all the right things, but the rest of the world is filing its fingernails.'[50] On 28 May, only hours after Clinton's last intervention, Pakistan detonated five nuclear explosions at the Chagai testing range in Baluchistan.

In announcing the tests, Nawaz Sharif claimed that Pakistan had been dragged into a nuclear arms race by India's actions and by the weakness of the international response to them. 'India', he stated, 'should have been condemned in the United Nations Security Council, but nothing was done.' He paid tribute to Pakistan's allies, particularly China, and urged his nation to unite and prepare for sacrifices in the face of imminent sanctions.[51] In effect, Pakistan had defied unremitting international pressure, placing its security concerns and its domestic pressures to respond in kind above exhortations from foreign governments. Although more vulnerable than India to external pressure as some 6% of its government spending is financed by foreign aid (compared with only 3.3% for India), Pakistan was already labouring under American sanctions and was unlikely to incur more severe penalties than those already imposed on India. While Clinton renewed his pleas to India and Pakistan to renounce further testing and sign the CTBT, doubts mounted over the likelihood of the US Senate ratifying the treaty following the intelligence debacle over the original tests. If the treaty was not verifiable, as sceptics argued, the US Senate was most unlikely to ratify it (and, on 13 October 1999, voted not to do so).[52]

Clinton's dilemmas stretched beyond the recalcitrance of the South Asian states, the lack of significant international support for America's response, and the limited diplomatic options at his command. Arguably his administration's policy of constructive engagement with China, imposing and later lifting limited sanctions over the export of missile technology to Pakistan, and failing to act over the Chinese export of ring magnets, may have fuelled India's fears of 'nuclear encirclement'. Atal Behari Vajpayee, the Indian Prime Minister, would claim that Pakistan's tests vindicated India's initiatives, proving that Pakistan had been pursuing a secret nuclear weapons programme, and that India faced a direct threat from China and Pakistan. He accused the former of having helped Pakistan to become a covert nuclear power, noting that India had fought both countries in the past 51 years and still had outstanding territorial and diplomatic disputes with them.[53] Moreover, the previous US efforts to impede India's nuclear testing in December 1995, when US officials revealed evidence of scientific and technical activity at the Pokhran test site from satellite reconnaissance, may have revealed sensitive information that India would use to disguise the testing programme in May 1998.[54] If correct, this would suggest that some exposures in the cause of preventing proliferation may only delay matters, and ultimately prove counterproductive and futile. Finally, intelligence failures of this magnitude raise questions about the viability of international nonproliferation regimes – and not merely the CTBT – that rely on intelligence surveillance to give timely warnings of covert activities. Unless states are confident that such activities can be detected, these regimes will hardly provide the deterrence and reassurance that their advocates and states parties expect.

However dismayed by events in South Asia, and by the response of friends and allies to the tests, the Clinton administration struggled to restore the credibility of its nonproliferation policy. Imposing sanctions with only limited international support, and continuing to denounce the actions on the Indian subcontinent, seemed a less than adequate response yet the administration cleaved to its nonproliferation assumptions. The South Asian tests, argued Secretary of State, Madeleine

Albright, far from discrediting the NPT regime, had illustrated 'its logic and its necessity'.[55] The administration sought to co-ordinate diplomatic pressure through the joint communiqué of the foreign ministers of the recognised nuclear powers (4 June 1998); the passage of UN Security Council Resolution 1172 (6 June 1998), reaffirming that neither India nor Pakistan can be accorded the status of nuclear powers under the terms of the Non Proliferation Treaty but calling on them to sign the NPT and the CTBT 'without delay and without conditions'; and G-8 support for denying international loans to India and Pakistan.[56] New Delhi has signalled that it wishes some accommodation, reversing its former opposition to the CTBT and indicating that it would enter talks on a Fissile Material Cutoff Treaty (which prompted Pakistan and Israel to follow suit and enabled the talks to begin in Geneva on 11 August 1998). India has also indicated that it would be willing to join the MTCR and the Nuclear Suppliers' Group as a full member, again reversing its former opposition to 'discriminatory ad hoc cartels.'[57] Nevertheless, even with these concessions, Washington will have to face the fact that the security of South Asia has changed fundamentally, and that the subcontinent has two *de facto* nuclear powers, outside the NPT. The South Asian security equation could change again if political relations deteriorated between India and Pakistan, and nuclear warheads were designed and fitted to the missiles of either side. So the military utility of weapons of mass destruction merits further review.

4
Military Utility of Weapons of Mass Destruction

In denouncing the nuclear testing of India and Pakistan, Anglo-American officials emphasised that both states had undermined their own security interests. While Robin Cook maintained that the tests 'do nothing to enhance Pakistan's security environment', Madeleine Albright insisted that the tests of both states had caused 'mutual insecurity' as they now faced the risks and costs of an arms race, would lack early warning of what the other will do, and so 'the risk of misinformation leading to miscalculation leading to disaster' was high.[1] As neither Britain nor the United States have evinced any desire to abandon their own nuclear deterrents, and have even reaffirmed (or would reaffirm in Britain's case) the security value of their reduced nuclear arsenals,[2] these admonitions seemed somewhat self-serving. However cogent the claims that established nuclear powers possessed more sophisticated methods of command, control and communications, better surveillance, intelligence-gathering and warning systems, and more reliable means of delivery, Prime Minister Vajpayee understandably argued that Western criticisms smacked of hypocrisy and double standards.[3] In fact, the Indian and Pakistani actions encountered widespread wrath because they countered the trend towards denuclearization – a de-emphasis of the role and utility of nuclear weapons as instruments of policy that had set in during the later years of the Cold War[4] and had gathered momentum thereafter. During Operation Desert Shield British Prime Minister John Major and French President François Mitterrand publicly rejected the option of nuclear retaliation, even if their forces were attacked with chemical weapons, while President Bush resolved not to retaliate with chemical or nuclear weapons, although the decision was kept secret and US threats left all retaliatory options open.[5] Whether other states will follow suit, and refrain from using or threatening to use their weapons of mass destruction, remains a matter of debate.

Nuclear weapons, particularly those with large yields (hundreds of kilotons or more) remain 'the most potent means of mass destruction'.[6] They could be used strategically in the hope of destroying an enemy's military infrastructure, economic base and even a significant portion of its population; tactical nuclear weapons could also be employed against concentrations of military forces, including tightly clustered groups of naval vessels operating in littoral waters, port, depot or air base facilities, concentrations of troops (whether in the front-line or reinforcements), massed formations of tanks and other armoured vehicles, and supply lines. In their analysis of the effects of one or two 20-kiloton nuclear strikes, air-bursted over a port such as Ad-Dammam, Greg Weaver and J. David Glaes (Science Applications International Corporation) found that the port might not be permanently destroyed, but that the damage to "softer" facilities (warehousing, mobile cargo-handling equipment and cargo stacked on piers) as well as the death or injury of nearly all the personnel in the area, was likely to disrupt severely any further near-term operation of the port facilities. They found that similar strikes over airfields such as Dhahran, Taif and Riyadh would cause extensive damage to above-ground structures, aircraft and personnel, effectively destroying 'the attacked facility for the purposes of the conflict at hand'.[7]

Admittedly new nuclear states are likely to acquire only small arsenals of nuclear weapons (i.e. a few to a few dozen), with relatively low yields (in tens and not hundreds of kilotons) in the near to mid-term. They may also lack the delivery systems to achieve the maximum destructive impact, and so their leaderships, even if uninhibited politically from using such weapons, may prefer to husband their limited resources for strategic purposes rather than use them in strikes that may not prove decisive. Tactical nuclear strikes may preclude follow-up military operations over the contaminated terrain and may cause large civilian casualties on both sides (either directly by means of radioactive fallout if the targets are near their own borders, or indirectly if subsequent retaliation is directed at the attacker's own cities).[8] Yet if a state possessed even a small nuclear arsenal, potential enemies could neither disregard this capability nor assume that it was only a weapon of last resort. During crises or the early stages of armed conflict, they might consider the options of launching pre-emptive strikes against these weapons and their likely deployment bases, especially if they lacked the conventional means with which to mount an effective counter-attack. If both sides possessed their own limited nuclear capabilities, the proximity of opposing nuclear forces, the vulnerability of such forces to a first strike, and their unsophisticated command, control, communications and intelligence facilities might cause miscalculation or tempt pre-emption. As Steve Fetter argues, 'Even if both sides prefer not to preempt, each may fear that the other will; consequently, both may decide to launch at the first (and perhaps) false indication of an attack.'[9] The mere possession of a nuclear arsenal by one or both sides would raise the political and military stakes and complicate the planning calculations of those involved, not least for any coalition forces intervening as a matter of choice.

Possessing a nuclear capability might prove useful if only to deter conflict or foreign intervention. If Walter Slocombe, US Under Secretary of Defense for Policy, can elegantly argue the case for retaining a nuclear deterrent by the United States, then other states with residual security concerns can also do so, *mutatis mutandis*.[10] Although their capabilities are likely to remain limited in size, numbers and accuracy, they could serve as part of a strategic threat in a regional context. Their value would be underscored by flexibility in the timing and routing of possible attacks, the nature of likely regional targets (probably few in number, poorly defended, and sometimes located close to mutual borders), and the high probability of target acquisition.[11] These capabilities might even serve as a means of inducing US intervention as South Africa had hopes of doing with its limited arsenal in the late 1980s. By detonating a nuclear device, or even making obvious preparations to do so at a known testing site (in this case, Kalahari), a state might aim to induce or accelerate American intervention to compose an imminent conflict.[12]

To underline that nuclear weapons retain a range of possible utilities does not mean that any proliferant could overlook the financial, political and security costs of developing and maintaining a limited nuclear capability. Quite apart from the costs of either keeping aloof from the NPT regime or of trying surreptitiously to develop a capability within the tightened safeguards of the regime (see Chapter 6), there would be costs in maintaining the safety of the system, developing effective command, control and communications arrangements, and conducting policy amidst deteriorating interstate relations. Accordingly the vast majority of states have refrained from seeking a nuclear option, but others, if lacking reliable great power allies and facing intractable security concerns, may regard the costs and opportunity costs of acquiring a nuclear capability as preferable to the costs and uncertainties of relying on conventional forces.

If compared with chemical or biological weapons, nuclear weapons are more destructive inasmuch as they can not merely kill and injure but also destroy equipment, facilities and military infrastructure. Their effects are more predictable and less dependent on meteorological and topographical conditions (although these will influence the distribution of fallout and radiological contamination). Furthermore, their military efficacy will not vary as much over time – after the initial use of nuclear weapons some defensive measures, such as the dispersal of forces, could be employed but much more effective protective postures and medical countermeasures could be adopted after the first use of chemical or biological weapons (depending in the latter case upon the agent involved and the scale and effects of the attack).[13] Nevertheless, if the state concerned had any reason to fear a prompt and overwhelming American intervention, this would almost certainly inhibit the use of nuclear weapons other than in the most extreme circumstances. The attractions of nuclear weapons reside primarily in diplomatic leverage, deterrence, and strategic independence.

Biological weapons may also seem more versatile and effective as an option than relying upon conventional weaponry. They can be employed to kill or injure humans, domestic animals, or crops, and infectious agents can be disseminated in various ways – by arthropod vectors, aerosol, and the contamination of food and water supplies – with the key requirement being an ability to disseminate the agent into the atmosphere in the right particle size. The most efficient method is by means of an aerosol – a stable airborne suspension of microscopic particles or droplets that can be inhaled into the lungs (with particles between 1 and 5 microns in diameter). So although BW agents could be dispersed from rockets, bombs or missiles, effective dissemination could be achieved by means of a relatively simple spray system, even an agricultural sprayer. The simplest method of area delivery could involve spray tanks mounted on manned aircraft, unmanned remotely piloted vehicles (RPVs) or low-cost, subsonic cruise missiles, which could release a large quantity of agent over a controlled line of flight. The agent would have to be discharged sufficiently slowly (either by air rushing past the spray tanks and forcing out the contents or by compressed air or carbon dioxide disseminating the agent) to generate a stable aerosol. Thereupon the linear cloud of agent, released from the "line source", could cover a larger area than a cloud released from a "point source" (although the latter would provide a higher saturation of a finite area).[14] The delivery attractions of cruise missiles for a BW attack have doubtless increased with the increased accuracy offered by commercially available (and affordable) guidance technology, such as the Global Positioning System (GPS). They are also less easily intercepted than slow-flying aircraft and less costly than manned aircraft or ballistic missiles.[15]

Meteorological conditions would influence the effectiveness of an area attack with a biological aerosol. As many micro-organisms are sensitive to sunlight, heat and humidity, a daytime attack would risk a higher rate of agent decay. An aerosol cloud could break up in the atmospheric turbulence and vertical air currents caused by bright sunlight, carrying particles and droplets up and away from the target area. BW attacks are likely to achieve the greatest coverage per unit of agent if launched at dusk or at night, when the ground and the layer of air above it are cooler than the higher layer of air (temperature inversion). By releasing BW agents in stable conditions prevents the vertical mixing of the cloud and keeps the pathogens or toxins at a low altitude where they can be inhaled. As the effectiveness of an area attack will also depend upon the prevailing speed and direction of the wind, the attack would have to avoid erratic or excessively strong winds that could cause the agent to miss its target or dissipate too rapidly.[16]

The scale and scope of such an attack, if efficiently delivered in the right conditions against an unprotected population, could be formidable. In such circumstances, argued the OTA, biological weapons 'would, pound for pound of weapon, exceed the killing power of nuclear weapons': a single aircraft could 'disseminate high dosages of biological agent over hundreds, or even thousands, of square kilometers by spraying a long line upwind from the target region'.[17] The United States had demonstrated this potential in the 1960s by a series of open-air biological tests, conducted secretly over four years in the Pacific Ocean downwind of Johnston Atoll, a thousand miles southwest of Hawaii. The results of those tests, particularly one of the largest conducted in the summer of 1968, removed any lingering doubts about the strategic potential of biological agents. As Dr William Patrick III, the former Chief of Product Development for the old US Army biological-weapons facility at Fort Detrick, Maryland, recalled, 'When we saw those test results, we knew beyond a doubt that biological weapons are strategic weapons. We were surprised. Even we didn't think they would work that well.'[18] The Soviets also appreciated the strategic potential of biological weapons, maintaining a capability for loading bacteria and viruses onto intercontinental ballistic missiles on several days' notice in the early 1980s.[19]

Within the context of regional conflicts, biological weapons could be envisaged as a cost-effective strategic deterrent against major powers, or against regional adversaries armed with weapons of mass destruction. 'An arsenal of such weapons', argued Victor Utgoff (Institute for Defense Analyses), 'could be a very powerful tool for intimidating neighboring states in peacetime or crises.'[20] To be effective such a deterrent would need a credible delivery system and an explicit means of communication to the adversary concerned. As the threat would involve an affront to international norms that not even Saddam Hussein was prepared to contemplate, regimes might only reveal such a deterrent as a weapon of last resort. In a regional "counter-city" role, a BW threat would raise the prospect of inflicting massive casualties and sowing the seeds of widespread terror and panic, especially as the population centres are unlikely to possess any means of detection and advance vaccination. Even the threat to hold civilians hostage in this manner could yield tangible military benefits, undermining civilian support for the imperilled regime and impairing its military preparations or other activities (not least by the breakdown of law and order and the mass flight of civilians from the target area). In a major theatre war, the threat or recourse to such escalation could have a serious impact upon allied or intervention forces supporting the state under biological attack[21] (and possibly upon the depth and duration of the allied commitment).

More specifically, a state armed with a strategic biological capability might employ it, as the US *Quadrennial Defense Review* forecast, in asymmetric attacks upon US forces or targets. Lieutenant-General Patrick M. Hughes, as Director of the DIA, explained that

> the perception of western political, economic, and especially military "dominance" means that many of our enemies will choose asymmetric means to attack our interests. ... At the "strategic" level, this probably means seeking to avoid direct military confrontation with US forces: at the operational and tactical levels it means seeking ways of "leveling (SIC) the playing field" if forced to engage the US military.[22]

The various ways could involve state-sponsored terrorist attacks on US cities, covert strikes on US bases overseas, attacks on the symbols of US power, and attacks on the cities and military bases of US allies. In all such actions, the weaker state might seek to sap American will by exposing divisions between the United States and its allies or by exploiting the apparent reluctance of sections of the American public to accept excessive casualties, thereby preventing or terminating prematurely US-led intervention.[23] Such strategies could prove counterproductive, stiffening American resolve and deepening the determination to seek a prompt and decisive military solution to the crisis.[24] Even so, a weaker state may feel that it had few better options. If unable to counter the conventional might of the United States and its allies, it probably could not pose a significant strategic threat with chemical weapons (in view of the tonnages which would have to be deployed on target) and, unlike the use of nuclear weapons, might be able to deny making a biological attack by launching one that looked like the normal outbreak of an infectious disease. The difficulty of differentiating biological attacks from naturally occurring epidemics or endemic disease[25] could enable the perpetrator to disclaim responsibility (or at least try do so until political divisions eroded the resolve of the United States or its allies).

Biological weapons might also be used in economic warfare against the crops or livestock of an enemy state. Plant and animal pathogens could be delivered against enemy crops and livestock to cause economic hardship or starvation (where the targeted state was heavily dependent on a particular crop) and to undermine civilian morale. In its BW programme Iraq examined the weapons potential of 'wheat cover smut', a naturally occurring fungal plant pathogen that produces a black growth on wheat and other cereal grains, rendering the contaminated grain useless as foodstuff. After small-scale production at Al Salam, larger-scale production was reportedly carried out near Mosul in 1987 and 1988, producing considerable quantities of contaminated grain. Although the concept was apparently not developed any further, and the stocks of contaminated grain were burnt,[26] the programme served as a reminder that the targeting of crops and animals has been a traditional objective in biological warfare (including the anthrax-filled cattle cakes that Britain prepared as a retaliatory measure during the Second World War), and that this form of economic warfare could have a devastating potential in certain countries.[27]

During the 1980s it was often asserted that biological weapons were too slow and too unreliable to be used as battlefield weapons,[28] but these claims simplified the requirements of battlefield weaponry and failed to allow for the range of agents that could be employed (and the delayed effects of some toxins are not much slower than those of mustard gas). Biological agents could certainly be used whenever immediate results were not required (as in a preparatory phase prior to the onset of hostilities) or where the danger to friendly forces was minimal (by attacking rear area units). If delivered in a covert pre-emptive attack, biological agents could produce widespread delayed effects that might be difficult to detect against forces in their peacetime locations. The possible targets could include reserve forces, formations massing for mobilisation, air bases, ports, and logistic centres. During Operation Desert Shield, some 80% of all air cargo was handled at five airfields in Southwest Asia and 86% of all sea cargo was unloaded at a single port – Ad Damman[29] – choke points that would delight a military planner.

These were not only large and valuable targets (and in the case of Ad-Damman, one that could not be readily replaced in the theatre), but they were also staffed by large numbers of unprotected civilians. Even an attack with incapacitants could prove highly disruptive in these areas, creating major medical and logistical burdens, causing demoralisation and possibly panic, and almost certainly diverting military resources to assist the afflicted civilians and decontaminate various facilities. If troops were forced by such an attack to wear protective kit and adopt contamination avoidance procedures, this would degrade their mobility and operational effectiveness, both individually and collectively, especially in hot weather. As Brigadier-General George Friel, commander of the US Chemical and Biological Defense Command, remarked,

> the biological threat has been recently singled out as the one major threat that still poses the ability for catastrophic effects on a theater-deployed force. Desert Storm solidified the perception in our country – in the Congress and among our military leadership – that [biological warfare] was something that third world nations considered a potential equalizer.[30]

Biological weapons might also be used in attacks on American power projection forces. The targets might include forces engaged in active combat or moving towards the theatre or deployed near the theatre or offshore. Once again logistic "choke-points" or points of embarkation or disembarkation might be likely targets and the surreptitious nature of biological weapons would add to their potential appeal. By using clandestine methods (such as launching the attack from another state that was not a party to the conflict or by employing non-state actors), and by using agents that produced an endemic disease, the perpetrator might not leave any clear "signature" of an attack. If efficiently delivered, such an attack might blur the distinction between strategic and tactical operations by disabling targets whose loss, even temporarily, could change the outcome of a putative campaign. In deep operational attacks against naval task forces, even US aircraft carriers could be vulnerable to biological (and chemical) attacks as they lack facilities to produce positive air pressure to expel contaminated air. Much would depend on the agent used, the effectiveness of any detectors and the response of crews to alarms, but there could be difficulties in monitoring the degree and extent of the contamination, in sustaining crew operations in contaminated conditions, in decontaminating exposed aircraft and flight deck, and in treating casualties. At the very least flight operations might be temporarily suspended and the rate of maintaining and servicing aircraft severely curtailed.[31]

In more oblique operational missions, including sabotage and clandestine attacks on high-value military targets, such as command, control and communications facilities, militarily important cities, overseas bases, and even targets in the United States itself, biological agents and toxins might again be the weapon of choice. The Soviets recognised the value of these weapons in *spetsnaz* or special forces operations, and anticipated that these weapons could be employed by saboteurs either in place or specially inserted during a crisis to carry out assigned sabotage missions before a war began.[32] This could form another variant of an asymmetric strategy by trying to disrupt the mobilisation and operational planning of US forces prior to their intervention in an overseas conflict. Local water supplies could be the targets in parts of the developing world by employing CB agents, such as anthrax, microcystin and cryptosporidium, that are capable of surviving in chlorinated water, or by injecting contaminants downstream of the monitoring point(s). Incapacitants might also be employed to create greater logistical and medical burdens (and hopefully preclude the option of "massive retaliation").[33] The psychological impact of these attacks would obviously be heightened if they could be conducted in a way that concealed the nature of the attack and the identity of the attackers.

The military and political utility of tactical attacks with biological and toxin weapons could be considerable. They would confirm that the adversary had learned from the blunders of Saddam Hussein and would not allow an intervention force the time and opportunity to deploy itself unmolested in theatre. If the attacks lacked any clear "signature" or clear attribution, they would almost certainly complicate political calculations at a domestic and possibly international level (especially if coalition forces were the victims). Were novel agents employed, they might prove difficult to detect and decontaminate, raising questions about how to avoid the contaminated areas and how to treat any casualties, including the civilians who might still be infected in a "tactical" strike. Above all, the attacks would confirm that their targets were highly vulnerable, that biological defence, though much improved since the Gulf War (see Chapter 7), can never be perfect, and that its weaknesses can be exploited. Whether those weaknesses will ever prove critical in a military or political sense depends on a whole range of factors, including the circumstances of the conflict and future developments in the offensive and defensive dimensions of biological warfare. Despite all the progress in US biological warfare defence, General Charles C. Krulak, Commandant of the US Marine Corps, would still admit on 26 February 1997:

> The one that keeps me awake at night, to be very honest, is chemical and biological capabilities, not just in armed forces, but in rogue hands. We as a Nation, I believe, can hold our own on the chemical side. We are absolutely in dire straits on the bio, because it is so difficult to detect...I think we will whip anybody else on the face of the planet, but if they have that kind of weapon of mass destruction, or a biochemical capability, we have problems.[34]

The reference to biochemical capability underlines the changing nature of the potential weapons systems in light of the rapid advances in molecular biology and biotechnology. These advances have tended to blur the basic distinctions between biology (concerned with naturally produced animate substances) and chemistry (concerned primarily with synthetically produced inanimate substances). The potential military significance of the breakthroughs in the use of recombinant DNA techniques in the 1970s, coupled with the legitimate civilian and industrial applications of these discoveries and the rapid growth and diffusion of the biotechnology industry, was all too apparent by the mid-1980s. Both commentators and governments increasingly sounded the tocsin over this issue, with the US government warning that advances in the industrial application of these discoveries 'have increased our ability to manufacture new substances or modify old ones, as well as making it easier and faster to produce these products'.[35]

The range of applications is immense. By transferring certain genetic traits into naturally infectious micro-organisms, new organisms of greater virulence, antibiotic resistance, and environmental stability could be created. The production process could alter the immunogenicity of the organisms, thereby rendering them difficult to diagnose and resistant to medical treatment. By bioengineering it may be possible to facilitate the poisoning of water supplies by creating chlorine-resistant strains of organisms or employ microencapsulation techniques to defeat the effects of chlorination and chlorine-depletion monitoring.[36] It is also possible to produce larger quantities of the altered compounds, and do so relatively quickly. Although genetic engineering is unlikely to increase the potency of naturally available toxins, it may facilitate the mass production of plant and/or fungal toxins, enhance the stability of toxins so that they can be disseminated more effectively as an aerosol, and alter the antigenic structure of toxin molecules, so countering the effects of existing antitoxins and thwarting antibody-based diagnostic techniques. Genetic engineering could also create "chimeric" toxins (combinations of two different toxin molecules) that are more capable of penetrating and killing target cells, or design novel toxins that are as poisonous as nerve agents but are small enough to penetrate the filters of current gas masks. The new toxins might have a range of specific military advantages over existing agents, namely novel sites of action, rapid and specific effects, the ability to penetrate the protective filters of gas masks, or the ability to incapacitate.[37] More effective incapacitants might also be developed by chemically modifying "bioregulators" – the small peptides that are normally present in the body in minute quantities and are active at very low concentrations, making their detection difficult. Bioregulators could be modified chemically (by changing their amino acid sequences) to enhance their physiological activity, stability or specificity, so affecting the mental processes or health of those incapacitated. Both the US and Canadian governments affirmed that 'Even a small imbalance in these natural substances could have serious consequences, inducing fear, fatigue, depression or even causing death.'[38]

In the early 1990s commentators generally argued that the possibilities of developing genetically modified agents will only be feasible for countries with an established background in biotechnology (and the ability to organise strong research teams). Although some of the conceivable innovations might take five, ten, or more years to accomplish, others including the cloning of toxin genes and the altering of the antibiotic resistance or the immunological characteristics of some agents, were already possible. If prospective proliferants were likely to follow the Iraqi approach and begin by producing anthrax and botulinum toxin,[39] reports on the potential of genetic engineering were becoming more specific. In 1997 the CIA claimed that 'Now, virtually any known disease-causing agent can be manufactured in a laboratory, and many can be produced on an industrial scale.'[40] The Pentagon also described how a gene could be spliced from a toxin or other lethal agent into an otherwise non-lethal, spore-forming bacteria so that the spore will reduce the rate of the pathogen's decay in the environment. Toxins or viruses could be protected by micro-encapsulation so that when particles are inhaled by victims, the polymer-encapsulating wall degrades initially and the pathogen is only released when in the lungs. Viruses could be modified to act as "carriers" for toxic compounds, so delaying the emergence of the symptoms of the toxic pathogen over an extended period of time and making diagnosis and treatment very difficult. Finally, toxins that were once discounted as potential threat agents because of their limited availability in nature might now be 'produced through genetic engineering techniques in sufficient quantities for an adversary to consider producing them as an offensive weapon'.[41]

US Secretary of Defense William S. Cohen asserted that the scientific community was 'very close' to being able to manufacture 'genetically engineered pathogens that could be ethnically specific'.[42] The potential impact of genetic engineering and biotechnology, as summarised by the Pentagon, could include the genetic alteration of benign micro-organisms to produce a toxin, venom, or bioregulator; micro-organisms resistant to antibiotics, standard vaccines and therapeutics; micro-organisms with enhanced aerosol and environmental stability; immunologically altered micro-organisms which could defeat standard identification, detection, and diagnostic methods; and combinations of any of the above four types. Each of these techniques, it noted,

> seeks to capitalise on the extreme lethality, virulence, or infectivity of biological warfare agents and exploit this potential by developing methods to deliver more efficiently and to control these agents on the battlefield.[43]

The revelations of the Soviet defector, Dr Kanatjan Alibekov, now known as Dr Ken Alibek, a former first deputy chief of research and production in the Soviet BW programme, have heavily reinforced these concerns. Alibek, who defected in 1992, has written a classified study of the Soviet programme for the US government and has spoken publicly about the scale and scope of the Soviet/Russian BW activities. He confirmed that the Soviet programme was vast, involving 32,000 scientists working for Biopreparat, the civilian company that served as a cover for BW work, another 10,000 in the Defence Ministry and thousands of others in other agencies, with an immense productive capacity and a missile-delivery capability. He revealed that it had already created genetically altered, antibiotic-resistant strains of plague, anthrax, tularemia and glanders, developed methods for genetically altering the smallpox virus while preserving its virulence (splicing VEE, or Venezuelan equine encephalitis, a brain virus, with smallpox), and refined techniques for cultivating the Marburg and Machupo viruses. He explained that research costs were not prohibitive: 'A few million dollars. This is what it cost us for making the smallpox-VEE chimera at Vector in 1990 and 1991.'[44] Following the orders of Gorbachev in 1990 and Yeltsin in 1992 to cancel the offensive BW programme, Alibek believes that some Russian scientists may have taken their expertise and samples abroad – 'Iran, Iraq, probably Libya, probably Syria, and North Korea could have smallpox' – and that a truncated BW offensive programme probably still exists in Russia, within the laboratories of the Defence Ministry.[45]

Given this continuing technological potential and the range of strategic, tactical and clandestine uses, biological and toxin weapons have a clear and continuing utility. When these factors are coupled with the relative ease and cheapness of agent production, the scope for clandestine manufacture using dual-use equipment and facilities, and the possibility of cultivating BW agents from seed culture into militarily significant quantities in days or weeks, then biological weapons emerge as the most cost-effective of the weapons of mass destruction. Although any recourse to biological warfare would constitute an affront to international norms, and uncertainty persists about the effectiveness of biological attacks (in the absence of any proven significant use in war), biological weapons remain an attractive option. On account of their potency, flexibility, and ability to be delivered against a range of targets, and possibly in a manner which leaves neither a clear "signature" nor obvious attribution, biological weapons are not simply a weapon of last resort. US government sources reckon that some 100 countries possess the indigenous technological capacity to launch BW programmes, and, as Jonathan Tucker claims, 'even relatively poor states can afford a BW capability. Biological weapons can inflict far more casualties per dollar of investment than either chemical or nuclear weapons.'[46]

Unlike other weapons of mass destruction, chemical weapons have been used extensively in war and most recently in the Iran–Iraq War

(1980–88). Chemical disarmers tend to discount this experience by claiming that chemical weapons have never proved decisive on the battlefield, although they could still prove an indiscriminate hazard to unprotected civilians. Victor Sidel asserted that 'it is generally agreed that chemical weapons are not only abhorrent but also have little or no effective use in war'.[47] Fortunately General Schwarzkopf and the other political and military planners during Operation Desert Shield did not agree. In devising their deterrent threats, bombing priorities, hospital provisions, and highly mobile manoeuvre strategy, they took account of the casualties that could be caused by the Iraqi CW capabilities (see Chapter 2).[48] Even the threat of chemical attacks had an impact; as Major-General Ralph G. Wooten recalled, whenever 'Scud missiles rained in on coalition forces, tens of thousands of soldiers went into full chemical protection for hours, slowing and disrupting unit operations.' Although the subsequent loss of operating tempo may not have proved crucial, he prudently warned that 'America's Army cannot accept this penalty in future operations'.[49] General John M. Shalikashvili added that the threat of chemical-tipped Scud missiles landing in Israel or among allied forces had a 'dramatic political and emotional effect. If a chemical attack had occurred, the Israeli and allied reaction could have resulted in a militarily significant outcome.'[50]

As chemical weapons have a limited area coverage, they are often described as primarily tactical weapons. They could only be employed strategically in wars where the belligerents lacked early warning facilities as well as adequate means of air and civil defence. Manned aircraft, carrying spray tanks, or cruise missiles would probably be the preferred mode of delivery to distribute the agent as a fine aerosol, with particles of less than 5 microns in diameter, and so maximise the likelihood of the particles being retained in the lung and absorbed into the bloodstream.[51] Theoretically eight F-16 aircraft, each delivering 0.9 tons of sarin under optimum conditions, could cover an urban area of some 25 km^2 and cause up to 50% casualities among unprotected civilians.[52] These effects would depend upon a host of variables, not least the total absence of civil defence provisions (which would be unlikely if the other belligerent was thought to possess a CW capability) and ineffective air defences. The agent would have to be dispersed accurately and this would involve releasing an appropriate mass of agent, taking account of its volatility, at the correct altitude (if dispersed at too high an altitude, the agent might dissipate and lose its lethality; if released too close to the ground, the aerosol cloud might not spread far enough). In mounting attacks against long-range targets, accurate meteorological data would be vital to ensure that the cloud drifted in stable conditions, at a steady speed and an appropriate mixing height and temperature.[53]

Whether the effects of a strategic CW attack would warrant the effort and the risks involved would depend upon the political/strategic calculations of the perpetrator. The contamination of certain areas by a persistent chemical agent (such as VX) might disrupt and slow down industrial and commercial activities for days or weeks, but it would leave the economic and transportation infrastructure of the city concerned intact. It might cause even less disruption to enclosed military facilities within the area of the attack. The perpetrator would also have to consider the political implications of such a conspicuous affront to the international norms underpinned by the Geneva Protocol and the Chemical Weapons Convention. Although Iraq was able to break the Protocol with impunity when it launched chemical attacks on Halabja (March 1988), this might not prove a precedent for the future, and, at the very least, the victim of a future attack could exploit its impact for propaganda purposes and seek external assistance. Nevertheless, it remains to be seen whether these factors would outweigh the potential impact of chemical attacks that could cause far more fatalities and injuries than similar attacks with conventional ordnance. They could also induce widespread terror and panic, and, if delivered (or even threatened) at an opportune moment, could have a psychological and political impact out of all proportion to their killing power. As Anthony Cordesman argued, 'chemical weapons had a critical effect on Iranian military and civilian morale by late 1987. ... Even when troops are equipped with defensive gear, they often feel they are defenceless and break and run after limited losses. Populations which fear chemical attacks may well cease to support a conflict.'[54]

Chemical weapons have been used extensively as battlefield weapons. Although their effectiveness has been questioned in some tactical contexts, especially when used against protected personnel (and even more so against protected personnel with a capacity to retaliate-in-kind), chemical agents can be delivered from a wide array of weapons (including mines, shells, mortars, multi-barrelled rocket launchers, bombs, missiles, rockets and spray tanks) and can be employed offensively and defensively in many tactical applications. While persistent chemical agents have been used to create or supplement 'barrier' defences and to protect the flanks of offensive operations, non-persistent agents have been used to disrupt enemy defences but still permit attacking troops to press through afterwards. Some chemical agents have also been employed as incapacitants, either as a precursor to an attack or in conjunction with it. The impact of such operations has always been difficult to measure as chemical warfare has never relied solely upon the lethality of particular agents. Chemical agents have been employed to harass enemy forces and civilians, complement the effects of conventional weapons, spread fear and disruption among untrained or ill-equipped troops, impose the burdens of NBC defence upon protected adversaries, kill or injure unprotected personnel (thereby adding to the burdens medical evacuation and treatment), and slow the tempo or movement of forces compelled to avoid contaminated areas. If never a war-winning factor (and relatively few forms of warfare ever have been in and of themselves), chemical warfare has proved a useful ancillary instrument for a military trained and equipped to employ it.[55]

Possessing an adequate stock of agents is a prerequisite for chemical warfare but this need not involve the accumulation of large and conspicuous stockpiles in peace, with all the technical difficulties associated with agent stability and storage. Iraq demonstrated that it was quite possible to produce and use chemical agent as and when required in the Iran–Iraq conflict,[56] but a large productive capacity could certainly prove useful. As the OTA claimed, 'the fact that chemical agents are usually disseminated as a wind-borne aerosol or spray means that many tons may be needed to produce many battlefield casualties' and even then, the actual impact would depend on how effectively the enemy was protected with gas masks, protective clothing and shelters.[57]

The quantity of agent required would depend not only upon the properties of the agent and its mode of dispersal but also upon the military effects desired against different types of target. General Shalikashvili has revealed the results of various studies, indicating that a quite diverse range of agent tonnages could be employed to achieve specific results in different contexts. A risk assessment conducted by the Joint Staff in 1987 indicated that if an aggressor could hit multiple targets, including key logistic nodes and airfields, several times a week for several weeks, with only 1,000 tons of persistent agent, he could degrade allied reinforcement and resupply operations, diverting shipping from ports and reinforcements from airfields, while causing delays in the transshipping at rail nodes. A similar study conducted by the US Army Concept Analysis Agency in 1989 found that several hundred tons of thickened persistent nerve agent could disrupt the arrival of military units in theatre. The Institute for Defense Analyses also demonstrated that tens of tons of agents achieved tactical successes during a one-month period in the Iran–Iraq War. Shalikashvili added that the mere threat of chemical-tipped SCUD missiles landing in Israel or among allied forces had a dramatic political and emotional effect, and that in some regional conflicts even one ton of agent could serve as a weapon of terror against an unprotected civilian population.[58] A Russian intelligence report concurred, observing that less than 600 tonnes of chemical weapons were thought necessary to wage a large-scale chemical war in Europe, whereas 'an average of about 100 tons of chemical weapons' would be required in a major and fairly prolonged regional conflict.[59]

The range of potential military effects extends far beyond the killing or injuring of unprotected personnel. In preparing for a potential chemical threat, logistic planners would have to make provision for protective equipment, displacing other equipment on cargo carriers, sufficient medical support to cope with the evacuation and treatment of chemical casualties, and NBC defence units. They would have to consider, too, the potential impact of rerouting reinforcements and supplies if their preferred ports, airfields and logistic nodes were rendered unusable and the time-consuming effects of large-scale decontamination. In operational planning, allowance would have to be made for the impact upon planned manoeuvres of contamination avoidance procedures and the possible dispersal of some formations (not only on land but also at sea if ships lacked collective protection facilities).[60] Above all, there would be the operational degradation at individual and unit level of personnel forced to discharge their duties in full protective kit (MOPP 4 in American parlance).

The degree of degradation is often given by Pentagon officials and senior US officers as in the range of 30–50% or above, with the more extreme results occurring at temperatures over 70 degrees Fahrenheit and afflicting units that could not practise contamination avoidance drills (including air and ground crews operating from static air bases).[61] The degree of degradation will vary with the nature of the task, the type of agent involved (persistent agents would pose greater problems than non-persistent), the length of time spent in MOPP 4, and the ambient temperature. Training may reduce the degree of degradation, but the training of élite professional forces cannot be emulated by conscript and reserve formations, for whom the degradation could be as bad if not worse than the American estimates. Some degradation will occur, and it will affect some missions more than others, particularly if the forces concerned are inserted into a chemical conflict in high temperatures without an opportunity to acclimatise. Moreover, the degradation need not affect both sides in a conflict – an enemy who did not have to fear retaliation-in-kind could choose the chemical agents, delivery systems and targets for his attack to create, as Frank Gaffney rightly claims, 'distinctly asymmetrical operating conditions for the two sides'.[62]

In a study of how VX could affect operations at ports and air bases in the Middle East, Weaver and Glaes reckoned that the limited accuracy and payload of Scud missiles were far less important when armed with a persistent nerve agent, like VX, than when carrying conventional ordnance. They found that chemical strikes would inflict fatalities, incapacitation, and visual impairment among unprotected civilian port workers at a port like Ad-Dammam, and that these effects would be compounded by the likely absenteeism among survivors, the impracticality of large-scale decontamination, and the negative impact of MOPP gear on port operations (reckoned by the Joint Staff to amount to approximately 80% at 85 degrees Fahrenheit or more). 'Chemical attacks', they concluded, 'can probably keep major ports closed indefinitely, limited only by the enemy's capability to keep contaminating the ports faster than the persistent chemical agent naturally weathers.'[63] They also reckoned that similar VX strikes on theatre air bases, if they could be sustained with successive attacks, could slow and severely disrupt combat sortie generation and airlift in a matter of days. A theatre air base commander under such an attack would lack good operational responses. Large-scale decontamination and operation in MOPP gear would probably prove impractical on account of the difficulty of decontaminating aircraft, munitions and the facilities of a large airfield. Relocation to other air bases would depend upon the availability, vulnerability and capacity of the latter, and the desirability of redeploying contaminated aircraft. Finally, the option of working and fighting in a contaminated environment could incur casualties and operational degradation, so reducing sortie rates. An analysis by Defense Technology Systems Inc. in 1995 found that the degradation effects from working MOPP kit at an air port of disembarkation would reduce the "throughput operations" by about 40% in temperatures between 50 and 84 degrees Fahrenheit, 'while such operations would virtually shut down at temperatures above 85 degrees Fahrenheit'.[64] Commanders would be able to relocate to bases out of range of the Scud missiles but this might impair some tactical air operations and require an even greater reliance on long-range bombing missions and smart munitions.

How effective such chemical attacks would prove either as a means of escalation in a war between regional states or as an attack on power projection forces would depend upon the ratio of chemical weapons to air bases and/or ports (which would be higher on the Korean peninsula than it was in the Gulf War), the ability of missiles to evade air defences, and the range of retaliatory or redeployment options for the forces under attack. Even well-timed strikes could prove massively counterproductive if they provoked a retaliation by the full range of US strategic air power.[65] An adversary, though, might reckon that the pre-emptive use of chemical weapons could assist in defeating or demoralising an ally of the United States before the latter intervened. Similarly the adversary might calculate that a limited strike with chemical weapons against a recognisable military target might not trigger a nuclear response, and if it also degraded US air power, might complicate the task of retaliating by escalating the air campaign.

In sum, chemical weapons, if not super weapons, are by no means negligible weapons. Like other weapons of mass destruction, they have a range of potential uses, even if the prospective user would have to consider the political, military and other risks (and costs) which might flow from their usage. Given this military potential and the understandable desire of most regimes to avoid a direct confrontation with the United States, attention has focused on the possibility of using these weapons unconventionally, and of exploiting their potential as instruments of terror.

5
NBC Terrorism

On the morning of 20 March 1995, commuters travelling on five trains towards Kasumigaseki station on the Tokyo underground railway system were attacked with the nerve agent sarin. Although the Tokyo attack was neither unprecedented nor unanticipated (a previous attack at Matsumoto on 27 June 1994 had killed seven and injured over 200 people),[1] it proved an immense shock. The Tokyo attack killed seven people directly, seriously injured another 122 (of whom five more would die), and prompted some 5,500 people to seek medical treatment in hospitals as a result of inhaling poisonous fumes. Widespread panic and disruption followed threats of further attacks, but the police raided the premises of the alleged perpetrators – Aum Shinrikyo (Supreme Truth) – seized large quantities of chemicals, and arrested many cult members, including the cult leader, Shoko Asahara.[2] It was also confirmed that the cult had experimented with biological warfare, had sent a team to Zaire in the hope of acquiring the Ebola virus as a possible biological weapon, and had mounted some nine abortive BW attacks.[3] In the United States several individuals and small extremist groups were discovered seeking access to, or planning the use of, biological agents and, in November 1995, Chechen separatists took credit for the first act of nuclear terrorism in the post-Cold War era. They placed a 30-pound package containing small amounts of radioactive cesium-137 at the entrance to Izmailovsky Park in Moscow, and, despite the lack of explosives to disperse the cesium, demonstrated a credible terrorist threat.[4] Questions were immediately asked about whether these incidents would serve as harbingers of similar acts to come, the implications of terrorism with NBC weapons, and the ability of responsible authorities to combat this form of terrorism effectively.

Jonathan B. Tucker (Center for Nonproliferation Studies of the Monterey Institute of International Studies) has argued that the Tokyo attack served as a 'wake-up call for policy makers the world over'.[5] If so, policy makers have overlooked a plethora of warnings from officials, scientists, and intelligence agencies about the potential attractions of weapons of mass destruction for terrorists;[6] the feasibility of terrorists handling or using these weapons, especially if trained to do so;[7] and the vulnerability of political, military and civilian targets in liberal democracies.[8] As late as 1994 Lieutenant-General James Clapper, a former head of the DIA, described the potential of mass-casualty weapons for terrorism as one of the 'most nightmarish concerns' that faced the United States and its allies.[9]

Paradoxically, this renewed concern arose at a time when the incidence of terrorism appeared to be declining. Compared with the mid-1980s, when worldwide terrorist incidents fluctuated in excess of 600 per annum, they had fallen to between 322 and 440 by the mid-1990s, even plummeting to 296 (a 25-year low) in 1996. Two-thirds of the recorded attacks in 1996 were minor acts of politically-motivated violence against commercial targets, which produced only a few casualties and no deaths, but the number of casualties was among the highest on record: 311 persons killed and 2,652 wounded (with 90 of the deaths and 1,400 casualties caused in a single bombing in Sri Lanka). Approximately a quarter of the attacks were directed against American targets (with 19 US citizens killed and some 500 persons wounded in the attack upon the Khobar Towers housing facility near Dhahran, Saudi Arabia, on 25 June 1996). The sustained decline in terrorist incidents may reflect political developments in some regions (notably Northern Ireland), economic difficulties bedevilling former sponsors of terrorism (Cuba), and the international isolation of others (Libya and Iraq). Iran remained the premier sponsor of state terrorism, but Osama bin Laden, the international terrorist financier, provided alternative sponsorship, while groups such as HAMAS and the Palestinian Islamic Jihad mounted major attacks in Israel. On account of the bombings in Dhahran, Tel Aviv and Jerusalem, the number of terrorist casualties in the Middle East nearly doubled from 445 in 1995 to 837 in the following year.[10]

Even more significant were the increasingly sophisticated operations mounted by international terrorists. Already apparent by the late 1980s, this trend prompted fears that a new breed of terrorist was about to emerge, one with far greater technological and organisational talents. Bruce Hoffman (Centre for the Study of Terrorism and Political

Violence at St Andrews University) described the larger scale of operations mounted in the 1980s, with more sophisticated conventional ordnance, timing mechanisms and precision-guided surface-to-air missiles.[11] The CIA noted that groups such as the Lebanese Hizballah and the Egyptian al-Gamaat al-Islamiyya had developed 'transnational infrastructures' for fund-raising, logistical support and cooperation with other terrorist groups.[12] The possibility of terrorists not only extending the geographical scope of their operations but also utilising the spread of dual-use technologies and expertise, thereby diversifying their choice of weaponry and tactics was all too apparent. Individuals and small groups have sought to acquire weapons of mass destruction, and have threatened or attempted to use them, albeit without inflicting mass casualties (apart from the poisoning of some 750 citizens in Oregon with salmonella by the Rajneesh cult in 1984).[13]

Compounding the fears aroused by these precedents is the emergence of terrorist groups motivated by religious fanaticism. Although the interplay between religion and terrorism has a long historical pedigree, its modern manifestation is comparatively recent. Whereas none of the 11 identifiable terrorist groups in 1968 could be described as religious, Hoffman identified 11 religious groups out of 48 terrorist factions in 1992, including Christian white supremacists, messianic Jews, radical Sikhs and Muslim fundamentalists. Apart from the difficulty of monitoring and penetrating so many terrorist groups, the religious terrorists pose particular problems for counter-terrorist agencies. Less concerned with making political points than with inflicting mass casualties as a means of 'purifying' society, religious cults and sects can contemplate massive acts of death in accordance with their beliefs that violence is a sacramental act or divine duty. Unlike secular terrorists, they may not be inhibited by political, moral, or pragmatic considerations, and may be willing to take great physical risks, even sacrificing themselves and/or killing 'non-believers'. If these groups feel isolated from a society whose norms they reject, and do not depend upon a target audience for funding or support, they may undertake terrorist acts for their own gratification, regarding violence as an end in itself, a means of fulfilling their own prophecies. A potential disaster, in this respect, may have been only narrowly averted in the bombing of the World Trade Center in New York (1993) when a radical Islamic group allegedly packed their bomb with sodium cyanide. According to a New York trial judge (whose assertion has not been corroborated), the plan only failed because the chemical agents burned during the explosion instead of disseminating through the building.[14]

There are also terrorists, gripped with hatred, vengeance or paranoia, who are determined to strike a devastating blow against a detested or despised enemy, such as government officials or another racial or ethnic group. Whether neo-Nazis, fascists, racial supremacists, or members of survivalist/militia groups in the United States, these terrorists may wish to inflict a massive blow against their various enemies. Some have already experimented with chemical and biological agents or weapons, notably the fascist Order of the Rising Sun, which was found to possess 30-40 kilograms of typhoid bacteria cultures in 1972; 14 white supremacists who were indicted in 1987 for plotting to poison the reservoirs in Chicago, Illinois and Washington, DC with cyanide; and the Confederate Hammer Skins who reportedly planned in 1987 to place cyanide crystals in the air conditioning unit of a synagogue in Dallas. In March 1995, two members of the Minnesota Patriots Council were convicted of planning to assassinate Internal Revenue Service agents and a deputy US marshall with ricin; in May 1995, Larry Wayne Harris, a member of the white supremacist organization, Aryan Nation, was arrested on charges of forgery after allegedly misrepresenting himself when ordering three vials of bubonic plague; and, in December 1995, Thomas Lewis Lavy was charged with trying to smuggle ricin across the Alaskan border into Canada.[15]

These reports were none too surprising. As terrorist incidents declined in number, terrorists may only gain publicity and expose the vulnerability of their targets by causing massive shock and inflicting horrendous levels of casualties (the car-bomb that killed 167 people in Oklahoma City on 19 April 1995, the suicide bombings that killed over 60 people in Tel Aviv and Jerusalem in 1996, the killing of 58 tourists at Luxor on 17 November 1997 and the bombing of US embassies, killing 12 Americans and some 300 Africans in Nairobi and Dar es-Salaam on 7 August 1998). Although some of these incidents proved counter-productive, leading to the arrests of the perpetrators, the tightening of anti-terrorist legislation, and massive reprisals by the victims (including cruise missile attacks on a Sudanese pharmaceutical plant and terrorist training camps in Afghanistan on 19 August 1998), the bombings in Israel provoked early elections and a change of government, while Luxor killings led to the dismissal of responsible ministers and had devastating effects on the Egyptian tourist industry. If terrorists wish to cause such an impact, then they may be attracted by the potential effects of weapons of mass destruction. They may also appreciate that only small quantities of materials are required to produce these effects, and that the designated targets are highly vulnerable.

Nuclear terrorism has long been an anxiety but its potential was underlined by the Chechen incident in November 1995 and the efforts of the Aum cult to mine uranium in Australia and buy Russian warheads.[16] Nuclear terrorism could take several forms, including the making or stealing of a nuclear weapon for detonation or blackmail; an attack on a nuclear weapons site or plant to spread alarm; the sabotage of a nuclear plant; the seizure of a nuclear plant or its personnel for blackmail; the theft or purchase of fissile material for blackmail or radioactive release; an attack on a transporter of nuclear weapons or materials; and the contamination or threat to contaminate a target with radioactive material. Some of these options are more plausible than others (attacks have already been made on nuclear plants in France, South Africa, Argentina, Spain and the Philippines) and much would depend on the motives, opportunities and expertise of the various groups.[17] Yet the potential effects of nuclear terrorism have always been formidable: if a group with sufficient skills was able to obtain about 30 pounds of highly enriched uranium, which is easily carried in a briefcase, or a small amount of plutonium (baseball size), and then spent some $200,000 acquiring readily available materials and equipment, it could build a nuclear device within a couple of months. Had such a nuclear device been in the mini van placed at the World Trade Center, it is estimated that 'the lower part of Manhattan would have disappeared up to Gramercy Park, all of Wall Street'.[18]

Formerly there were thought to be two main impediments to nuclear terrorism: the technical knowledge on how to build a bomb and the acquisition of fissile material. While the manufacture of a nuclear bomb is far from the easy proposition sometimes depicted (and is more demanding than the construction of chemical or biological weapons), much of the requisite technical knowledge is now in the public domain. In the mid-1980s an international task force reported that the manufacture of a crude nuclear device is within the reach of terrorists with sufficient resources to recruit a team of three or four technically qualified specialists and to acquire both the chemical high explosives and a sufficient quantity of weapons-usable nuclear material.[19] This places an even greater premium on ensuring the security of fissile material, particularly, if not exclusively, in Russia at a time when it has become more difficult to do so. Many of the institutional mechanisms that once prevented the spread of nuclear materials, technology, and scientific knowledge no longer exist or are only present in a weakened form, while new methods of control have only just been introduced. Estimates of how safe the Russian stockpile is vary considerably,[20] but the evidence of small scale thefts (see Chapter 2) indicates that illicit diversion is possible. John Deutch drew attention to the possible loss of weapons-usable materials from non-MOD facilities, especially in view of the inadequate accounting procedures, and the risk posed by an "inside job" from a nuclear-weapons facility. As an example, he observed:

> A knowledgeable Russian has told us that, in his opinion, accounting procedures are so inadequate that an officer with access could remove a warhead, replace it with a readily available training dummy, and authorities might not discover the switch for as long as six months.[21]

Fundamentally, the security of Russia's nuclear stocks is inextricably linked with the country's deepening political, economic and social predicament. Unless confidence in the country's political and legal institutions can be restored, the economy bolstered, and the crime syndicates suppressed, nuclear-trafficking whether by individuals or by organized crime remains a possibility.

A terrorist group would not necessarily need to obtain fissile materials for its purposes. Depending upon the group's objectives, non-fissile (but radioactive) materials, such as cesium-137, strontium-90 and cobalt-60, could suffice. If dispersed by conventional explosive, or even released accidentally, these materials could contaminate some water supplies, business centres, government facilities or transportation networks, causing social, political and economic disruption. Although non-fissile materials would be unlikely to cause significant casualties, they could interrupt economic activity and require post-incident clean-up. They could also cause extensive panic or psychological trauma among a work force or local populace.[22] Whether terrorists would wish to detonate such devices is a moot point. Brian Jenkins (deputy chairman, Kroll Associates) has claimed that terrorists would be more likely to 'brandish it [a nuclear capability] as a threat than detonate it'. They would still have to establish the credibility of the threat (conceivably by using a similar device as a demonstration) and persuade governments to negotiate (which could depend upon the points at issue, the character of the government, and the options other than making concessions).[23] While more traditional terrorists, with established sponsors, might be more fearful of the quantum leap involved in 'going nuclear', not least the likelihood of provoking a concerted international response and the alienation of their supporters, the new breed of terrorists, motivated by feelings of revenge, hatred and religious fervour, might be more ready to consider this option.

Chemical or biological weapons might be preferred to nuclear weapons, if only because their materials are more readily available and affordable, much of the equipment and technology can be legitimately acquired as it is genuinely dual-use in its application, and the process of producing the agent is relatively simpler (although devising an effective means of dissemination is hardly a trivial task). From a terrorist's perspective, argued Deutch, the likeliest threats would be 'chemical first, biological second, nuclear third',[24] not least because the methods of producing CW agents are documented in the open literature and the tasks are feasible within covert laboratories. The Aum effort was particularly well funded (with a reported $30 million spent on the production of sarin). The cult gathered the requisite expertise, procured vast stocks of over 200 chemicals, and purchased filters, pipes made of hastelloy (a corrosion-resistant alloy), a fluorine treatment process, and computer-controlled equipment. Cult scientists synthesised a range of chemical agents, including mustard gas, sodium cyanide, LSD, and nerve agents such as tabun, sarin, soman, and VX.[25] Even if other terrorist groups failed to emulate the scale and sophistication of the Aum enterprise (which still suffered several lapses of security, involving accidents that injured personnel, produced emissions of toxic fumes and discoloured nearby vegetation),[26] they could obtain the requisite materials and equipment, and conceal their production facilities.[27]

State-sponsorship, coupled with training in how to use chemical weapons against civilian targets (as the Stasi, the former East German secret police, used to provide), might serve as an alternative source of supply. If the terrorists had access to Russian sources, they might also be able to buy the services of underemployed or underpaid scientists, or acquire chemical weapons illicitly from the seven storage sites in Russia, where there are genuine concerns about physical security provisions (around perimeters and storage buildings), accountability standards, and the local response and recovery procedures.[28] If unable to manufacture, steal or acquire chemical weapons, terrorists could still obtain, with an exterminator's licence, toxic insecticides like TEPP or parathion which are almost as toxic as their military counterparts. The accidental release of 30 tons of methyl isocyanate – a chemical some hundred times less deadly than modern nerve agent – at the Union Carbide plant, Bhopal, India (3 December 1984), killed some 6,000 people, confirming the high toxicity of some industrial chemicals.[29]

Effective dissemination would be crucial as terrorists (unless they had state-sponsorship) could rarely disperse a bulk supply of chemical agent over a chosen target. The CIA reckons that 'a rough rule of thumb is that one ton (or about 55 gallon drums) of agent' is required to contaminate effectively 'one square mile (2.6 km^2) of territory if properly disseminated'.[30] Terrorists could mount attacks by poisoning a person or persons (the Aum cult tried several chemical assassinations, using phosgene and VX, while Tajik terrorists laced champagne with cyanide, killing six Russian soldiers in January 1995). They could also contaminate air-dissemination systems in aircraft, trains and buildings, or poison foods and pharmaceuticals (but a municipal water supply might prove too demanding in view of the volume of water involved as well as the filtration and purification processes).[31] In the Tokyo attack the methods were fairly primitive, relying on the puncturing of plastic bags and the volatilisation of liquid nerve agent (from an original two gallons' solution of about 30% sarin). The diluted nerve agent and lack of aerosol generators probably accounted for the relatively low death toll, but this was a rushed operation, conceived on a Friday (to pre-empt an imminent police raid), prepared over a weekend (replacing stocks of sarin destroyed in a cover-up following the Matsumoto incident), and implemented on a Monday morning. Had the cult been able to wait several months as originally planned, they might have mounted a more effective operation (they had already produced 30 kilograms of sarin in February 1994, had plans to produce 70 tons of sarin, and had purchased a Russian Mi-17 helicopter and two pilotless drones to disseminate large amounts of chemical or biological agents).[32] Terrorists, though, do not need highly sophisticated means of delivery: they could use items 'as complex as a timed generator device or as simple as a container equipped with a hand-operated atomizer'.[33]

Chemical weapons could be an attractive option, if the terrorist group wished to inflict or threaten to inflict large numbers of casualties, cause panic, and disrupt society (as happened when Asahara predicted that a 'horrible' event would happen in Tokyo on 15 April 1995, nearly paralysing the city).[34] They could also be used to impose economic costs on particular corporations by poisoning their products, to punish dissidents or defectors, and undermine the authority of a government and its law-enforcement agencies. If used against a foreign military base or a political target of high symbolic importance, chemical agents could be an instrument of revenge. Even if the usage was only threatened or was minimal but required extensive inspections, the economic costs could be considerable (the poisoning of two grapes due for export from Chile in 1989, reportedly cost Chile $334 million).[35] Above all, the recourse to chemical agents might be seen as a means of shocking an audience that has become increasingly inured to terrorist actions. Given the proliferation of terrorist groups, the recurrence of terrorist incidents, and the increasing efficiency of counter-terrorist units, some groups might regard chemical weapons as a means of regaining the initiative, shocking their target audience, and undermining confidence in the political authorities under attack. Chemical weapons may not provide the explosive and destructive spectacle associated with conventional bombings, but the psychological impact of a successful chemical attack, reviving all the fears of poison gas, should not be overlooked. The effects are likely to be even more significant, if political élites continue to follow the example of Presidents Bush and Clinton and claim that the Chemical Weapons Convention will either ban chemical weapons 'from the face of the earth', or make 'chemical terror like the tragic attack in the Tokyo subway, much, much more difficult'.[36] If public confidence is boosted by such ill-considered rhetoric, then the reaction to a subsequent chemical attack will be all the greater.

Biological weapons might appear even more attractive, inasmuch as a very small quantity of agent, if effectively dispersed, could in theory injure and kill far more people than conventional, chemical or radiological weapons. The agent production is easier, cheaper, and more easily concealed than the production of chemical or radiological weapons. If disseminated as an aerosol, the agent would be invisible, silent, odourless and tasteless, and, as it could not be detected, the first signs of an attack could be hundreds or thousands of ill or dying people (see Table 3). On account of the delayed effects, possibly over several days, the perpetrators could have fled the country. Admittedly, the lack of "signature", and the difficulty in some cases of distinguishing between a natural outbreak of disease and a terrorist act, might not appeal to those wishing to make a political statement, but an appropriate choice of agent and target should obviate this difficulty. In essence, biological agents would appear to offer the attractions of extreme potency over considerable distances from a relatively small amount of materials, while enabling the perpetrators to flee from the scene of the attack.[37]

The raw materials for the production of biological agents can be readily obtained. Cultures of *Bacillus anthracis* can be found in research, clinical and veterinary laboratories, and in the soil of cattle country; *Clostridium botulinum* can also be found in nature (as Aum

Table 3 Hypothetical dissemination by aeroplane of 50 kg of biological agent along a line 2 km upwind of a population centre of 500,000 under optimal weather conditions.

Biological agent	Downwind reach (km)	Dead	Incapacitated
Rift Valley Fever	1	400	35,000
Tick Valley Encephalitis	1	9,500	35,000
Typhus	5	19,000	85,000
Brucellosis	10	500	100,000
Q Fever	>20	150	125,000
Tularemia	>20	30,000	125,000
Anthrax	≫20	95,000	125,000

Source: W[orld] H[ealth] O[rganisation], *Health Aspects of Chemical and Biological Weapons* (WHO, 1970) reproduced in Lt-Col. E.M. Eitzen, Hearings on *Global Proliferation of Weapons of Mass Destruction*, Part 1, before the Permanent Subcommittee on Investigations of the Committee on Governmental Affairs United States Senate, 104th Congress, first session (31 October 1995), p. 117.

managed to do from a wilderness near the Tokachi river on the northern island of Hokkaido), stolen from research laboratories, or acquired for notional research purposes by mail orders from professional scientific and medical journals. To cultivate the bacteria, the Aum cult purchased vast amounts of a growth medium, peptone (some 160 drums, each having a capacity of 18 litres, were found at the Mount Fuji headquarters) and standard laboratory equipment, including four fermenters, a vacuum dryer and milling machine. Having worked on the production of anthrax, botulinum toxin, Q fever (a highly infectious rickettsial disease), and possibly others, Seiichi Endo, the senior microbiologist, planned to develop the BW programme by applying advances in biotechnology. He intended to equip a four-storey concrete facility at Naganohara, which was almost built by the time of the Tokyo attack, with a "clean room" possessing specialised ventilation systems and a sealed room for protecting cultivated bacteria from leaking. In short, the cult had demonstrated the ease with which clandestine research can be undertaken.[38]

However, the Aum BW programme was bedevilled by laboratory accidents and at least nine attacks failed (using agents such as botulinum toxin and anthrax), so indicating that the efforts of the cult were hardly a model for biological terrorism. Aum was an extraordinary terrorist group, flourishing as a registered religious sect in Japan, where the police are very reluctant for historical reasons to interfere with religious groups, but, despite financial resources in excess of $1 billion, front companies, overseas contacts, scientific expertise, and the intent of its leadership, it failed to disseminate BW agents effectively. State sponsorship might be a prerequisite for the effective use of BW agents by terrorists, as biological warfare, in the opinion of Professor Milton Leitenberg, 'isn't all that easy for an untrained group to produce'.[39]

Karl Lowe (Institute for Defense Analyses) explained that the process of moving beyond the laboratory phase is 'laden with unexpected twists'. The multi-skilled operation involves the dangerous and demanding task of converting agent from a liquid slurry into a dry powder in milled particles of an appropriate size for aerosol dissemination. It requires calculations about the efficiency of the delivery system and the right amount of agent to inflict casualties over the target area, followed by the reconnoitring, planning, and mounting of the attack itself. The lone terrorist, he affirms, is less likely to master all these tasks than the terrorists benefiting from state-sponsorship.[40] Although terrorists could try to disseminate liquid agents as aerosols, they would probably have to do so by forcing gaseous energy through a narrow orifice and so run the risk of plugging the orifice (which reportedly happened to the Aum cultists) – a problem which can be overcome with the appropriate processing of the agent. A dried agent would be much more effective (and could be easily stored and transported without much risk of detection,[41] and disseminated from devices that require only small amounts of energy), but the process of drying (whether freeze, spray, drum, or azeotropic distillation) would require skilled personnel and sophisticated equipment.[42]

Whether these skills and equipment are beyond the reach of contemporary terrorists is a moot point. Lieutenant-Colonel Edward M. Eitzen, Jr, Chief of the Preventive Medicine Department, Medical Division, US Army Medical Research Institute of Infectious Diseases, observed that the equipment for freeze drying or spray drying has been available in industry for a number of years. While accepting that state sponsorship could provide the requisite expertise for the production of sophisticated biological weapons, he insisted that 'There are numerous people with the technological knowledge necessary to develop crude biological weapons.'[43] These weapons could be dispersed as aerosols from aeroplanes, ships, trucks or canisters, or employed in the sabotage of foods and other products (for which unsophisticated agents such as salmonella and more common bacteria might be used) and in the spreading of disease among animals or plants. Dr Graham Pearson, the former Director General of the Chemical and Biological Defence

Establishment, Porton Down, rightly emphasised that terrorists could face difficulties in mounting aerosol attacks in the open air against a target population. The attacks would face the vagaries of local micro-meteorology, and could suffer from a lack of civilian or military expertise in the dissemination of C/B materials, possibly posing the greatest risk to the terrorists themselves.[44] All these points may explain why the vast majority of terrorists prefer the immediate and (seemingly pre-dictable) effects of conventional bombings. Nevertheless, Aum demon-strated that bio-terrorists can determine where, when, and how to launch an attack, and, if it fails, return to their clandestine facilities, produce another agent or another means of dissemination, and try again. Aum not only mounted several attacks (possibly failing because they chose harmless strains of anthrax)[45] but they were never detected in doing so and were not deterred from further experimentation. Other groups could emulate Aum's determination but recruit adherents with more expertise in the dissemination of aerosols in the open air.

Aspiring terrorists may not plan to undertake large-scale operations, requiring relatively sophisticated delivery systems. They could employ very small amounts of agent for the purposes of assassination and the intimidation of potential defectors, or for the sabotage of foods and other products, coupled with well-publicised threats to damage the rep-utation and/or the commercial viability of the corporations affected. They may realise, too, that even a partially successful aerosol attack (say in a crowded thoroughfare, building, subway or holiday resort) could produce serious effects, including a delayed but burgeoning number of casualties. Compounding the plight of the victims could be the creation of mass panic, the disruption of economic and social activity, the exposure of the government's inability to protect its citizens from biological attack, and the revelation of any medical shortcomings (including possible delays in diagnosis, growing waiting lists of patients, and insufficient beds, isolation wards, and stocks of antibiotics in local hospitals). The potential effects of such an attack, especially if coupled with threatened or follow-up attacks, could be extremely damaging to the authority of the government concerned. They fully justify the concern that the threat of biological terrorism is growing, and that it may not be a question of whether biological agents are used by terrorists but when they will be used.[46]

Hitherto terrorists have displayed a preference for well-tried, conven-tional weaponry which is simpler to use, more reliable, less expensive and requires less risk in obtaining, handling, and using. They may be inhibited about the handling of NBC materials and the process of weaponization if that is desired (and in some cases it may not be, as simply producing and disseminating large quantities of agent may suffice).[47] They may also dislike the uncertainties of dissemination or the delayed effects of biological or radiological attacks. If terrorists wish to create an incident with an immediate and dramatic impact, and one over which they can retain control, they may prefer an explosive device that produces a limited number of casualties, without a legacy of lingering illnesses.[48]

Complementing these technological concerns are the political risks associated with recourse to weapons of mass destruction. Just as states have been reluctant to use such weapons because of adverse political costs, it is hardly surprising that terrorists, most of whom have sought to gain a political following, have not employed weapons of mass destruction.[49] Nor have the states known to sponsor terrorism proved ready to distribute these weapons, doubtless fearing that any retaliation might be directed at themselves and not the terrorists. The terrorists themselves might calculate that the employment of NBC weapons would be disproportionate to their demands, either alienating supporters or provoking a massive retaliation by the government concerned (but if the United States is going to retaliate massively against conventional terrorism, as in August 1998, then fear of provocation may be less inhibiting). Escalation to NBC weapons might still seem potentially counterproductive if, as Brian Jenkins observed, terrorists prefer to see 'a lot of people watching, not a lot of people dead'.[50] As major conventional operations can still attract media attention, and possibly provoke disproportionate responses, states would be ill-advised to become so preoccupied with the potential of NBC terrorism that they neglected their defences against conventional terror.[51]

Despite this caveat, the prospects for NBC terrorism including radiological terrorism, have increased because of the greater diffusion and accessibility of expertise, materials, and more sophisticated, dual-use technology. The likelihood has been further enhanced by the changing nature of international terrorism, with its more diversified range of motives, transnational infrastructures, and capacity to mount complex and coordinated attacks. State-sponsorship might be necessary to undertake some forms of NBC terrorism, especially those involving sophisticated delivery systems, but sponsorship would not be essential for less sophisticated operations such as the poisoning of food or the releasing of a volatile agent within an enclosed building, subway or aircraft. Even when these operations fail (as in the Aum case), they can prove dangerous, cause panic, and expose both the vulnerability of those under attack and the limitations of their law-enforcement authorities. There is every reason to assume that other terrorists will study the efforts of the Aum cult and consider how to apply their methods more effectively.[52] Bruce Hoffman was in no doubt that

> We've definitely crossed a threshold. This is the cutting edge of high-tech terrorism for the year 2000 and beyond. It's the nightmare scenario that people have quietly talked about for years coming true.[53]

In responding to the Aum revelations, President Clinton was not alone in believing that the first priority should be the ratification of the Chemical Weapons Convention. Ratification, it was claimed, would bolster the Geneva Protocol (1925) and the Biological and Toxin Weapons Convention by establishing legal norms against the development, production, stockpiling, transfer and retention of chemical weapons. It would also criminalise the development, production and possession of such weapons under the national legislation required of each state party (so assisting law-enforcement authorities in their investigation, arrest, and prosecution of transgressors). It would inhibit the diversion of chemicals placed on the schedules of the CWC by monitoring and inspecting activities at designated facilities, and require companies to make declarations about their international transfers of certain chemicals. In view of all these benefits, argued Jonathan B. Tucker, it was 'not surprising that the Japanese government's first policy response to the Tokyo subway incident was to ratify the Chemical Weapons Convention and pass domestic implementing legislation'.[54]

It was perhaps none too surprising that the much-criticised Japanese government felt that it had to do *something* in the wake of the Tokyo incident, and that ratifying the CWC was thought to be a suitably reassuring response. However, arms control agreements may not have much effect on terrorist groups, especially religious terrorists, for whom violent attacks may be seen as sacramental acts or a divine duty. Secular terrorists may also respond to the ratifying of the convention in differing ways: while some may remain content with their conventional ordnance and regard escalation as counterproductive, more extreme groups, and those sponsored by states outside the CWC, may regard escalation as an even more tempting means of causing shock and panic. Nor would they necessarily feel inhibited by the terms of the convention, particularly if they planned to employ chemicals from the wide range of dual-purpose toxic chemicals with legitimate civilian applications. When Dr Gordon C. Oehler, Director of the Non-proliferation Center, CIA, was asked whether the Aum cult would have found it harder to make chemical weapons had the CWC been in force since 1993, he flatly disagreed. He emphasised that Aum had not imported any chemicals or chemical weapons across an international border, and that domestic laws were unlikely to curtail the internal movement of chemicals to customers without a criminal record.[55] A US Inter-Agency Report on Terrorism subsequently stated that 'In the case of Aum Shinrikyo, the CWC, the Chemical Weapons Convention, would not have hindered the cult from procuring the needed chemical compounds used in its production of sarin', a view endorsed by George J. Tenet, when acting Director of the CIA. He confirmed that although a determined group might find that the CWC made it more difficult and costly to acquire chemical weapons, they could circumvent its provisions.[56]

These doubts fully reflected the assumption that arms control agreements, however comprehensive in scope, were inherently limited instruments of policy. Although a firm advocate of the CWC, Major-General William F. Burns, when Director of ACDA, frankly admitted that 'conventions don't work against terrorists'.[57] Similarly the safeguards provisions of the IAEA, designed to provide for the timely detection of diversion of significant amounts of nuclear material from peaceful nuclear activities to the manufacture of nuclear weapons, were regarded as basically a means of providing reassurance about the nuclear programmes of non-nuclear weapon states of the NPT and not a barrier to nuclear terrorism.[58] Even the enhanced safeguards of the additional protocol approved by the IAEA Board of Governors on 15 May 1997, were designed primarily to provide as complete and correct an account as practicable of a state's production and holdings of nuclear source material, its activities in the further processing of nuclear material, and specified elements of its infrastructure that directly supported a state's current or planned nuclear fuel cycle. While this may ensure that the NPT continues to impede access to fissile materials on the open market, sovereign states remain responsible for the physical security of their facilities and for protecting materials against sub-national adversaries. In Russia domestic provisions, bolstered by bilateral US and Russian initiatives, remain the prime means of addressing this problem.[59] Finally, the proposed verification regime for the Biological and Toxin Weapons Convention, irrespective of its other attributes, is most unlikely to serve as a tool for detecting clandestine activity by biological terrorists. The proposed regime could not expect the wide-ranging inspection rights enjoyed by the UNSCOM inspectors – rights which produced mandatory declarations, numerous intrusive routine and challenge inspections over four years at 80 biocapable facilities but which failed to uncover 'incriminating evidence that would identify any of these sites as linked to a proscribed BW programme'.[60] On-site inspections, in short, may not detect illicit activities by those who are outside the convention.

The Tokyo subway incident also raised questions about the readiness of modern societies, not least the United States – the target of about one quarter of all terrorist attacks worldwide – to meet the threat posed by terrorists armed with weapons of mass destruction. Questions were asked about the efficacy of US intelligence activities when the CIA admitted that it neither monitored religious cults in general nor the Aum cult in particular, even after the Matsumoto attack; the failure to share information between agencies; and the lack of international cooperation despite the anti-American rhetoric of Aum and the presence of large US bases in Japan (two of which Aum tried to attack with botulinum toxin). Concerns were also raised about the organisation and training of response teams (prompted by the sight of Japanese civilian responders entering subway unprotected alongside military and other government officials encased in modern protective CBW uniforms) and about assurances that all would be well in Western subways, although some authorities never conducted exercises geared specifically to the CBW threat.[61] Numerous reports and papers were written, advocating the reform or enhancement of the provisions for combating terrorism,[62] but any national scheme had to recognise certain caveats. Just as governments cannot guarantee the safety of all their citizens, or even their political, military and judicial élites, from conventional terrorism, they cannot protect all their citizens from attacks with weapons of mass destruction. In modern times only a few, relatively small states have ever made provisions for civil defence on a nationwide basis, and, in the absence of reliable biological detectors, even these provisions are unlikely to be adequate. Nor can a civil defence programme readily counter an episodic terrorist threat in peacetime other than in planning to cope with a potential crisis and manage its consequences. A nationwide distribution of respirators is only feasible on the brink of war (as in Israel from October 1990 onwards) but the distribution could still cause panic and, in the absence of an imminent threat, could invite public indifference, misuse of equipment, and even ridicule (as in Britain during the Second World War).[63]

Rather than await terrorist attacks, it is obviously preferable to pre-empt and prevent such actions. To apprehend international conspirators will require coordinated diplomacy, intelligence and law-enforcement efforts, but any counter-terrorist successes (and there were apparently several during the Gulf War)[64] will receive far less publicity (for fear of revealing the methods employed) than terrorist incidents. Moreover, coordinating international action before an attack occurs, and without the threat of war, is always likely to encounter difficulties. In the absence of utterly conclusive information from defectors or other 'inside' sources, allies may not have the same levels of concern about a particular terrorist group, may not share the same anxieties about the new forms of terrorism, and may have differing views about the treatment of the sponsors of terrorism. They may also recoil at the burden-sharing implications of pre-emptive action (where the costs might be measured politically, economically, or in strains upon their domestic legal procedures). Finally, if a state responds to terrorism by retaliatory bombing, it may find that the action is far more popular domestically than internationally. Despite precision bombing with minimal collateral damage, the action may secure only limited international support unless the evidence is convincing that the correct target was struck and the response was appropriate.[65] Combating terrorism, however elaborately organised, funded, and managed, is a highly complex process and one riddled with political choices and daunting uncertainties.

Nevertheless the task cannot be neglected, especially by the United States as it conducts its national security planning out to the year 2020. Within this time span, the United States may face not only challenges to deployed forces, military bases and embassies overseas but also, and possibly increasingly, transnational threats to the US homeland from international terrorists, organized crime and narcotics smugglers. These adversaries, particularly international terrorists, pose a different and difficult challenge to the United States because they are difficult to deter, may be willing to employ NBC weapons, and do not respect any boundaries, whether political, organisational, legal or moral. Any terrorist attacks within the United States (as elsewhere) will have an immediate impact locally, and may require state and federal assistance (with the latter coming from any or most of 40 designated federal agencies, departments, and bureaux).[66] Although the US government has considerable assets at its disposal for combating terrorism, it has been criticised for failing to develop a comprehensive national strategy, or even a capacity for long-range planning to address this problem.[67] Presidential interest has been desultory, leaving a significant gap between Presidential Decision Directive(PDD)-39 of June 1995 and PDD-62 and PDD-63 of May 1998 – with Clinton's interest belatedly revived in late 1997 and early 1998 by the continuing Iraqi crisis, Alibek's revelations, intelligence reports that 17 states were now undertaking BW research, and, reportedly, the reading of Richard Preston's popular science fiction novel, *The Cobra Event*.[68] Meanwhile policies and analyses had been driven by activist legislators (Defense Against Weapons of Mass Destruction Act of 1996 or the Nunn-Lugar-Domenici (NLD) legislation), the Pentagon (with its plans to inoculate all serving personnel against anthrax) or specialist committees (with studies by the Defense Science Board Summer Study on Transnational Threats and the National Defense Panel issued in December 1997).

US policy, as adumbrated in PDD-39, aimed to deter, pre-empt, apprehend and prosecute terrorists; to work with friendly governments in combating terrorism; to identify and isolate sponsors of terrorism, making them pay for their actions; and not to make any concessions to terrorists. To meet these aims, it required an interagency effort coordinated by the National Security Council. The State Department acted as the "lead agency" for overseas incidents and the Department of Justice, acting through the Federal Bureau of Investigation (FBI), had a similar responsibility for domestic incidents. Although state governments retained primary responsibility for managing the consequences of terrorist incidents, the coordination of federal support lay with the Federal Emergency Management Agency (FEMA) and, since October 1998, with the National Domestic Preparedness Office (NDPO). Intelligence from the various agencies was shared in an interagency committee, with the Director for Central Intelligence's Counterterrorist Center at the CIA compiling reports on terrorist groups and issuing monthly classified reviews of international terrorism. The FBI monitored the activities of suspected domestic groups and individuals, and conducted surveillance on suspected foreign terrorists under the Foreign Intelligence Surveillance Act.[69] The effectiveness of this intelligence monitoring is possibly moot: at a conference of US law enforcement officials in Honolulu (September 1998), a CIA official described the agency's 'reliable monitoring' of nuclear trafficking as 'limited and fragmentary'.[70]

The US organisation for combating terror, with its multiple layers of federal involvement, has been appraised in several reports,[71] and criticised by several commentators, including senior state and local officials at a 'Stakeholders' Forum' in Washington, DC (August 1998), for being incoherent, confusing, excessively bureaucratic and prone to duplication.[72] Hence the creation of the NDPO to assume overall responsibility for coordinating the federal government's efforts to prepare American communities for terrorist incidents involving weapons of mass destruction. At the same time federal funding for counter terrorism has swollen dramatically after the bombing of the US embassies in east Africa (August 1998), with $2.8 billion requested to fight terrorists armed with germs, chemicals and electronic devices, and the grant for domestic preparedness growing from $12 million in 1998 to a projected $171 million for the year 2000.[73]

However demanding and costly these requirements, the US conceptual approach remains instructive. "Anti terrorism" is a prime consideration, namely defensive measures to reduce the vulnerabilities of personnel and facilities at home and overseas. Protecting military personnel, their families, facilities and equipment involves not merely physical security and protection procedures at various bases but also a widespread training and awareness programme. Civilian protection is a more diverse activity, with the Secret Service responsible for protecting the president, visiting heads of state and other US officials as defined by statute, the State Department responsible for protecting US diplomatic posts and persons overseas, the Federal Aviation Administration the security of civilian aviation (for US airports and US-flagged carriers as well as proffering assistance and recommendations for foreign airports served by US carriers and foreign-flagged carriers with routes to the United States), and government-private sector arrangements for the protection of key elements in the US national infrastructure (financial services, water supply, telecommunications and others).[74]

In "counter-terrorism" – offensive measures used to deter, disrupt or respond to terrorist acts – the United States disseminates threat warnings through the CIA and FBI, utilises economic sanctions (through the Department of the Treasury's Office of Foreign Assets Control and the Customs Service) against the sponsors and supporters of terrorism, and employs both covert and retaliatory military action against terrorist targets. International cooperation can both support and facilitate such action, notably the joint declarations of the G-8, conferences and the joint ministerial and expert-level meetings devoted entirely to countering terrorism. There are also nine key international treaties and conventions against forms of terrorism, expanding the legal basis for bringing terrorists to justice. When the United Nations imposed sanctions on Libya after the destruction of Pan Am flight 103 over Lockerbie, this was the first time that it had imposed sanctions on a country because of its links with terrorism.[75]

Should a terrorist act occur, the United States plans to respond by means of crisis management (attempts to resolve the incident) and consequence management (efforts to alleviate the effects of the incident). The FBI would direct an operational response to a domestic incident. Each of its 56 field offices has contingency plans for WMD incidents, with further support from the FBI Critical Incident Response Group (including the Hostage Rescue Team) and specialist assistance from other federal agencies. In the event of a nuclear incident, the Department of Energy (DoE) would activate its Nuclear Emergency Search Team (a body that has been in existence since 1975) to assist in the assessing the threat, conducting search operations, disabling any device (once the military had rendered it safe) and removing nuclear materials. Arguably, the FBI and local police could benefit from a chemical and biological equivalent of NEST,[76] but in its absence have to call on various federal agencies. Several Department of Health and Human Services (HHS) bodies could provide threat assessment, consultation, agent identification, epidemiological investigation, hazard detection, decontamination, and medical, pharmaceutical, and public health support operations.[77] The Environmental Protection Agency (EPA) could assist in identifying contaminants, sample collection and analysis, on-site safety and the issue of permits for the custody, transportation and transfer of chemical materials. The Department of Defense (DoD) could provide assistance from some rapid-response groups, a 24-hour command centre, and the US Army Technical Escort Unit with its capacity for sampling, identifying, rendering-safe, disposing, escorting and mitigating the hazards associated with weaponised and non-weaponised CB materials. Contingency planning by these departments and agencies for special events such as the 1996 Olympic Games in Atlanta, Georgia, revealed the need for improvements in communications equipment, the distribution system for antidotes to WMD agents, and the surveillance system for reporting illnesses associated with a chemical or biological attack.[78]

Generally crisis and consequent management would occur concurrently, with local and state authorities assuming responsibility for the latter but with the NDPO coordinating any federal support. Ten Army National Guard Rapid Assessment and Initial Detection (RAID) teams have been established in selected cities to respond to NBC incidents (other units will be formed to assist in surveillance and decontamination). The Chemical/Biological Incident Response Force (CBIRF) established by the Marines in February 1997 consists of approximately 375 marines and sailors, with a 120-man Rapid Response Force on a four-hour alert able to be reinforced within 24 hours. The "first responders" – local fire, police, and emergency medical personnel – would remain the key elements in an emergency. They would have to identify any agents involved, decontaminate, treat, and transport victims; establish a controlled perimeter around the incident; and assume all the preliminary burdens before support arrived from a regional Metropolitan Medical Strike Team (largely composed of off-duty local fire, police, and emergency medical personnel) and later, if required, the second wave of more highly trained specialist federal support. Under the Nunn-Lugar-Domenici legislation the DoD was required to 'train the trainers' in the country's 120 largest cities by fiscal year 2001 (and loan equipment to state and local authorities for training purposes).[79] In view of similar training courses provided by FEMA and the Department of Justice, GAO depicted these provisions as 'evidence of a fragmented and possibly wasteful federal approach'. Echoing the criticisms of state and local officials, it questioned the value of the city-by-city approach in the absence of any threat analysis, the failure to exploit the potential of regional instruction where cities are clustered together and share emergency services, and the value of the RAID units as other federal support units (the Army's Technical Escort Unit, the Marines' CBIRF and the HHS' National Medical Response Teams) would arrive more quickly and provide a range of specialist assistance.[80]

Undoubtedly US policy could benefit from a more coordinated approach – a much-publicised plan (22 May 1998) to stockpile vaccines at strategic sites across the country was postponed within a month, pending the possible development of cheaper and more effective vaccines.[81] The NDPO may improve the overall organisation, but US policy has had to evolve cautiously, avoiding the risk of over-reacting and of taking action that would compromise legitimate personal liberties and freedoms. It had to take account of local, state and federal jurisdictions and of legal statutes, not least the Posse Comitatus Act, prohibiting the use of the armed forces to enforce domestic law. It also deserves some credit for perceiving the threat from new forms of terrorism, for proposing and funding some important initiatives (particularly the training programmes for "first responders"), and for raising awareness about the possibility of NBC terrorism in a way that few allied governments have emulated.[82] Nevertheless, the threat from NBC terrorism has to be kept in proportion, particularly in view of the continuing threat from terrorists armed with conventional ordnance. International efforts aimed at pre-empting and preventing terrorism remain crucial, but they have to be correlated with other nonproliferation policies, especially arms control and export controls, to establish norms of international behaviour.

6
Multilateral Control Regimes: Their Role and Impact

Multilateral regimes, whether focused on legally binding arms control or disarmament treaties or on consensual agreements about export controls, have sought to curb the spread of weapons of mass destruction. As a core element in preventive diplomacy, the regimes have served a multitude of purposes. The arms agreements and their periodic review conferences have established, reinforced, and sustained various norms of international behaviour. By expanding their membership, these treaties and conventions have demonstrated enduring concerns about the weapons involved and their potential for development, acquisition and use. The regimes have also indicated that these are matters of international concern, and that multilateral commitments are an appropriate and necessary response. The export control regimes (principally the Australia Group, the Zangger Committee, the Nuclear Suppliers' Group (NSC), and the Missile Technology Control Regime) have all broadened their memberships, expanded and refined their lists of controlled items, and greatly enhanced their coordination.[1] Nevertheless, proliferation has persisted, cases of non-compliance with various treaty regimes have occurred, and doubts remain about the intentions and activities of certain states despite their membership of multilateral regimes. What then have these regimes accomplished in the transition from a bipolar to a multipolar world; how far are they challenged by technological and political developments; and how much are they dependent upon the leadership, initiatives, and sustained commitment of the United States?

All these regimes responded to the revelations of the vast NBC programmes of Iraq. They had to take account of Iraq's ability to import a large volume of materials and equipment (much of it dual-use) to sustain its NBC programmes, and of the abject failure of the IAEA inspectors to notice anything amiss in their monitoring of safeguarded nuclear materials. This was even more galling as Iraq never conducted its activities in a totally clandestine manner. David A. Kay, the former head of the evaluation section of the IAEA and a chief inspector in Iraq after the Gulf War, explained:

> In fact the Iraqis did something quite different. Their major nuclear weapons research program was conducted at exactly the same site that was inspected twice a year by the International Atomic Energy Agency. The safeguards had simply missed it.
>
> What had happened is that the technology had changed, the diversion, deception and denial techniques that were used by the Iraqis were far more advanced than anyone gave them credit for in the 1980s, and they fooled and defeated the international inspectors.[2]

The Iraqis had exploited the fact that the NPT regime was essentially a co-operative arrangement whereby non-nuclear weapon states had accepted regular inspections of their declared nuclear materials to confirm their safeguards undertakings. By co-operating with the inspectors, they built confidence in their 'peaceful' nuclear intentions, and benefited from the technical assistance that the IAEA provided to 'peaceful' nuclear programmes. In other WMD areas the Iraqis had by-passed export controls to import materials and equipment (including chemical precursors, chemical reactors and heat exchangers), thrived on the absence of multilateral controls on biological exports (importing fermenters, spray dryers and pathogens), and employed external expertise, illicit materials and advanced Western commercial technology to extend the range of several SCUD missiles and build their own SCUD-type missiles.[3]

The Iraqi revelations, far from eroding confidence in the value of arms control regimes and export control arrangements, merely encouraged governments to improve the existing regimes. New agreements were concluded – the CWC in 1993 and the Comprehensive Test Ban Treaty (CTBT) in 1996 – and efforts were made to improve or provide verification for existing regimes (the $93 + 2$ safeguards arrangements for the IAEA and discussion of a new protocol for the Biological and Toxin Weapons Convention). New items were also added to existing control lists (including biological pathogens and equipment to the chemicals listed by the Australia Group), domestic licensing processes were tightened up (the Enhanced Proliferation Control Initiative (EPCI) of the Bush administration), and domestic legislation enacted (the British

Biological Weapons Act of 1994 and the American Antiterrorism and Effective Death Penalty Act of 1996). New regimes were formed (notably the Wassenaar Arrangement on Export Controls for Conventional Arms and Dual-Use Goods and Technologies in 1996), and the membership of multilateral regimes expanded (gaining Russia as a member of the NSC and the MTCR, France and China as members of the NPT, and China as purportedly observing the guidelines of the MTCR).

All these developments were hailed as major achievements in the task of countering proliferation. Despite the nuclear tests of India and Pakistan, the NPT regime was still regarded as having succeeded 'beyond the expectations of its founders'.[4] Some commentators applauded the resolve of the IAEA's Board of Governors to use special inspections (or try to do so in North Korea) and to launch the $93 + 2$ enhanced safeguards programme (which it would ultimately approve in May 1997). They also praised the willingness of the 1995 Review Conference to make the NPT permanent without formal opposition; the signing of the Bangkok and Pelindaba treaties, establishing nuclear-free zones in South-East Asia and Africa; the conclusion of the CTBT as a substantive move by the nuclear-weapon states towards honouring their commitments under Article VI of the NPT; and the continued expansion of the NPT's membership towards near-universality. By 1998 the NPT had 187 members, including the five declared nuclear powers and other members like Argentina, Belarus, Kazakhstan, South Africa and the Ukraine who had abandoned their nuclear weapons and/or nuclear explosives programmes in the 1990s.[5]

There were similar plaudits for the CWC, a non-discriminatory treaty unlike the NPT, that entered into force on 29 April 1997. Within its first year, John Gee, the Deputy Director-General of the Organization for the Prohibition of Chemical Weapons (OPCW), claimed a 26% growth in membership from 87 to 110 states parties. 'No other multilateral disarmament agreement', he added, 'has enjoyed such strong support from the international community so soon after its entry into force'.[6] By September 1998, when inspectors of the OPCW had completed some 250 inspections and 117 states had ratified the CWC (of whom eight declared existing or past chemical weapons capabilities), this was hailed as 'one of the most significant achievements in international disarmament of the past year'. Huang Yu, Director of External Relations for the OPCW, now claimed that 'the tide has been turned and the possession of chemical weapons is no longer seen as acceptable in the majority of countries around the world' (apparently overlooking the fact that 109 states parties had apparently never possessed chemical weapons anyway).[7]

The BTWC has moved more slowly, attracting fewer ratifications than the NPT and a derisory response to the requests at the review conferences of 1986 and 1991 for politically-binding confidence-building declarations (only 35 from a treaty membership of about 120 by September 1992). The states parties to the BTWC established two Ad Hoc Groups (the first composed of governmental experts on verification and known as VEREX). The VEREX group reported on these measures in 1993, and a special conference (19–30 September 1994) established the second Ad Hoc Group to examine how these verification measures could be incorporated into a legally-binding document, as well as procedures and mechanisms for implementing them and investigating incidents of alleged usage. The draft provisions included a range of off-site measures, notably mandatory declarations of facilities, programmes and relevant events; exchange visits; remote sensing whether from satellites, aircraft or ground-based off-site systems; data-exchange; and the sharing, monitoring and checking of information through an independent BWC organisation. They also referred to on-site measures, including random and clarification visits (if they can be conducted without a loss of commercial proprietary information), auditing, sampling, identification of key equipment, and investigations of allegations of use and/or unusual outbreaks of disease, whether involving humans, animals or plants. In July 1997 the Ad Hoc Group produced a rolling text for this prospective protocol (23 articles, eight annexes and five appendices), and began the tortuous process of seeking collective agreement at subsequent meetings. Graham Pearson argued that 'It is evident that there are verification measures that have at least a finite possibility of detecting noncompliance, and such measures in combination have a very significant deterrent effect.'[8]

Complementing this deterrent effect are the multilateral export control regimes, all of which share the premise that the export of certain materials and equipment may facilitate proliferation, and can be impeded or at least delayed and made more expensive, if major producers agree to impose controls. These regimes differ considerably in scope. Although they are not formally linked to any multilateral arms conventions or nonproliferation treaties, the Australia Group supported the universal aims of the BTWC and the CWC, and both the Zangger Committee and the NSG have sought to assist in the implementation of the NPT. Conversely, the MTCR is not supported by any multilateral treaty or convention, restricting the possession or use of ballistic missiles or any international agency monitoring compliance with its provisions. It also lacks enforcement mechanisms or even institutionalised arrangements for regular meetings. Nonetheless, all the supplier cartels have sought to broaden their memberships in the 1990s, and, in the case of the Australia Group and the MTCR, to dilute the impression that they simply served the interests of Western industrialised nations. The regimes have brought in most of the former members of the Warsaw Pact, the European countries that were neutral or non-aligned during the Cold War, and states such as Argentina and South Africa.

All the regimes have refined their lists of controlled activities following the revelations of Iraq's successful procurement efforts. In March 1991 the NSG met for the first time since 1978 to update its list of controlled items and did so again in January 1992, when it included a wider range of nuclear-related dual-use equipment and adopted the longstanding US policy of requiring "full-scope" safeguards for all nuclear exports (requiring the purchasers of nuclear technology to open all their nuclear facilities to inspection and not just the facility due to use the imported item). The Zangger Committee updated its list of nuclear export items, whose transfer would "trigger" a requirement for the application of IAEA safeguards to ensure that the items were not used to make nuclear explosives. The Australia Group added biological materials and equipment to their list of controlled items, while the MTCR, in January 1993, issued revised guidelines to limit the risks from the proliferation of missile delivery systems for all weapons of mass destruction: chemical and biological as well as nuclear weapons.[9]

While the multilateral export control regimes are regarded as a useful forum for informal discussion, the exchange of information, lobbying, and bargaining in support of national policy objectives, the general aim of their discussions is to build a consensus on the conditions and items of technology transfer. Thereafter the regimes rely upon states to administer export controls independently through national export codes and legislation if necessary, and, ultimately, upon a degree of collaboration between governments and industries to implement these policies. Given the increasing diffusion of scientific and technological knowledge and the growth of industrial infrastructures within the developing world, as well as the existence of suppliers from outside the multilateral regimes,[10] the controls and embargoes are essentially buying time. As David Fischer, a former Assistant Director-General of the IAEA, has argued, this can be crucial, enabling regimes to change their minds or be persuaded to do so, with Argentina, Brazil and South Africa serving as important examples.[11]

Even so, technology denial has tended to succeed when combined with diplomatic initiatives, security guarantees, and regional confidence-building measures (CBMs). Walter Slocombe, US Under Secretary for Defense for Policy, has reasonably claimed that US 'strong security relationships have probably played as great a role in nonproliferation over the past 40 years as the NPT or any other single factor'.[12] Technology denial was almost certainly a secondary consideration in the switch of policies by Argentina and Brazil, where the return of civilian leadership in both countries proved the decisive factor, with their mutual wish to gain greater access to advanced technology and foreign trade. Both countries set up a joint system for the accounting and control of their nuclear materials on 18 July 1991, which entered into force on 12 December 1991. This paved the way for a Quadripartite Agreement between the two states, the joint agency, and the IAEA (13 December 1991), enabling the nuclear materials in all of their nuclear facilities to come within "full-scope" IAEA safeguards. Economic pressure (notably the German threat to terminate all nuclear relations by 1995 unless Brazil adopted full scope safeguards) probably contributed towards the ratifying of this agreement by the Brazilian Chamber of Deputies, but economic inducements, especially the prospect of access to advanced technology, may have been crucial in securing the necessary votes.[13]

By any measure, preventive diplomacy has had notable successes: international norms have been preserved and strengthened (more conspicuously for nuclear and chemical weapons than biological); the regimes have responded to various "shocks" (more fully to the Iraqi revelations than the North Korean defiance of the NPT); and a new international organisation (OPCW) has come into existence. Multilateral regimes appear to have made a successful transition from a bipolar to a multipolar world, even if export controls are still regarded as essentially discriminatory, exacerbating 'North–South' divisions. Critics characterise the controls as perpetuating the division between nuclear 'haves' and 'have-nots', as undermining the pledge of Article XI of the CWC to facilitate 'the fullest possible exchange' of chemicals and equipment between states parties, and as impeding the space programmes and technological development of various states. They also describe the regimes as ineffective and counterproductive, merely stimulating drives towards self-reliance and indigenous development.[14] Nevertheless, multilateral export controls, implemented quite legitimately at national level, seem firmly embedded in the international arena, and have benefited from the active involvement and diplomatic endeavours of the Bush and Clinton administrations.[15]

Arms control has confounded forecasts that it was no longer necessary or particularly relevant in the wake of the Cold War. Although 'tending arms-control agreements', as Brad Roberts avers, 'has rarely attracted the same energy or public enthusiasm as creating them', this has been a conspicuous feature of the 1990s, with the United States engaged as facilitator, monitor, and guarantor at both global and regional levels.[16] International organizations have also been active in promoting their regimes: the IAEA Director-General made a timely visit to Brazil during its ratification debate and the OPCW's Director-General, José Bustani, made his first visit to the Russian Federation, which had yet to ratify the CWC but soon did so (on 5 November 1997).[17] In short, the 1990s has witnessed a surge of preventive diplomacy aimed at curbing the proliferation of weapons of mass destruction; it has prompted claims that a process of reversing proliferation was well under way.[18]

For the participating states, the multilateral arms control regimes have a continuing momentum. Committed to periodic review conferences (and now in the case of the NPT, preparatory commissions in each of the three years prior to the 2000 review conference), states not merely reappraise their various treaties and conventions on a regular basis but also consider ways of strengthening their implementation and broadening their base of support. However, strengthening existing regimes, introducing new inspection procedures, and, where appropriate, devising new treaties such as the CTBT, will not necessarily curb the activities of determined proliferators. The belief that the mere signing of the CTBT on 24 September 1996 would establish a powerful norm against nuclear testing (even in advance of its ratification by all 44 nuclear-capable states of the Conference of Disarmament)[19] was swept aside by the nuclear tests of India and Pakistan in May 1998. Similarly the introduction of more intrusive inspection measures, particularly the 93 + 2 safeguards, will not necessarily transform the nature of an arms control regime that is essentially co-operative in scope and operation. Historically, the NPT has taken the form of a tacit political bargain, with agreement upon the ultimate norm that states should not possess nuclear weapons, requiring the five declared nuclear states to seek ways to divest themselves of their nuclear stocks while the others are guaranteed access to civilian nuclear technology. Safeguards have served primarily to demonstrate the peaceful intentions of the states concerned, and the introduction of more intrusive inspection procedures encountered resistance from the IAEA's Board of Governors.[20] The additional protocol, though devised in 1995, was not approved until May 1997 and would only be applied to states that volunteered to adopt its provisions. Despite the readiness of the nuclear states to participate in the additional protocol, opening up much, if not all, of their non-military industry to inspection (as the protocol is designed to detect new proliferators), only 32 states had signed the protocol or were soon expected to do so by September 1998. Whether the states causing most concern will accept the new safeguards remains doubtful, and in the meantime the regime will be monitored by inspectors operating under two different safeguards procedures.[21]

States parties may also believe that preserving the integrity of their treaty regimes remains an absolute priority and so any disputes should be resolved, if possible, by arbitration in a non-confrontational manner. Traditionally the IAEA inspectorate sought to resolve anomalies or possible violations of the NPT by moving through prescribed review channels, with discussions between the Agency and the state concerned. Operating on the assumption that states joined the treaty out of self-interest, and submitted themselves to IAEA safeguards to demonstrate their compliance with their international undertakings, the Agency sought to resolve any anomalies or discrepancies quietly and "in-house".[22] Whether the IAEA can sustain this approach is arguable, following the revelations of calculated non-compliance and deception by Iraq and North Korea's refusal to permit special inspections of its nuclear facilities. The Agency may try to rely on co-operation as far as possible, especially as efforts to upgrade its safeguards system could be limited by a reluctance of members to increase the IAEA's budget.[23]

The OPCW may encounter somewhat similar problems as the Executive Council wrestles with the conflicting requirements of transparency and confidentiality. The early reports of the OPCW – both the Director-General's *Status of Implementation Report* (SIR) submitted to each session of Council and the annual *Verification Implementation Report* (VIR) – were general in scope without specific information on particular states parties (not even mentioning the names of the states concerned). At the ninth meeting of Council (21–4 April 1998) some Council members pressed for more specific information in future reports, and, by 20 May, 18 states parties had requested information about other states, or a particular state (but only 12 of them had provided details on how they would handle such information in accordance with paragraph 4 of the Confidentiality Annex of the Convention). Bustani recommended that the SIR and VIR should include as much information as possible within the provisions of the Confidentiality Policy and the Media and Public Affairs Policy, but, at the next meeting of Council, he conceded that only a few states had volunteered to be named.[24] Although preserving confidentiality may facilitate the maximum degree of co-operation among existing and prospective members of the CWC, and underpin assurances about the protection of commercial information, confidence in the Convention will only be enhanced by more transparency in the dissemination of data.

The regimes will also have to respond to technological challenges, especially those which might enable states to develop "virtual" weapons capabilities that might not breach the terms of treaties but would enable states to break out of a treaty at relatively short notice. For example, the NPT obliges non-nuclear weapon states not to manufacture nuclear weapons but it does not define 'manufacture' with any precision (and simply precluding the final assembly of a completed nuclear weapon would be too late in the process). The treaty hardly clarifies the status of design work and planning for nuclear weapons or the implications that could be involved by the acquisition of sensitive nuclear technologies or new advances in enrichment technologies. Even if potential proliferants were unable to exploit advanced enrichment technologies, they might import dual-use equipment to upgrade their capacities in machining, computations, diagnostics, chemical processing, simulating aspects of weapons design, and in improving the guidance and propulsion of delivery systems. In their pursuit of an EMIS programme at Tuwaitha, the Iraqis employed unclassified data from the Manhattan Project, developed several generations of prototype devices to optimise the design of production equipment, and incorporated modern microprocessor, fibre optic and computer-assisted controls into the system to achieve gains in reliability, precision and availability. These gains were not proven in full-scale production but they may explain why intelligence and other circles underestimated the military potential of Iraq's EMIS programme.[25]

Technological developments have also transformed the potential of biological warfare (see Chapter 4). In the mid-1980s US officials warned that biological production technology had proceeded to a point where large quantities of biological products could be rapidly produced in small facilities, so obviating the need, in some cases, for long term storage. The DIA claimed that anthrax agent could be produced from seed culture in 96 hours using batch fermentation or continuous fermentation, and that both systems could be computer-controlled.[26] Production could exploit advances in mammalian cell culture (which can be grown on the surface of minute beads instead of the surface of glass roller bottles, thereby simplifying the production of viruses); continuous flow fermenters, dramatically increasing productivity; new compact ultrafiltration methods, greatly reducing the time required to separate and reconstitute products; and hollow fibre technology that occupies less than a twentieth of the volume of previous technology and 'permits a far greater concentration of cells with a markedly increased rate of recovery in a shorter time than previously obtained using roller bottles'. Although these developments have tended to erode the distinction between small laboratories and production facilities,[27] questions of intent are not the only means of distinguishing between offensive and defensive BW programmes, both of which employ common laboratory techniques at the outset. There are likely to be observable differences between offensive and defensive BW programmes (with the former involving research on the mass production and storage of large quantities of micro-organisms, stabilisation in an aerosol, possible improvements in virulence or persistence, and in methods for dissemination and weapon development).[28] Potential proliferants, nonetheless, may be able to explain away freezers full of seed stock and a production facility which normally produces agricultural or medical products, while retaining 'the ability to produce militarily significant quantities of BW from seed stock within a month or so'.[29]

Rapid acquisition of chemical warfare (CW) agents is also technologically possible for the purposes of immediate usage (as distinct from long-term storage for the purposes of a deterrent). Whether a surge capacity, as the Iraqis developed, would meet the military requirements of other states would depend upon how large and pressing those requirements were. It has often been claimed that any pharmaceutical or pesticide plant could produce CW agents, and that much of the equipment, including special alloys and glass-lined vessels required in the production of highly corrosive CW agents, is genuinely dual-use as it meets current health, safety, environmental or commercial practices. It has also been asserted that these production plants could be converted within 24 hours, or less, to appear as legitimate civilian plants, removing all traces of CW production,[30] (so possibly thwarting a challenge inspection). These claims have been questioned as either untested generally, or at variance with the results of trial inspections at multi-purpose batch plants, or as too sweeping for the production of the more toxic nerve agents, like sarin, for which only a minority of pesticide plants might be convertible.[31] Much of this debate about the feasibility of rapid conversion, without leaving traces of illicit activity, must remain speculative until tested by challenge inspections (and none of these were mounted in the first 18 months of the OPCW's existence). CW agents could certainly be produced in chemical plants outside the CWC regime, and, even within the regime, states could try to maintain a "virtual" CW capability by planning to divert chemicals from perfectly legitimate stocks produced in civilian facilities, either older CW agents, such as phosgene and hydrogen cyanide, or a key precursor such as thiodiglycol (TDG) from which mustard gas can be produced (in a one-stage production process, involving a reaction with a chlorinating agent such as phosphorous trichloride or thionyl chloride or hydrochloric acid which is, according to Professor Ronald Sutherland, 'extremely simple').[32]

Alternatively, states might plan to maintain a small covert capability either by producing agents, such as tear gas and mustard gas, in 'minimum' facilities,[33] or by planning to convert production periodically at civilian plants in small uneconomic quantities, and, possibly following the Iraqi precedent, by paying scant attention to safety requirements (although they would have to be more careful in environmental matters, lest a mishandling of waste products attracted external attention). They might even request the design of new multipurpose plants that could facilitate rapid changeovers in production[34] (and while this capability might seem highly suspicious, it might not constitute evidence of non-compliance in the absence of CW agents or their precursors on site). Finally, states might simply retain a small undeclared stockpile of CW agent either in bulk form or in filled munitions. Russian intelligence has argued that

> detecting 100 or 500 tonnes of concealed chemical weapons in any country is practically impossible. Chemical compounds and agents may be stored in containers smaller than regular barrels and may even be continuously on the move, in a number of instances.[35]

Neither export controls nor arms control are likely to solve all these problems. Although maintaining multilateral export controls may serve political purposes (indicating that the governments concerned are not condoning proliferation and are attempting to deter such activity by imposing additional costs and delays on proliferators),[36] the process may have only a limited effect on the diffusion of technology. In the first place, some states may join supplier cartels to exploit the benefits of the trading arrangements within the cartels and not necessarily to uphold the constraints on external trade. In spite of multilateral agreements on nuclear and missile exports, Russia has proffered assistance in the construction of Iran's Bushehr reactor, advice on the mining and processing of uranium in Iran, and missile components and materials to several regimes, including India, Iraq and Iran.[37] Problems have also arisen within the Australia Group over the unauthorised transshipments of restricted goods and technology, which can be traded among the members of the group without export licensing requirements. As unlicensed shipments cannot be properly monitored, critics maintain that countries such as Iran and Iraq have evaded export controls through multiple transshipments from group members.[38]

Secondly, controls are more feasible in some areas than in others. They are more difficult to apply where alternative suppliers operate outside the regimes, the components are small and relatively inexpensive, and items are dual-use and so easily hidden under the guise of legitimate civilian programmes. The export of missile technology and equipment, so easily justified for space launch programmes (or jet engines purportedly for aircraft development but actually for cruise missile programmes) may be less easily inhibited than nuclear-related exports, while chemical and biological materials and equipment may be even less susceptible to export controls. John Deutch candidly conceded that monitoring chemical and biological programmes posed particular difficulties:

> It's a lot more uncertain ... because of the fact that much of the technology used in those programs is dual use, so the equipment and the technology can be procured for another purpose and then be diverted. It's hard to track it, it doesn't require large facilities, it doesn't require special nuclear materials, it doesn't require tremendous electricity or other signatures.[39]

Thirdly, many aspects of WMD programmes can be produced indigenously, thereby bypassing export controls altogether. Iraq produced all the components for its EMIS facility, upgraded and refined many of its imported missiles, and could have developed a chemical and biological weapons capability from its own resources had it been forced to do so. Export controls will neither inhibit a determined proliferator from producing some weapons, particularly First World War vintage ones such as mustard gas,[40] nor impede terrorists, like Aum Shinrikyo, from obtaining their materials and equipment domestically.[41]

Maintaining export controls also involves hidden costs. The mere existence of controls may induce complacency that proliferation is being addressed effectively, may incur financial costs as other suppliers meet the demands for restricted goods and technology, may forego the intelligence and influence that might have been gained from trading with the potential recipients, and may prove politically divisive.[42] Of these costs, the potential economic losses are possibly the least significant. As indicated in a report for the Chemical and Biological Arms Control Institute, the volume of exports in nuclear, chemical and biological goods from the developed to the developing world is vast (in chemicals, the value of this trade increased from $33 billion in 1980 to $57 billion in 1991, and the US alone approved 54,862 licenses for nuclear-related exports (worth $29 billion) to 36 countries of proliferation concern from 1985 to 1992, one-half of which went to countries that have or are seeking nuclear weapons. US licenses for the export of micro-organisms and toxins grew from 90 in 1991 to 531 in 1994, with application denials numbering one in 1991 and four in 1994). Export controls may actually enhance trade by creating confidence among suppliers that their recipients will use their products for peaceful, non-military purposes.[43]

While Gary Milhollin agrees that the volume of trade towards the developing world has not been severely restricted by export controls, he doubts that US exporters should be too confident that the existing arrangements will prevent their exports from assisting various WMD programmes. He notes that the European Union has refused to join the United States in a complete trade embargo against Iran, and that there are some 22 Iranian companies operating in Dubai's free-trade zone, the main purpose of which is to handle reexports to Iran. Although US exporters may not deal with these companies directly, they cannot be certain that the latter are not securing US products by retransfers from other countries.[44] Iran demonstrates that states can pursue the 'full range of weapons of mass destruction, missile delivery systems, as well as advanced conventional weapons' despite the collective resolve of various export control regimes. It has sustained links with key suppliers, notably Russia, China and North Korea, exploited opportunities for the import of retransferred goods, and benefited from a continued supply of sensitive dual-use equipment from several states including Germany.[45] Multilateral export controls may be preserved for political and symbolic purposes, even legitimising a large and expanding body of trade and investment that could suffer in their absence, but they will hardly curb the widespread availability of many materials, technology, and dual-use equipment used in the manufacture of weapons of mass destruction.

Nor will arms control necessarily prove a panacea. The UNSCOM and IAEA inspections of Iraq may have been a timely indicator of the strengths and limitations of on-site inspections as a means of detecting and deterring non-compliance by a determined proliferator. These inspections were a uniquely focused undertaking, backed by the author- ity of the UN Security Council, and charged with implementing a coer- cive peace settlement under the threat of resumed military attacks. Accorded unprecedented rights of entry and access (see Chapter 2), UNSCOM was hardly a model for inspections under multilateral regimes but it was a highly innovative body, utilising devices such as cipher locks, secure communications, and hand-held global position- ing systems.[46] In its early years UNSCOM demonstrated the vital role of team leaders, the physical, psychological and technical demands upon inspectors, the priority of technical competence over national balance in team membership, the medical, transportation and logisti- cal requirements for inspections, and the equipment and operational procedures involved in the collection, handling and analysis of sam- ples.[47] The inspectors also showed that information could be employed from a diverse range of sources, including declarations, interviews, import/export data, sampling, 'indicators' of proscribed Iraqi BW activity (namely evidence from several countries about undisclosed production and the imports of large quantities of growth media and fermenters), intrusive inspections, and the analysis of their findings by knowledgeable experts.[48]

Nevertheless, UNSCOM could not fulfil its mandate. Despite a remark- able record of achievements, it encountered a wide range of obstruc- tion (confirming the difficulty of mounting effective responses to low-level harassment),[49] and, periodically, major confrontations with the Iraqi authorities. By all these endeavours, Iraq eroded the resolve of UNSCOM's supporters. Rifts emerged within the Security Council, and prompted China, France and Russia to press for an easing of the UNSCOM inspection demands (both France and Russia would benefit from an end of sanctions as the former is owed $5 billion from Iraq and the latter $7 billion). Russia sought changes in the staff com- position, reporting process and oversight committee of UNSCOM, and tried to enhance the role of the 21-member Special Commission, an oversight board of nonspecialists, at the expense of the UNSCOM exec- utive chairman.[50] Even worse, when UN Secretary-General Kofi Annan intervened in the crisis over access to eight presidential sites and secured a Memorandum of Understanding between the UN and Iraq (23 February 1998), he undermined the authority of the UNSCOM process. The MoU reaffirmed Iraq's obligations to co-operate fully with the UNSCOM and IAEA inspectors but required UNSCOM to 'respect the legitimate concerns of Iraq relating to national security, sovereignty and dignity' and established a special group of senior diplomats and experts from UNSCOM and IAEA to agree procedures for initial and subsequent access to the presidential sites. By diluting the principle of unannounced and surprise inspections (as the arrival of the diplomats served as an early warning for Iraq), the MoU diminished the authority of UNSCOM and opened a parallel diplomatic channel for the Iraqi leadership.[51]

When the MoU eventually unravelled, with Iraq refusing to co-operate over the inspections (5 August 1998), UNSCOM was ordered to resume its work in Iraq regardless. On 26 August 1998 Scott Ritter, an experienced weapons inspector, resigned, citing a lack of support from the United States and Britain (a view subsequently endorsed by a senior British arms inspector, Chris Cobb Smith).[52] In his half-yearly report to the Security Council (6 October 1998) Richard Butler, the Executive Chairman of UNSCOM, conceded that

> Iraq had successfully implemented concealment on a large scale. Examples exist in all weapons areas. Programmes which were hidden include: indigenous missile production programme, the VX programme and the entire biological weapons programme.

He added that the Security Council may have to consider the implications of the inability of UNSCOM to 'provide 100 per cent verification of the claimed fate or disposition of prohibited weapons'.[53]

Admittedly when Saddam over-reached himself and tried to sever all links with UNSCOM on 31 October 1998, the United States and Britain could threaten air strikes with little overt opposition from the Security Council or from Iraq's neighbours. Although Saddam's capitulation on 14 November 1998 frustrated military intervention, Iraq's subsequent failure to cooperate fully with UNSCOM was used by the United States and Britain to justify Operation Desert Fox. Quite apart from the effectiveness of this operation as a counterforce strike (see Chapter 7), the integrity of the inspection process seemed fatally compromised when some of the collusion between UNSCOM and the United States was brought to light. The confirmation that intelligence gathered during UNSCOM inspections had been passed on to the CIA (in violation of UNSCOM's mandate), and thence to the Pentagon to assist in its targeting for Operation Desert Fox, damaged the credibility of Richard

Butler and exacerbated relations between the UN and the United States. It confirmed Iraqi claims that some UNSCOM inspectors had engaged in espionage, gave Saddam another propaganda triumph, and raised questions about the viability of the weapons inspection process.[54]

If UNSCOM with all its advantages struggled to enforce its mandate, then multilateral disarmament regimes may have even more difficulties in dealing with calculated acts of non-compliance. For these regimes, verification provisions will largely confirm the compliant behaviour of most states parties, build confidence in international norms, and aim to deter acts of significant non-compliance (as distinct from technical violations such as the failure of numerous states to sign safeguards agreements for the NPT or to supply all the requisite declarations and notifications to the OPCW). Whether regimes can meet all their verification objectives, or even be perceived to do so, is doubtful (and hence the sustained campaign by the United States to dissuade countries from assisting the nuclear programme of Iran despite the fact that it has repeatedly met the safeguards criteria of the NPT).[55] In spite of the rhetorical claims that the CWC will eliminate an 'entire class of weapons of mass destruction' and reverse proliferation,[56] many informed observers, including James Woolsey, have candidly admitted that the convention will not eliminate all chemical weapons.[57]

The CWC may be able to monitor the destruction of declared stocks of chemical weapons and production facilities, and detect large-scale production, filling and stockpiling of chemical weapons. It may also augment the costs and increase the difficulty of concealing illicit facilities, not least in preventing the defection of 'whistle-blowers'.[58] Nevertheless, some proliferators may not join the CWC, while others, if they do join, will still have access to CW agents – the dual purpose agents, such as chlorine, phosgene and hydrogen cyanide, that are permitted for legitimate industrial purposes. Some may also believe that they can sustain a small scale, clandestine CW programme. US intelligence authorities have repeatedly admitted that they may not be able to detect small-scale CW activity at undeclared sites (that is, 'up to a few hundred tons of chemical agent'), still less detect and confirm the production of new binary chemical agents.[59] As a consequence, the regime may either induce a false sense of complacency (and hence a reduced willingness in some states to sustain their funding for research, procurement and training in anti-chemical defence) or uncover evidence of non-compliance that may be ambiguous in detail, intent, or perceived significance. How states respond to such evidence will be crucial, especially after the failures to act on infractions of the Geneva Protocol, most notably during the Iran–Iraq War.[60]

However daunting the difficulties in the case of the CWC, they pale by comparison with those involved in verifying the BTWC. These difficulties derive less from the specifics of the proposed protocol (notably the debates over routine inspections, threshold quantities for agents and toxins, and the prospects of increasing co-operation between states parties and the lifting of export controls),[61] than from the task of detecting evidence of non-compliance in BW production and weaponization. Detecting production will be particularly difficult as it could be conducted in small laboratories, with no distinguishing features for overhead reconnaissance. Production need only involve a small number of people (so reducing the likelihood of defections), use growth media and equipment that could be indigenously produced, and avoid stockpiling large quantities of agents over long periods of time. Both the testing of agents and the filling of munitions could be conducted in nondescript facilities, while operational training, involving the distribution of masks and instruction in use, could be explained as purely defensive in intent. As George Tenet conceded, 'biological developments are small, they are easily hidden. They are not like big nuclear developments that have big signatures that everybody understands. ... It will be easy to cheat.'[62] Given the BW difficulties of UNSCOM – both the lack of accurate intelligence until a fortuitous defection and the limitations of anywhere/anytime inspections – the proposed protocol has been described as primarily a confidence-building measure in its own right and as only one of several measures within a broader 'web of deterrence'.[63] Even so, several American authorities understandably query whether the proposed measures can detect or verify conclusively evidence of non-compliance, and they worry that the protocol could compromise the protection of commercial proprietary information and induce a false sense of confidence about the functioning of the treaty.[64]

Whatever changes or refinements are made in the multilateral regimes, much will depend on how they are upheld. American leadership will be crucial in this respect. Just as the promotion of nonproliferation is only one of several issues on the US foreign policy agenda (see Chapter 3), so the maintenance of multilateral control regimes had to be considered in light of Madeleine Albright's desire to forge 'a set of partnerships' which will assist 'the sole remaining superpower in dealing with the problems of the world'.[65] As this policy placed a premium upon diplomatic meetings, summits and personal deal-making, particularly with political leaders in Russia and China, the Clinton administration became increasingly reluctant to impose public strains on those relationships even in response to Russian and Chinese assistance to proliferant regimes. Spokesmen asserted that imposing sanctions on Russia would prove counterproductive and impair 'key' programmes intended to promote democracy and market reform, as well as insure that the process of disarmament proceeded in a safe, secure and accountable manner. They claimed, too, that sanctions would not necessarily be appropriate when these countries were endeavouring to create export control regimes, and that they would undermine the flexibility desired by the White House and the State Department in their dealings with both powers. Conversely they insisted that both countries have significantly improved their policies on nonproliferation, responding positively to diplomatic approaches from the United States, including periodic démarches sometimes employing the threat of sanctions.[66]

These diplomatic priorities were coupled with a desire to ensure that the United States profited from the growing volume of international trade, with American companies remaining competitive internationally and operating within controls that are reasonable and enforceable. In 1993 the Clinton administration began a review of US export controls, seeking to make such adjustments as seemed necessary in light of the end of the Cold War, the global diffusion of increasingly sophisticated technology, and the growth of indigenous capabilities in the developing world.[67] In March 1994 it abandoned COCOM, the Coordinating Committee for Multilateral Export Controls, a group of Western nations that had limited the flow of weapon-related technology to the Soviet bloc and China, and took two years to replace it with the Wassenaar Arrangement (by which each member state can determine whether an export may proceed, in contrast with COCOM in which a consensus among member nations was required before an export could take place). The administration sought unsuccessfully to modify the EPCI controls imposed by the Bush administration in the 102nd and 103rd Congresses, and so diluted these controls by altering the regulations to reduce their effects on US companies, lifting license requirements on high performance computers and other goods, and streamlining the inter-agency review process to the benefit of the Commerce Department. By 1997 the United States was issuing only 8,000 licenses per annum – about one tenth of the number issued during the Bush administration, and down from 150,000 per annum a decade previously when the volume of international trade was approximately half that of the late 1990s.[68] Dr William Schneider, a former Under Secretary of State (1982–6) who was responsible for the Department's export controls, argued that the process of decontrol in the 1990s had 'gone to the point where the export control system is, in effect, abetting proliferation rather than containing it'.[69]

The abrupt change of tack in March 1999, when the Clinton administration proscribed the sale by the Hughes Electronics Corporation of two $450 million satellites to China, following revelations that China may have conducted successful espionage activities at Los Alamos and other US weapons laboratories,[70] provided scant reassurance. It hardly dented the impression that the United States, by reducing its national controls in the 1990s, had restricted its ability to verify how dual-use exports were being used or whether end-users were complying with restrictions on the use of these items. Intelligence gathering, and the American ability to monitor WMD developments, may have suffered, so increasing the possibility that surprises might occur in connection with emerging capabilities. Nor were other leading suppliers of goods and technologies likely to support such an inconsistent US policy, thereby impairing the residual trading embargoes imposed by the United States against a regime such as Iran. While other states might join the United States in expressions of concern about Iran's WMD programmes, they have not curtailed all their trading practices. Notwithstanding the profits to be earned from this trade, other states have doubtless perceived that US export control policy, despite protestations about the priority of nonproliferation, lacks a global remit. The inconsistent policies towards China and Russia, while setting aside embarrassing intelligence about their sales to proliferant states, and repeatedly accepting their recantations as binding commitments on nonproliferation, was hardly reassuring.[71]

Similarly US policy in support of multilateral arms control has been anything other than a model of consistency. Despite the Clinton administration's rhetorical support for the CWC, it was slow to press for ratification of the treaty, saw one attempt flounder in 1996, and only secured the Senate's "advice and consent" after making numerous 'clarifications' about the treaty and concessions in other areas of foreign policy. Even afterwards, the administration failed to press for the necessary implementing legislation to require US chemical companies to declare treaty-relevant data and accept on-site inspections, so leaving the United States in technical violation of the treaty for another 18 months.[72] The administration had concentrated upon nuclear arms control, helping to secure the indefinite extension of the NPT and the agreement on the CTBT, but it made important concessions on the verification of the CTBT (accepting the Chinese requirement that at least 30 of the 51-member Executive Council of the proposed CTBT Organization would have to approve an on-site inspection before it could take place). As the DIA has formally admitted that 'The on-site inspection (OSI) provisions and voluntary CBMs are less far reaching than the US had originally sought', and US intelligence agencies failed to detect the Indian nuclear tests, the administration would fail to secure the ratification of the CTBT by the Senate in October 1999.[73]

Nevertheless, in response to any incidents of non-compliance with arms agreements, US leadership will remain crucial. Its role in response to the North Korean crisis (see Chapter 2) reflected the reluctance of other states to support the IAEA (either because they were not sufficiently interested or fearful of the issues involved, or lacked the means to intervene, or, in the Security Council, could not agree upon sanctions).[74] Any dissatisfaction with the subsequent accord has to be tempered with the realisation that unless the US had intervened, the alternatives were fairly stark, including the possibility of a regional war. Less reassuring was the launching of cruise missiles by the United States against the al-Shifa pharmaceutical factory in Khartoum (20 August 1998) in response to the terrorist bombings of the US embassies in Nairobi and Dar es Salaam. The Clinton administration justified the attack because the plant was reportedly linked to Osama bin Laden, whom it blamed for the embassy bombings, and because the facility was manufacturing (or storing) Empta (an intermediate in the manufacture of VX). Quite apart from the non-involvement of chemical weapons in the embassy attacks, and the violation of Sudanese sovereignty, the widespread scepticism about the bombing reflected the timing of the bombing (three days after the video-taped testimony of President Clinton before a grand jury in the Paula Jones case); the apparent reliance of the administration upon the evidence of one soil sample analysed in one laboratory, without peer review; and the subsequent revelation of gaps in US intelligence (ignorance of the medical products made at the factory, the similarity of Empta's structure to other pesticides used in the Sudan, the theoretical possibility of using Empta for commercial purposes, and a bin Laden connection that was later described as 'indirect').[75] This scepticism was far from universal (42 US Senators approved of the attack after hearing a classified briefing from Cohen and Tenet),[76] but there were reportedly doubts about the decision within the administration as well as in foreign capitals, and considerable support for Sudan's call for an official inquiry by the UN.[77]

What these examples indicated were not only the controversies that could be aroused by unilateral action (be it diplomatic or military) but also the problems that could arise from dealing with particular cases, and limited evidence, in an *ad hoc* manner. In planning to deal with treaty infractions in the future, or evidence of proliferation involving weapons of mass destruction, the US will have to insure that it has a credible case, if only to carry an appropriate degree of domestic and international support. It will also need an array of military instruments to support its diplomacy or implement its initiatives whether acting on behalf of specific regimes or undertaking unilateral action.

7
Counterproliferation

When US Secretary of Defense Les Aspin launched the Defense Counterproliferation Initiative (DCI) on 7 December 1993, he drew attention to the need to learn lessons from the Gulf War and apply them to armed forces that were being significantly reduced and restructured in light of the "Bottom-up Review". He indicated that the United States had to improve its intelligence on the proliferation of NBC weapons and ballistic missile capabilities, to enhance its ability to detect weapons of mass destruction, locate mobile missiles, penetrate underground installations, destroy stocks of chemical and biological weapons without causing collateral damage, and improve defences, particularly against biological weapons.[1] As Dr Mitchel B. Wallerstein, Deputy Assistant Secretary of Defense for Counterproliferation Policy, added, these requirements assumed a further significance for armed forces required to fight and win two Major Regional Conflicts (now known as Major Regional Wars). In such conflicts there was still a high probability that US and allied forces could encounter the use or the threat of using weapons of mass destruction. Wallerstein prudently observed that this was an evolving problem, and that it could not be addressed by 'a single acquisition-oriented program within the Department'. Looking forward to 2010, the Pentagon had to develop plans to cope with various WMD threats, improve operational intelligence on the WMD stocks, facilities, deployment plans and capabilities of proliferant states, and provide a focus for its own research, development and procurement programmes. It had to infuse the military leadership with a greater understanding of the political and military implications of WMD threats and correlate these efforts with potential allies, especially in NATO.[2] To gauge the effectiveness of this programme will require an understanding of how strategic thinking has developed since the early 1990s, including notions of deterrence and operational planning (with Operation Desert Fox being a test case of the latter), and of how NBC-related research, development, procurement and training is faring amidst the reductions of defence expenditure during most of the 1990s.

In the post-Cold War period the United States, like most though not all NATO allies (Greece and Turkey are exceptions), has had to refine its military planning in light of steadily decreasing defence budgets and much smaller force structures. By February 1997 the US armed forces were 33% smaller than in 1985, defence procurement had declined by 63%, and the defence budget of $250 billion was approximately 38% smaller than in 1985, representing only 3% of the US gross domestic product – the lowest proportion since before the Second World War. The *Quadrennial Defence Review* envisaged further cuts which, if implemented fully, would reduce the force structure by another 3%.[3] These cuts reflected not only a desire to exploit the so-called peace dividend but also to adapt armed forces to a broader range of missions in peace and war and exploit the technological assets so conspicuously displayed during the Gulf War.

Just as Britain's *Strategic Defence Review* (1998) anticipated that Britain's much smaller and heavily stretched armed forces would perform or prepare for a diverse range of eight missions – the 'most demanding' of which would no longer be all-out war in Europe but 'a major regional crisis involving our national interest, perhaps on NATO's periphery or in the Gulf'[4] – so General Shalikashvili admitted that the US military 'is performing more missions, in more places than it did during the Cold War, and is doing so with significantly fewer personnel'.[5] He was still convinced that US forces could cope with multiple mission tasks and meet future challenges by virtue of the Joint Vision 2010 programme, intended to harness the full potential of the "Revolution in Military Affairs" and exploit an information superiority. Thereupon, US forces could utilise "total battle space awareness" to execute the evolving concepts of dominant manoeuvre, precision engagement, focused logistics and full-dimensional protection with the aim of achieving "full-spectrum dominance" over any enemy or enemies. While these new operational concepts and organisational arrangements would guide forward planning for each of the armed forces, they afforded even more scope for joint operations, with or without coalition partners. By exploiting US information superiority, William Cohen expected that US forces should be able to

> deploy lighter; require fewer weapon platforms and fewer munitions; be capable of directing both lethal and non-lethal fires to the

right targets; and be able to descend on the scene early in a conflict, take the initiative away from a numerically superior foe, and end the battle quickly on our own terms.[6]

Accordingly US military planners have evinced an understandable concern lest future adversaries seek to counter US dominance in the conventional military arena by unconventional operations (including terrorism and information warfare) and/or mount asymmetric attacks, using nuclear, biological or chemical weapons. The latter might be employed in the early stages of a regional conflict to disrupt US operations and logistics, and attempt to delay or deny access to key facilities such as ports and airfields.[7] When NATO evaluated the possible threats posed by the proliferation of NBC weapons and missiles, particularly by countries near the southern periphery of Europe, the Senior Defence Group on Proliferation (DGP) – one of three senior proliferation groups established in the wake of the Brussels summit of January 1994[8] – highlighted a range of possible implications. It noted that the behaviour of proliferants could be less predictable than the patterns established by the former Warsaw Pact states, that their command, control, communications and release procedures could be less effective, and that the weapons have different characteristics and so might be used for different military effects. The DGP was particularly concerned about the threat to deployed NATO forces, especially when they were entering a region of conflict. If a potential adversary had the ability to hold key targets at risk, such as ports, troop concentrations, staging areas, or even population centres, it might believe that it could coerce regional host countries or influence NATO's decision-making and operations. Even if proliferant states lacked the ability to defeat NATO forces, their NBC weapons and missiles could alter the military balance in the region, degrade NATO capabilities (either by causing casualties or by forcing NATO forces into their protective posture for extended periods of time or by exploiting the uneven defensive capabilities of NATO allies and coalition partners), and complicate NATO's operations by causing panic among the local civilian community. The loss of civilian labour on the docks could hamper reinforcement and supply; the diversion of military resources, including missile defence systems, to defend civilian communities could detract from coalition defences; and large-scale movements of civilians could impede military operations. In short, NBC and missile capabilities could be seen as *political* weapons usable for purposes of coercion, or as *military* weapons, whose use, even on a limited scale, could counter NATO's superiority in conventional weaponry.[9]

The United States and its allies would prefer, if possible, to deter asymmetric challenges. In 1991, after the end of the Cold War, NATO adopted its New Strategic Concept, stating that an appropriate mix of nuclear and conventional forces was essential to prevent war or coercion of any kind. 'Nuclear weapons', it added, 'make a unique contribution in rendering the risks of aggression incalculable and unacceptable. Thus, they remain essential to preserve peace.'[10] The Clinton administration endorsed the balanced approach in its Nuclear Posture Review (September 1994) and *Quadrennial Defense Review*, but emphasised that conventional forces would and should assume a far larger share in the deterrent role in the post-Cold War circumstances. On 12 February 1997 Walter Slocombe summarised official US deterrent policy:

> Of course, nuclear weapons are only a part of the broad range of capabilities by which we seek to prevent, deter and if necessary defend against threats from weapons of mass destruction. Passive defences, improved intelligence, diplomatic efforts, active air, cruise missile and ballistic missile defense capabilities, each have key roles to play, but nuclear weapons also play a part.[11]

Relying on nuclear and conventional forces reflects confidence in the safety and security of US nuclear command and control arrangements (with the last accident almost 20 years ago, and none that have ever produced a nuclear detonation or a nuclear yield),[12] and the flexibility, range and precision of nuclear and conventional delivery systems. David Omand, when Deputy Under-Secretary of State (Policy), Ministry of Defence, even argued that Britain could respond to external aggression by launching Trident missiles in limited and highly selective sub-strategic strikes.[13] However, the mix of nuclear and conventional options also reflects the lack of any in-kind retaliatory deterrents to the threat of chemical or biological warfare. As the United States unilaterally renounced its in-kind retaliatory options (for BW in 1969 and CW in 1991), and subsequently joined multilateral disarmament conventions (the BTWC and the CWC), it could not revoke these commitments without risking a revival of interest in in-kind deterrents and hence a greater proliferation of chemical and biological weapons.[14] There was, too, a widespread belief that the US had successfully deterred any recourse to chemical warfare in the Gulf War, and had done so by making ambiguous threats to retaliate, if attacked with CW, in an 'absolutely overwhelming' and 'devastating' manner.

Henceforth, argued Deutch, the Pentagon could support 'giving up the ability to retaliate with CW because we have an effective range of alternative retaliatory capabilities'.[15] US forces would plan to thwart any CW attacks by relying primarily upon their full range of chemical and biological defensive measures, coupled with an 'overwhelming' conventional capacity. 'We believe it worked in Desert Storm', claimed General Shalikashvili, 'we believe it will work in the future.'[16]

Yet the efficacy of these deterrence provisions has been questioned in several respects. The role of nuclear weapons has been contested in an upsurge of abolitionist writings and reports in the 1990s – all seized by the belief that the opportunity now exists to press towards the long-term objective of eliminating nuclear weapons by reducing existing stockpiles, an approach embraced not merely by longstanding nuclear disarmers but also by some notable politicians, former diplomats and retired senior military officers.[17] Critics assert that nuclear weapons have a declining political and military utility as a means of deterring aggression, and that threats to use them against developing states would be incredible. They contend that any nuclear retaliation in response to chemical or biological attacks would be disproportionate and uncertain in its effects (possibly even prompting more CBW attacks as the adversary would have nothing more to lose). A nuclear response would also break a taboo on nuclear usage that has existed since 1945, possibly stimulating nuclear proliferation, and contradict the negative security assurances that the US and other nuclear powers have made not to use nuclear weapons to attack non-nuclear weapon states (most recently in the attempt to secure an indefinite extension of the NPT).[18] Finally, critics claim that nuclear weapon states possess such an overwhelming superiority in their conventional forces that a combination of defensive measures and high-precision conventional weaponry should be sufficient for purposes of deterrence or retaliation.[19] Nevertheless, as long as nuclear weapons exist – and none of the reports envisage their rapid elimination – many critics accept that the United States will have to retain a smaller nuclear arsenal to deter nuclear threats against the United States, its forces overseas, its allies and friends, and to deter other states from producing and acquiring such weapons.[20]

Conventional weapons may not always serve in all contingencies as an effective means of deterring or retaliating against chemical and biological attacks. Whether they deterred Iraq during the Gulf War is debatable as Tariq Aziz has affirmed that Iraq was far more concerned about the possibility of US nuclear retaliation (see Chapter 2). While

US and allied conventional capabilities may suffice in some or even most conflicts, they could be stretched if employed in two simultaneous major wars. Moreover, if conventional capabilities are fully utilised at the outset of a campaign, they may not be perceived as sufficiently awesome or certain in their effects as a means of retaliating against chemical or biological attacks. Further large-scale retaliation may also be stymied by logistical problems, and factors of time, expense (in possible casualties as well as cost) and enemy countermeasures.[21] Expanding the war aims or diversifying the number of targets under attack would depend on the political resolve of the allies involved, the readiness to risk collateral damage, and the ability to locate and attack key facilities (especially if the latter were buried underground or were highly mobile). If the US had developed reliable means of attacking such targets, it would have to demonstrate that it was able to do so – a deterrent objective which may contradict the military's desire to preserve surprise and its battlefield advantages.[22] The careful calculus of conventional retaliation could be set aside by public rage and a desire for vengeance in response to CBW attacks, or by allied political leaders alarmed lest the CBW attacks had created a military imbalance or inflicted unacceptable military or civilian casualties. Should the allies need a decisive response to avert defeat (and its devastating political consequences) or show that illegal CBW attacks were neither acceptable nor effective, they might invoke the international legal doctrine of 'belligerent reprisal' and use nuclear weapons. In short conventional weapons, though central to US deterrent strategy, have their limitations and precluding nuclear weapons altogether would remove a key element of uncertainty. As Michael Moodie (president of the Chemical and Biological Arms Control Institute) observes, 'Doubts must remain in the mind of the proliferator that an egregious attack, including one involving chemical and biological weapons, not necessarily will, but could provoke a nuclear response.'[23]

Whatever means are employed in contemporary deterrence, the concept that evolved during the Cold War should be adapted to the challenges currently posed by chemical and biological warfare. If deterrence formerly involved an attempt to dissuade an adversary from certain decisions or actions by clearly communicating a credible threat to impose unacceptable punitive costs, this may now be more difficult to apply. Compared with the Cold War, there are many more actors involved, with differing values, goals, and susceptibility to external pressure (and some are not nation states but amorphous transnational groups, with bases and facilities in different countries). They possess very different WMD capabilities, ranging from modest and possibly experimental programmes to more diversified and advanced capabilities, and, in a few cases, fully-fledged WMD arsenals with long-range delivery systems and operational doctrines. They may have different perceptions about the utility of these weapons – in some instances regarding them as weapons of last resort, in others as operational weapons of first use. They may also envisage employing these weapons in strategic, tactical, counter-insurgency or covert roles and may reasonably distinguish between the potential effects of chemical and biological weapons, possibly seeking to exploit the anonymity of the latter or to employ either as instruments of state-sponsored terror. Above all, their calculations may vary according to their differing geo-strategic circumstances, regional rivalries, and external relations (whether in periods of relative stability, crisis, or conflict).[24]

However complex these factors, the United States will have to protect its citizens, territories, and forces overseas, as well as allies and friendly states, and may wish to begin by deterring CBW attacks. A broad declaratory statement, promising to respond decisively to the acquisition or use of such weapons might be prudent, but it could not be prescriptive about the method of response.[25] While some states might be deterred from acquiring these weapons by diplomatic methods, economic pressure or pre-emptive military attacks, others might not prove susceptible to external pressure. A purely punitive threat might not work if the enemy placed a higher premium on certain values. Saddam Hussein appeared to summarise this dilemma prior to the Gulf War:

> We know that you can harm us, although we do not threaten you. ... You can come to Iraq with aircraft and missiles, but do not push us to the point where we cease to care. And when we feel that you want to injure our pride and take away the Iraqis' chance of a high standard of living, then we will cease to care, and death will be the choice for us. ... Because without pride life would have no value.[26]

Whether this statement reflected genuinely different cultural values or mere bluster would require a careful intelligence assessment before choosing an appropriate response. In Iraq and elsewhere US policy requires an element of proportionality and international support. Threats to punish disproportionately any use of chemical or biological weapons might seem incredible if US and allied interests were not directly involved (and in some cases the usage could be unclear – if part of counter-insurgency operations in remote localities – or if alleged by an enemy in its black propaganda).

The United States and its allies may have to move away from their Cold War priorities and place greater emphasis upon deterrence by denial. In making credible threats, any proposed course of action should be carefully chosen, employing a range of instruments and options and should be commensurate with the interests at stake (in many regional conflicts these may be far less fundamental than those at issue during the Cold War). If an adversary had acquired WMD capabilities with a view to deterring a US-led intervention, then simply intervening might suffice. If US-led forces encountered a limited and largely ineffective CW attack in an isolated sector, it might prove sufficient to demonstrate that coalition forces could operate effectively in their protective posture and deny any tactical advantages from the original attack. If they incurred larger and more systematic attacks, they would still have to consider the consequences of a massive response (any nuclear use could prompt other states to seek nuclear weapons or justify their existing nuclear programmes, while a wide-ranging conventional response could cause bitter recriminations and complicate the postwar settlement). They would also have to consider the implications of not responding lest this undermined the credibility of the US deterrent for future occasions.[27]

Whether in a retaliatory or a pre-emptive strike, the United States might be tempted to employ its counterproliferation assets (as it did to some extent in the Sudan and Iraq in 1998). When Aspin launched the DCI, emphasising the need for 'improved non-nuclear penetrating missions', he aroused concerns about the compatibility of this initiative with the nonproliferation priorities of the State Department and ACDA. He apparently caused service concerns about the mission requirements involved and the funding implications, encountered a lukewarm reception from some NATO allies, and provoked external scepticism about the propriety and practicality of the new undertaking.[28] The more thoughtful commentators stressed that this was hardly an unprecedented policy (the allies sabotaged and bombed the German heavy-water facility at Rjukan, Norway in the Vemork raid of 1943, and Israel bombed Iraq's nuclear plant at Osiraq in 1981). The Gulf War had also exposed limitations in the coalition's intelligence, targeting and strike capabilities that needed correction. Even so, the emphasis upon acquiring new technology and counter-force capabilities not only caused unnecessary alarm but also seemed premature before any threat analysis had been completed, mission requirements determined, and operational responsibilities established.[29]

In April 1994 Ashton Carter admitted in congressional testimony that 'Frankly, I don't think we have done a very good job of explaining what we mean by counterproliferation.'[30] Clarification followed in the so-called Deutch report (May 1994) which eased interagency tension by recognising the primacy of the National Security Council as manager of all counterproliferation and nonproliferation issues. Counterproliferation would be described as a multi-tiered response to the threat posed by proliferation. It encompassed 'proliferation prevention' (through inspection, monitoring, verification and enforcement support for nonproliferation treaties, export controls, and assistance in identifying potential proliferants); strategic and tactical intelligence and battlefield surveillance (to detect, identify and characterise NBC and missile (NBC/M) forces of emerging proliferant states or groups); counterforce (the planning, targeting, interdiction or destruction of enemy NBC/M forces and their supporting infrastructure); the provision of active and passive defences to protect US, allied and coalition forces and noncombatants; and the countering of paramilitary, covert and terrorist NBC threats.[31]

Within the Pentagon the 'Missions and Functions Study' (1995) of the Chairman of the Joint Chiefs of Staff determined that regional commanders-in-chief should be responsible for implementing DoD counterproliferation policy. A Counterproliferation Council, chaired by the Deputy Secretary of Defense, began to monitor DoD-wide efforts to train, exercise, and equip US forces for the counterproliferation mission. The DGP, co-chaired by the United States, largely reassured NATO allies by establishing counterproliferation as a priority for NATO and making recommendations for improved Alliance capabilities (June 1996). In December 1996, NATO Defence Ministers approved new counterproliferation force planning targets. NATO and the national intelligence agencies reassessed the threats from NBC weapons, and the Alliance incorporated the risks posed by such weapons into NATO's exercises and training. The DGP recommended that NATO's operational doctrine, plans, training standards, and exercises should be adapted to ensure that military operations can be conducted effectively despite the presence, threat, or use of these weapons.[32]

Major threat analyses of the impact of CBW environments upon US and allied operations have also been conducted within the Pentagon and by the US Air Force. A General Officer Steering Group completed a classified report (March 1998), and the US Air Force conducted studies on *Sustaining Air Mobility Operations in a WMD Environment; Counter Chemical and Biological Warfare Operations Counterforce*; and *Fighting the Base*. A group of senior retired officers from all four services reviewed the potential impact of CW/BW upon joint operations in the political and military circumstances that might pertain in the year 2010. It found that the projection of US forces could be delayed and disrupted if deployment facilities, prepositioned matériel or key reception sites were attacked by chemical or biological agents. Accordingly the *CB 2010 Study* recommended that DoD policies, service doctrine, and CBW defence programmes should be broadened to recognise and redress these vulnerabilities, including the possibility of attacks within the United States.[33]

Finally, in a major organisational change, counterproliferation was brought within the remit of the Defense Threat Reduction Agency, established on 1 October 1998. This agency consolidated three major agencies (the Defense Special Weapons Agency, the On-Site Inspection Agency and the Defense Technology Security Administration) as well as various offices engaged in NBC activities. It would have eight directorates – Nuclear Support, On-Site Inspection, Cooperative Threat Reduction, Technology Security, Special Weapons Technology, Chem-Bio Defense, Counterproliferation and Force Protection. The new agency, asserted Dr John Hamre (Deputy Secretary of Defense) would become 'the central nervous system for America's counterproliferation plans and preparation'.[34]

Notwithstanding these efforts to set counterproliferation within a much broader context, both as an adjunct to "proliferation prevention" and as a means of countering threats to US and allied forces, the counterforce element remained as controversial as it did originally. Critics questioned whether pre-emptive aerial strikes would necessarily locate and destroy all their targets, especially if the latter involved small, easily concealable or highly mobile facilities. They feared that these attacks, however accurately delivered, might produce collateral damage in the release of toxic substances or nuclear radiation or have unwanted consequences (either prompting retaliatory attacks or possibly precipitating a major regional war in a theatre such as Korea or simply prompting an adversary to invest even more resources in deep underground concealment). They also recognised that counterforce attacks, unless conducted during a war, were of doubtful validity in international law and carried political risks for their perpetrators. As Janne E. Nolan observed, 'The idea that a few states have the right to eliminate military capabilities in states of which they disapprove will not help Western credibility in its quest for international acceptance of nonproliferation objectives.'[35]

Compounding these doubts were a range of technological problems. Prior the Gulf War, the US had experimented with ways of destroying CW/BW weapons without causing significant collateral damage, and by the 'timing of attacks and choice of munitions' planners were able to minimise the chances of chemical or biological agents being released. Seven years after the war, the US Air Force's Agent Defeat Weapon Program was still in its concept exploration and definition phase, with extensive testing required to evaluate alternative concepts for neutralising and eliminating CB agents.[36] Similarly, the capacity to identify and destroy hard and deeply buried targets, recognised as a key limitation during the Korean nuclear crisis (see Chapter 2), was still to be resolved five years later. The 2,000 pound, GBU27 and GBU28 bombs, available during Operation Desert Fox had only a limited penetrative capability, and several more advanced weapon concepts, including the Tunnel Defeat Demonstration Programme at the Nevada Test Site, were under evaluation for their ability to detect, identify, target and attack hardened, deeply buried, and tunnel complexes.[37]

In the task of detecting, tracking and attacking mobile or camouflaged missile launchers, many of the requisite weapon systems exist, including laser-guided bombs, the GPS-Aided Munition carried by B-2 stealth bombers and the Army Tactical Missile System (ATACMS). For laser-guided munitions, a new generation of lightweight laser designators for use by special forces are under development (including the UK's LF28 man-portable laser designator/rangefinder). However trials at the US Joint Camouflage, Concealment and Deception Center, opened in October 1996, indicated that the crew of attacking aircraft, using precision-guided munitions, engaged the correct target on only 48% of occasions when camouflage, concealment or deception (CCD) measures were employed, compared with 78% without these measures.[38] Hence the US Defense Advanced Research Projects Agency (DARPA) has funded research on advanced surveillance sensors, including the foliage-penetration radars, and information exploitation technologies to defeat CCD practices and track mobile targets. Like other counterforce research and development programmes, the programmes on countering mobile and camouflaged weapon systems are scheduled to continue into the early years of next century.[39]

Yet the controversies that erupted during and after Operation Desert Fox did not derive from the weaponry employed. Although at least one eminent historian of strategic bombing, Max Hastings, questioned the

efficacy of the counterforce campaign, arguing that it would only succeed if followed up by a large ground force operation to remove
Saddam from power,[40] scepticism focused upon the political and international repercussions. Critics deplored the timing of the strikes on
the eve of President Clinton's impeachment vote in the House of
Representatives, the propriety of the bombing (using previous Security
Council resolutions as a justification at a time when Russia and China
were adamantly opposed to the military attacks), and the repercussions
of the attacks.[41] If the exact effects of the bombings cannot be fully
measured by external observers, a massive aerial assault (involving 300
night-strike sorties and over 415 Tomahawk cruise missiles) launched
with the maximum of surprise, could have significantly damaged Iraq's
manufacturing, maintenance and delivery capabilities. Even so, the
bombings were limited in scope to avoid losing the lives of pilots and
to minimise collateral damage and reportedly exempted concealed
WMD stocks because of targeting difficulties and the risk of any inadvertent release chemical and/or biological agents.[42] Cohen disavowed
any intention of destabilising the Iraqi regime, but this seemed disin-
genuous as many of the buildings bombed (military intelligence headquarters, the headquarters of the Ba'ath party and the barracks of the
Republican Guard) were both involved in controlling Iraq's weapons of
mass destruction and were vital to Saddam's protection and security.[43]
Saddam, nonetheless, remained in power and, in the absence of inspectors, could start rebuilding his military infrastructure. Meanwhile the
Security Council appeared even more divided than before, with specu-
lation about the future of sanctions and any monitoring regime to
replace the UNSCOM inspectors in Iraq.[44]

Ultimately any counterforce strike, if launched unilaterally or even
bilaterally in peacetime, is likely to prove politically contentious. However precise the weaponry employed and the care taken to minimise
civilian casualties, the operation may not seem particularly credible if
it is based upon intelligence that cannot be revealed publicly in a full
and convincing manner. Similarly, it is likely to remain controversial if
the punitive justification begins to unravel under press scrutiny, if the
attack is thought to have served ulterior political motives, and if the
effects of the attack are not as clear as the perpetrators claim. Even less
dramatic actions such as intercepting ships reportedly carrying NBC
cargoes can prove highly embarrassing if the intelligence is flawed (in
1993 the Clinton administration had to apologise after its inspectors
fruitlessly searched the Chinese freighter, *Hin Ye*, for chemicals to manufacture nerve gas).[45] More covert operations (for example, extracting

civilian scientists, sabotaging enemy NBC installations, or disrupting their operations by electronic warfare) could also cause serious domestic and international repercussions if discovered in peacetime. All counterproliferation options are, as a Congressional Research Service report concluded in 1994, 'risk-laden. Some may be infeasible. All seem unattractive,' but, as the report prudently added, the risks of inaction could prove even worse if proliferant states used the intervening period to develop and deploy weapons of mass destruction.[46] In these circumstances the political embarrassments caused by the Sudanese and Iraqi bombings of 1998 could either induce more care in the planning of future operations (especially in the handling of intelligence, the timing of such actions, and the cultivation of international support), or they might induce future administrations to err on the side of caution, with potentially disastrous long term consequences if a war subsequently occurred.

Whatever choices are made, selective punitive strikes are unlikely to become commonplace and will hardly remove all the laboratories, production facilities and arsenals causing concern. Preparations must be made to ensure that US and allied forces can, if necessary, enter, operate, and prevail in military environments where there is a threat or actual use of weapons of mass destruction. In these circumstances confidence in missile and NBC defences will not only underpin any nuclear or conventional deterrence posture but will also be crucial if the United States and its allies plan to show that they cannot be coerced by the threat of NBC weapons. These defensive capabilities will enhance the efforts of allied governments to reassure coalition partners and host countries that they can respond to, or protect against, NBC attacks. They may also bolster political support domestically by demonstrating that every effort has been taken to minimise the risk of casualties. The mere deployment of missile defence systems, notably the US Patriot system in Israel during the Gulf War and in South Korea during the crisis of 1994, can serve political purposes and demonstrate a degree of strategic reassurance.[47]

Militarily, theatre missile defences (TMD) are essential because of the burgeoning scale of missile proliferation. By 1996, 30 non-NATO countries possessed thousands of theatre-class ballistic missiles (and nine of those countries were reportedly developing new missile systems), 77 states possessed cruise missile systems (mainly anti-ship cruise missiles), and 13 states were developing land-attack cruise missiles.[48] As counterforce systems cannot guarantee locating and intercepting missile launchers, TMD are required to protect deployed forces and population centres, to counter short-range "militarily insignificant" missiles, to prevent any missiles being used in escalatory or destabilising attacks, and to diminish the perceived utility of missiles generally, thereby conceivably boosting the prospects for non-proliferation.[49] Several countries have either purchased TMD systems (particularly Patriot after the Gulf War) or joined in multi-national development projects (notably the Medium Extended Air Defense System (MEADS) involving the US, Germany and Italy) or developed their own systems (most notably Israel which is planning to deploy its Arrow 2 system in two fixed-site batteries – one near Tel Aviv, the other near Haifa, protecting some 85% of the country's population). Several NATO allies have also participated in the European-based TMD assessment exercises that have been held annually since 1996. The 1998 exercise not only covered all aspects of TMD but also Combined Air Operations and Offensive Counter Air operations to assess the integration of TMD with general warfare activities.[50]

The US TMD programme involves the development of a "family of systems" to counter a diverse range of threats and provide a defence in depth, utilising lower-tier systems – those that intercept at relatively low altitudes in the atmosphere; upper-tier ones that intercept missiles at longer ranges and outside the atmosphere; and potentially boost-phase intercepts, involving programmes such as the Air Force Airborne Laser which aim to intercept ballistic missiles early, while they are still over the enemy's territory. The lower-tier systems include the upgrades to Patriot, notably the upgrade to the Patriot Advanced Capability-2 (PAC-2), which expanded by about eight times the volume covered by PAC-2 in the Gulf War, and then PAC-3 with its enhanced radar, communications system, remote launch capability and other improvements. In addition there are plans to install the Navy Area Defense system, employing Standard Missile-2 Block IVA interceptors, aboard AEGIS ships which can move into theatre and provide protection for coastal cities, ports and airfields, and to develop MEADS, the only genuinely mobile land-based system which could provide manoeuvre forces with 360° protection against the threat of short-range ballistic missiles, cruise missiles and unmanned aerial vehicles. The upper-tier systems include the Navy Theater Wide Defense and the more advanced programme, the Theater High Altitude Area Defense (THAAD). The latter is planned to enhance area coverage significantly, engage longer-range more sophisticated theatre ballistic missile threats, and utilise a 'shoot-look-shoot' capability.

All these programmes are under development but only the PAC-3 system (a limited point defence system that looks out at about a

60-degree angle in one direction, and is not particularly mobile) is likely to be deployed before 2000. The Navy Area Defense system is supposed to be deployed in 2002, but neither the upper-tier systems nor the MEADS are likely to be deployed before 2005. Despite extensive funding (with $12.5 billion requested for fiscal years 1998 to 2003) and Congressional support, the programmes, especially the upper-tier ones, have struggled with immense technological challenges (THAAD failed in its first four intercept flight tests) and cannot afford a high leakage rate, if NBC submunitions are involved.[51] In the near term the potential of theatre missile defences is limited by delayed availability and doubts about their effectiveness, but, in a decade or so, they may be making a more significant contribution to NBC deterrence and damage limitation. They will only do so if they can meet the technological challenges posed by the development of increasingly sophisticated and longer range missiles that may pose a threat to the United States, its allies and its forward-deployed forces. In January 1999 the Clinton administration belatedly announced plans for a limited national system of missile defence, at a proposed cost of $10.5 billion over six years.[52]

Even if only a few missile, aerial or covert attacks took place, involving chemical or biological weapons, the aerial, ground or naval elements of an intervention force could be compelled to operate in contaminated conditions. The Gulf War had revealed serious deficiencies in the CB defences of US and allied forces. The Pentagon catalogued a whole array of shortcomings, including the lack of any BW detection system, inadequate stocks of drugs, vaccines and collective protection facilities, little emphasis on the medical management of casualties caused by biological agents, and protective kit that 'dramatically impedes crew performance', restricting or distorting vision, hindering communications, and impairing both the use of equipment and close cooperation between crews during high-speed combat. In the absence of early and reliable warnings, some US forces anticipated chemical or biological attacks and assumed the full mission oriented protective posture (MOPP), despite its debilitating effects on operational efficiency (see Chapter 4).[53] Even the British forces, who entered the war with some excellent protective kit and equipment (the S10 mask, M4 suit, the Chemical Agent Monitor (CAM) and nine prototype BW detection systems), could neither detect mustard gas nor employ any specific medical countermeasures against it. They had to purchase medium-scale decontamination apparatus, use FUCHS NBC reconnaissance vehicles from Germany, and found that despite the high standards of NBC training within the Royal Air Force, shortcomings in CB defence awareness and training persisted within some Army units, at both individual and collective levels, and among crews on Royal Fleet Auxiliary ships.[54]

Extensive programmes have been launched since the Gulf War to repair many of these deficiencies, particularly in the United States where the consolidation of funding resources at DoD level in 1995 enhanced the management of the programme, its cost-effectiveness, and the degree of "jointness" in determining key requirements and overall coordination.[55] To facilitate contamination avoidance, improved point and stand-off detectors are being procured, including the M21 Remote Sensing Chemical Agent Alarm (RSCAAL) – a stand-off system able to detect nerve and blister agent vapour clouds out to 5 km; the M22 Automatic Chemical Agent Detector Alarm; and the Improved Point Detection System (to detect nerve and blister agents at low levels on ships). The 123 FOX reconnaissance vehicles are being upgraded to carry the RSCAAL, with an automatic warning and reporting capability networked digitally to the command and control system. In 1996 the US Army also fielded its first biological point detection systems – 38 truck-mounted Biological Integrated Detection Systems (BIDS) – with plans to receive another 86 upgraded systems in 1999. The US Navy fielded 25 Interim Biological Agent Detectors and the 310th Chemical Company received three Long Range Biological Standoff Detection Systems (LR-BSDS), designed for use with helicopters, to provide long range/large area aerosol cloud detection, tracking and mapping out to 30 km (an improved version will be able to scan out to 50 km).[56]

However, the Pentagon candidly admits that these are limited and, in some cases, interim deployments – the chemical and biological detectors cannot detect all threat agents, the first generation BIDS system is not automated and takes 45 minutes to identify an agent, while the LR-BSDS only differentiates between natural and man-made clouds and cannot detect the presence of a BW agent. The upgraded BIDS will be able to identify specific BW agents in 15–30 minutes and the Advanced Concept Technology Demonstration (a BW point defence system for ports and air bases) will be able to make a presumptive identification of a BW agent in 15 minutes. Nevertheless, as US forces lack any biological (and possess only a limited chemical) stand-off detection ability able to detect, identify the agent, and give timely warning before the arrival of the agent cloud, research priorities include the development of a biological stand-off detector (the Joint Biological Remote Early Warning System) and a joint biological point detection system that will provide a fully automatic operation and warning of a positive BW detection.[57] Although some 19 countries produce chemical detectors, very few produce even basic BW detectors. The United Kingdom plans to replace its NAIAD nerve agent detector with up to 2,000 man-portable chemical detectors from the year 2000 to 2001 and to introduce an Integrated Biological Detection System, costing some £11 million, from 1999. As an automated continuous-flow monitoring system, capable of identifying biological agents in two to three minutes, it is probably a generation ahead of the BIDS due to its automation.[58]

As NBC hazards cannot always be avoided, US forces have excellent protective kit, including the M40 series of masks which provide a very high standard of protection against aerosol threats from CBW agents, toxins and radioactive fallout particles. The M40/M42 masks replace the elderly M17 masks worn by the Army and Marine Corps in Desert Storm (the M40 for dismounted warriors, the M42 for combat vehicle crewmen). The M45 mask replaces the more expensive pressurised masks for aviators (but the M48 mask will still be worn by aviators in Apache helicopters and the M49 mask by Korean aviators), while the MCU-2A/P with its improved fit, comfort and visibility compared with earlier masks, has been adopted by the Navy and Air Force. US forces are also receiving the M41 Protective Assessment Test system to assist in validating the maintenance of their masks at individual and unit levels and to ensure their fit and serviceability. As all US services require lighter and less bulky protective clothing, the Joint Service Lightweight Integrated Suit Technology (JSLIST) has been developed, aiming to produce lightweight protective garments (overgarment, undergarment and duty uniform), improved gloves, and multipurpose boots. While the first generation JSLIST, currently being introduced, will provide a 45-day garment that provides 24 hours of chemical protection, the preplanned improved version is intended to be lighter, less expensive, and more durable (60 days field use and retain its chemical protection after eight launderings).[59] Even the highly commended British M4 suit has been found to cause unacceptable heat stress levels in the hot and humid conditions of northern Australia, prompting the development of the Australian lightweight Chemical Biological Combat Suit.[60]

More significant shortcomings persist in the areas of collective protection, decontamination and medical countermeasures. Funding rather than technological design appears to be the main impediment in meeting the larger collective protection facilities required by the Air Force; the much greater filter requirements of the Navy (as it plans to retrofit collective protection systems into all its close-in support ships by 2000); the integrated vehicular systems and tactical field shelters of the Army and Marines; and the specialist requirements for protecting Army and Air Force field hospitals, thereby enabling them to sustain medical operations in a chemically-protected environment for 72 hours. NATO has recognised that despite the availabilty of a wide range of European-produced collective protection systems (both the liner systems developed by the British and the French and the containers of the Norwegians), NATO forces need more collective protection facilities to support forward deployments, not least in "bare-base" air operations.[61]

Decontamination poses more technical challenges for although existing systems are effective against a variety of CB hazards, many are slow and labour-intensive, cannot be used on sensitive electronic equipment, consume large amounts of water, and present logistical, environmental and safety burdens. In order to facilitate "contamination control" US and allied forces need to minimise the amount of time that personnel have to spend wearing their protective kit, prevent the spread of contamination, and reconstitute personnel and equipment more quickly for combat purposes. If contamination cannot be avoided or offset by natural weathering for less persistent or non-thickened agents, decontamination may be necessary on an immediate basis (for individuals, their own equipment or to save lives), operationally (on hatches, latches, locks and levers to limit the spread of contamination) and thoroughly (to eliminate the need to wear protective kit and restore units as fully effective combat formations).[62] The technical challenges involve replacing the DS2 decontaminant solution now used by US forces with one that is non-aqueous, noncorrosive, and effective against a broad spectrum of agents (some of the enzymes currently being studied could detoxify nerve agents but not mustard),[63] as well as one that is both environmentally safe and safe to use on the interior of aircraft and other vehicles. Decontaminants would also have to be packaged in several forms to be easily transportable, and to sustain large area decontamination centres for forces landing at forward airports or seaports that may have been targeted for CBW attack. Despite considerable research on potential decontaminants – the French firm GIAT Industries has developed a new vehicular decontamination system (Système de Décontamination Approfondi) and, in combination with Alfred Kärcher, a system for decontaminating sensitive items (Système de Décontamination des Matériels Sensibles) – new decontamination systems for US forces may not be available before 2003 at the earliest.[64]

Medical countermeasures, so necessary not simply to avoid fatalities but also to sustain or restore combat effectiveness, are gradually being improved. Although nerve agents can be countered by a pretreatment drug (pyridostigmine) and post-exposure treatment by an injection of atropine, P^2S, and the anti-convulsant diazepam, research is underway to improve these treatments (the Canadians have developed a drug, HI-6, to protect against all known nerve agents). There are also projects to counter vesicant agents, produce a nerve agent multi-chambered autoinjector, and counter the threat from novel CW agents or combinations of chemical agents.[65] For BW agents, there are a range of potential responses – vaccines as a preventive measure, antidotes for forward treatment after exposure, and casualty care, including diagnosis, therapy and casualty management. Having eventually established a Joint Vaccine Acquisition Program, the Pentagon has issued contracts for the development of 18 new vaccines to meet the 'most probable' BW threat agents. In 1998 it began to inoculate all service personnel with an anthrax vaccine, licensed by the Food and Drug Administration, and plans to spend some $320 million in developing 18 vaccines over a period of five years.[66] However, the anthrax vaccination programme which involves six inoculations in the first 18 months, followed by annual boosters thereafter, will prove administratively difficult to monitor (maintaining accurate records on 2.4 million people) and may not cope with all anthrax threats (as the Soviets had developed both a multi-strain blend and a genetically engineered form of anthrax). Ken Alibek has suggested that US programme of focusing on the 'most probable' threats may not account for some 100 different forms of plague, smallpox, glanders and other diseases developed by the former Soviet Union, and that the development of immune system boosters to counter all threats might be more appropriate (but this option could take at least five years to complete and cost billions of dollars).[67] To explore the possibilities of a revolutionary approach to BW-related research, DARPA is currently funding research projects that could detect and identify BW agents in real time (within one to two minutes) and could diagnose the presence of any pathogen in the body in real time and in the absence of recognisable signs and symptoms.[68]

Notwithstanding the accomplishments and potential of NBC defensive research, the equipment has to be procured in sufficient numbers and service personnel have to be trained to use it effectively. NATO allies have different organisations – the US and German armies have chemical corps, while the British forces, despite the recent acquisition of an NBC reconnaissance regiment from the the Royal Armoured

Corps, rely on delegating informed risk-taking as far down the chain of command as possible. Many have specialist NBC schools (Winterbourne Gunner in the United Kingdom, Fort McClellan, Alabama – soon to move to Fort Leonard Wood, Missouri – in the United States) and patterns of detailed training for forces about to enter high-threat areas. At Fort McClellan's Chemical Defense Training Facility – often described as the world's only live-agent CW training facility – over 40,000 US and allied troops have been trained since its opening in 1987.[69] Nevertheless, as armed forces were reduced and defence budgets fell in the 1990s, spending on NBC defence – less than 1% of the Pentagon's budget – fell from $750 million in 1992 to $504 million in 1995. Procurement programmes were cut (only about half of the 210 FOX reconnaissance vehicles were bought), and unit commanders concentrated their spending on higher priority items. In March 1996 the GAO published a devastating indictment of the CB defence readiness within the US Army. In inspected units (both rapid-reaction and reserve units earmarked for early deployment), it found wholesale shortages of individual and collective protection kit; inadequate stocks of patient treatment and decontamination kit; derisory attendance by physicians in the advanced medical and casualty management courses on the treatment of chemical and biological patients; and serious weaknesses in CB defence training at individual, unit and joint exercise levels. Only 10% of joint exercises in 1995 included training to defend against CBW agents, and only 15% of such exercises were planned to do so in 1996. The GAO attributed the deficiencies in CB defence awareness to 'a lack of emphasis up and down the line of command in DOD'. It found that officers at all levels said that:

> training in chemical and biological preparedness was not empha-
> sized because of higher priority taskings, low levels of interest by
> higher headquarters, difficulty working in cumbersome and uncom-
> fortable protective clothing and masks, the time-consuming nature
> of the training, and a heavy reliance on post-mobilization training
> and preparation.[70]

Major-General Friel agreed that commanders were probably not emphasising NBC defence because 'they make decisions to spend those limited operational dollars on things that are of importance to them at the moment'.[71] Congress found additional funds for immediate procurement needs and, in the wake of the priority accorded to CBW in the *Quadrennial Defense Review*, the Pentagon announced an enhanced level of funding over the five years to 2003, with a subsequent augmentation of the planned expenditure by approximately $1 billion over this period.[72] In its next report (March 1998) the GAO welcomed the additional funding, and noted that several regional commanders-in-chief had increased their stocks of defence equipment and had incorporated more CB defence scenarios into their major military exercises. It noted that there were still deficiencies in high-threat areas, namely a lack of vaccines, BW detection capabilities, and collective protection facilities, and drew attention to inadequacies in doctrine and policy regarding CB defence of overseas airfields and ports, the protection of essential civilians in high-threat areas, and equipment questions regarding the return of contaminated aircraft or ships.[73]

The US armed forces have at least had the benefit of a heightened awareness of the potential NBC threat at home and abroad and the political willingness to allocate more resources towards countering this threat. Despite the agreements reached with NATO's DGP, it is by no means clear that all allied governments will meet the requisite costs (at a time when many are reducing their defence expenditures) and improve their NBC defences. Most have gaps particularly in BW defences, whether in equipment, doctrine or training, and none appear able to emulate Britain, Canada and the US in maintaining an integrated system that correlates a comprehensive set of capabilities with realistically defined threats. Joint programmes on medical countermeasures could ease the political and economic difficulties of particular governments, but policy questions have to be resolved about the protection of essential civilians and the indigenous populations in high-threat areas, as well as collaboration with non-NATO countries that might join coalition forces in the developing world.[74] Counterproliferation, in short, is still an evolving concept, but its development will doubtless depend on how the risks are evaluated in the proliferation of weapons of mass destruction.

8
Proliferation: Risks and Challenges

Despite all the endeavours to establish nonproliferation norms, impede the free flow of weapons and dual-use technology and deter recourse to weapons of mass destruction, the continuing spread of these weapons appears all too probable. This may not prove a particularly rapid phenomenon as the political attractions of these weapons are limited by their sheer lethality, the limited competence of some military organisations, and their limited appeal for a number of democratic states with liberal values and interdependent commercial interests.[1] The continuing international leadership of the United States in the 1990s (upholding and reshaping alliance commitments, maintaining extended deterrents, and promoting nonproliferation in multilateral arenas) has probably dissuaded allies (if any were so minded) from reconsidering the nuclear option. Several former proliferants, doubtless prompted by changes in their domestic political priorities and external relations, and possibly influenced by diplomatic démarches, have displayed more confidence in (and a willingness to abide by) nonproliferation treaties. Even so, several states have persevered with their WMD programmes (some of which derived from the Cold War era), even more are apparently undertaking research on biological weaponry,[2] and some have adhered to nonproliferation treaties in name only, deriving benefits from membership of the regimes while covertly developing weapons of mass destruction. The weapons could serve a range of political and military purposes, and the biological and toxin weapons are capable of considerable refinement. Some of these weapons have been employed in recent memory and they could be used again, not least by terrorist groups. So the risks involved in this phenomenon, both in the development and potential use of these weapons, and the challenges that they pose for the US and allied governments, as well as for regional neighbours, merit further consideration.

Proliferation is only one aspect of the much broader diffusion of scientific and technological expertise that was under way well before the end of the Cold War.[3] Whether measured by the growth of defence industrial infrastructures within the developing world or the sales of advanced conventional weapons, weapons platforms and delivery systems, proliferation has continued across various fronts in the 1990s. Although the global volume of arms sales may have slumped by some 30% since the late 1980s, there is a growing demand for arms in Asia and the Middle East – with three of the largest recipients of arms in 1997 – China, South Korea and Taiwan – all located in North-East Asia.[4] The range of systems included advanced-technology weaponry (high-performance aircraft, surface-to-air missiles, precision-guided munitions and anti-ship cruise missiles) and satellite services in imagery, navigation and communications (as well as capacities to jam GPS signals). While these capabilities by themselves, or in combination with weapons of mass destruction, could be employed in attempts to impede the movements of US-led intervention forces,[5] the proliferation of conventional weapons could heighten regional tensions and stimulate the demand for weapons of mass destruction. If a small state, lacking reliable allied support, finds itself confronting a hostile neighbour or neighbours, with much larger economic and demographic resources (and hence the capacity to acquire large stocks of conventional weapons and/or highly expensive, advanced-conventional capabilities), it may respond by seeking a WMD capability.[6]

The spread of nuclear weapons, whether stimulated by external or internal pressures (or a combination of both), may not necessarily be a disastrous development. Some scholars, following the pioneering writings of Kenneth Waltz, argue that this may be a positive phenomenon, establishing new deterrents between regional adversaries. Waltz does not claim that nuclear weapons, once acquired, will never be used but he disputes the ethnocentric view that regimes in the developing world will prove more reckless and irresponsible in charge of such weapons. He contends that nuclear weapons induce caution, and that 'the weaker and the more endangered a state is, the less likely it is to engage in reckless behaviour'. States with small nuclear arsenals, he asserts, have every incentive to protect them from pre-emptive attack or accidental use. They can deter adversaries effectively, and their deterrent threats, backed by second-strike nuclear forces, raise the costs of conventional war to such heights that it becomes unlikely. 'Nuclear weapons', he observes, 'have not been fired in anger in a world in which more than one country has them.'[7] After the end of the Cold War, several scholars endorsed this theme, arguing that the spread of nuclear weapons could enhance regional stability, that the United States should tolerate a selective degree of proliferation (either by long-standing allies, such as Germany or by weak states such as the Ukraine facing a more powerful neighbour), and that nuclear weapons could render war between their owners less and less likely, even stabilising inter-state relations in regions such as the Middle East (where Israel has an assured second-strike capability in its nuclear-capable *Lance* and *Jericho* missiles, high-performance fighter-bombers and air-to-ground missiles).[8]

James Woolsey, when Director of the CIA, disagreed. 'I can think of no example,' he wrote, 'where the introduction of nuclear weapons into a region has enhanced that region's security or benefited the security interests of the United States.'[9] Many scholars shared his pessimism. They argued that the stable deterrence in East-West relations during the Cold War derived from unique cultural, historical and geo-strategic circumstances. In his seminal study of the "Long Peace" John Lewis Gaddis identified seven factors that contributed towards the remarkable stability of the Cold War era: bipolarity; the independence of the United States and the Soviet Union from each other, geographically and economically; domestic constraints on foreign policy; nuclear weapons; advanced reconnaissance technologies that reduced the fear and risk of surprise attack; ideological moderation; and the evolution of an implicit set of rules for the superpower 'game'. Of all these factors, admitted Gaddis, 'what has really made the difference in inducing this unaccustomed caution [in superpower relations] has been the workings of the nuclear deterrent'.[10] Nevertheless, this deterrent was distinctive (at least from a Western perspective) inasmuch as it embodied the peculiar requirements of extended deterrence, and reflected the legacy of strategic bombing during the Second World War and the assumptions of a just-war tradition.[11]

Proliferation is occurring in regions of the developing world that are anything but stable, especially those divided by deep religious, ideological and cultural differences as well as lingering border disputes. Vulnerabilities are heightened by the close proximity of high-value targets (Islamabad and New Delhi are both within four or five minutes of a missile attack); the unpredictable behaviour of some political and military élites (not least in North Korea); uncertainties in intelligence-gathering; and recent histories of pre-emptive strikes (or near pre-emption, as in the so-called 'Brasstacks' crisis between India and Pakistan in 1986–87). These difficulties could be accentuated by fallibilities in early warning systems, unreliable command and control arrangements, and local asymmetries (while all Pakistan will fall potentially within range of the *Agni* 2 missile, only part of India will fall within range of the *Ghauri*, so raising the possibility of "inadvertent escalation", namely the launching the *Ghauris* in the event of a conventional war).[12] For a new state, such as the Ukraine, which 'inherited' a nuclear capability (but not its operational control), these risks could have been compounded by disputes over the ownership of the weapons, the lack of organisational expertise that normally accumulates over the long lead times associated with the acquisition of nuclear weapons, custodial dangers regarding the safety of the arsenal, and political instability both within the Ukraine and in its relations with Russia.[13]

Proliferation pessimists accepted that proliferants will try to preserve their weaponry and that deterrence will not necessarily fail during regional crises, but they maintained that the risks associated with nuclear proliferation are unacceptability high compared with the alternative of nonproliferation. They argued that the superpowers were more vulnerable to crisis instability during the Cold War than is commonly realised, and that their records of accidents and 'near accidents', which continued long after the early years in which their forces were 'crudely designed', reflected the risks inherent in maintaining nuclear forces. If these forces rendered deliberate war less likely, they may have enhanced the risk of accidental war because of shortened warning and response times to perceived attacks, the vulnerability of command, control and communications systems, the delegation of alert and launch authority to lower levels in the chain of command, and the constant readiness of modern nuclear forces (especially modern missile forces).[14] Whether the risks of accidental war during the Cold War were as serious as some commentators have implied is a moot point (and even they admit that there never was an accidental detonation, still less an accidental nuclear war),[15] but these risks are certainly greater for new proliferants. Unlike the established nuclear powers, proliferants may lack the numerous political, technical, and organisational factors that have been developed – at immense expense and over many years of organisational effort – to reduce the likelihood of pre-emptive, unauthorised, accidental or inadvertent use of nuclear weapons. If they also lack reliable early warning and intelligence-gathering capabilities, they may find that their first-generation nuclear weapons are more vulnerable to accidental detonation and unauthorised use.[16] Bruce Blair is convinced that the proliferating states will 'cut corners in their pursuit of warning, introducing high rates of error and leaving themselves and the world vulnerable to inevitable intelligence failures. The operational postures of these nuclear rivals are virtually certain to become accidents waiting to happen.'[17]

Whether the logic of organisation theory is any more useful than the logic of deterrence in predicting the stability of relations between proliferant states is debatable. A state possessing a small, first-generation nuclear arsenal and delivery systems of limited accuracy, is likely to adopt a countervalue (or countercity) and not a counterforce nuclear doctrine. It would therefore not require a first-strike capability[18] but only a small number of nuclear warheads that could be delivered against an enemy after the latter had attempted a first strike. As General Sundarji wrote, 'With minimum deterrence and targeting confined to cities, hair-trigger readiness to respond is not essential.'[19] These states could also follow the precedent of other proliferants and address their survivability problems in highly innovative ways. China hid missiles in tunnels and caves and created a defence industrial base in its remote southwestern hinterland; Israel created an entire rocket-launch facility in a cave-studded hill about 14 miles west of Jerusalem; North Korea concealed both weapons and industrial plant in hardened underground facilities; and South Africa stored the nuclear and non-nuclear components of its nuclear devices separately in concrete and steel vaults.[20] The small size of these arsenals, coupled in some cases by the small size of the states concerned, the proximity of potential adversaries, the lack of any clear natural borders, and the sharing of the same weather systems and water drawn from the same river basins, placed a premium upon tight control. Questions of escalation, radiation and contamination remained matters of acute concern, and the maintenance of unassembled arsenals reduced the possibilities of accidental or inadvertent nuclear launch. In the South African case, the devices could only be assembled for testing by applying four codes held by separate officials, and only the head of state knew the fourth code.[21]

The South African model could be anomalous and, in other examples, basic design faults could have caused their own problems. The IAEA inspectors described the design of the Iraqi bomb as 'highly unstable', requiring 'the cramming' of 'so much weapon-grade uranium into the core … that the bomb would inevitably be on the verge of going off – even while sitting on the workbench'.[22] Even states armed with more reliable weapons and intent on maintaining a minimum deterrent, with the weapons earmarked for a second-strike mode, would need to be confident that they could detonate them in the required manner: air burst or ground burst. They might also require a capacity to respond-in-kind lest an adversary attacked with a low-yield tactical nuclear weapon for which a response with a much larger nuclear response would seem disproportionate. In 1994, Major-General Kotera M. Bhimaya predicted that

> It is naive to expect India and Pakistan to settle for a minimum deterrence posture vis-à-vis each other. The momentum of "weapon dialectics" will simply drive these countries inexorably toward expanding their nuclear arsenals.[23]

When India and Pakistan conducted nuclear tests four years later, they tested both potential battlefield nuclear weapons (sub- or very low kiloton devices) and larger atomic bombs with the power to devastate a medium-sized city (a 12 KT device by India and a 15 KT device by Pakistan). India also tested a 43 KT hydrogen bomb (registered by foreign sources at about 20 KT).[24] The leading scientific advisers of both countries – Drs A.P.J. Abdul Kalam and A.Q. Khan respectively – claimed that each state has ballistic missiles (the *Prithvi* and *Agni* for India, the *Ghauri* for Pakistan) capable of carrying nuclear warheads or 'any type of warhead' in India's case.[25] These capabilities were confirmed by the test-firing of the *Agni* 2 and the *Ghauri* 2 missiles by India and Pakistan respectively on 11 and 14 April 1999.[26]

The risks of proliferation are likely to heighten in times of regional crisis or pre-crisis, when the potential capabilities of rival nuclear arsenals may exacerbate rising tensions. Scott Sagan fears that in states where the military has a particularly influential or even predominant role in decision-making, it will give priority to operational readiness (over safety or second-strike concerns). Arguing from the basis of organisation theory, he maintains that military officers, if left to themselves, may not construct invulnerable nuclear arsenals. They will cleave, he believes, to inflexible routines, traditions, and war-fighting plans rather than consider the costs (and the opportunity costs in foregoing expenditure on other weapons) involved in the building of secure facilities (citing the example of China's Second Artillery Division, which controlled China's missile forces and pressed for missiles with longer ranges, better accuracies, improved reliability and enhanced operability but left strategic requirements and matters of survivability to others).[27] Sagan maintains that military officers are more likely than civilians to perceive war as likely or inevitable in crisis situations, especially if the latter occurred during the early transitional phase of nuclear development between rival powers. These officers may conceive of 'victory' in peculiarly narrow terms, favour offensive and decisive action, and focus upon the requirements of war-planning in the short term, without being unduly concerned about the longer-term political and diplomatic implications of preventive war. Extrapolating from the US experience during the early years of the Cold War, and from the recent history of Pakistan, he feared that the new proliferants might experience similar pressures.[28]

Sagan's pessimism may or may not be vindicated by future events, but pessimism derived from generalised theories about the behaviour of military organisations or civil-military relations in the United States (and elsewhere) during the early Cold War years, may not shed much light on the decision-making of the new proliferant states. As there is little 'reliable information' about command and control in these states,[29] these extrapolations may or may not apply. In some states civilian control appears to predominate (to a greater or lesser degree), especially as several of the proliferant states are long-standing democracies or states accustomed to civilian rule.[30] Even in states where military opinions are more influential, senior military leaders will not necessarily favour offensive action and preventive war during crises. Cautious military advice has often occurred in times of crisis (not least during Operation Desert Shield) and civilian leaders have sometimes proved rash, bellicose and unpredictable (notably in Pakistan during some of the Indo-Pakistan crises).[31] In any event, past behaviour may provide little guidance about future decision-making, especially if the state concerned is facing an enemy armed with nuclear-tipped ballistic missiles.

If making these nuclear capabilities as safe and secure as possible, particularly in times of crisis, is a high priority for the United States, it could assist proliferants and thereby minimise the risks of accident, theft or unauthorised use.[32] There are precedents, namely American assistance to the United Kingdom and France,[33] and more recently Russia, under the Cooperative Threat Reduction programme. US administrations have been willing to assist allies (and thereby reap political and diplomatic benefits) or reduce nuclear instabilities, where this seemed in the interests of the United States. Nuclear-sharing, though, has always aroused anxieties lest it undermine nonproliferation and reward proliferants, while alienating neighbouring states.

It would have to overcome political reservations, including fears lest the process compromise US security interests and a reluctance on the part of proliferants to seek assistance for fear of revealing the depth of their organisational difficulties. By addressing specific safety issues, the policy might also prove counterproductive if it enabled proliferants to adopt higher states of nuclear readiness. Finally, any US government could not ignore domestic inhibitions, namely the requirements of US legislation, export controls, international commitments under the NPT and the MTCR, strategic arms treaties, and Congressional opinion.[34]

Even so, the United States has an unrivalled experience in developing the technology and procedures to enhance nuclear safety and security, and could advise proliferants on these matters formally or informally. Formal assistance is more likely when it can be proffered in a covert manner and the recipient is perceived as a friendly and stable power. Informal assistance, avoiding any transfer of technology, could be proffered more generally (as it was in the 1960s when the United States was worried about the custodianship of Soviet nuclear weapons, and so publicised the value of its permissive action link (PAL) technology and the use of coded locks to ensure proper control).[35] The transfer of accident-prevention technology might be incompatible with the requirements of the NPT, especially if the systems were associated with the requirements of weapons design (such as the environmental sensing devices that prevent detonation unless a weapon has experienced the physical parameters associated with its means of delivery). Yet the United States could utilise appropriate international gatherings or bilateral meetings to emphasise the safety value of storing the fissile core of a nuclear weapon separately, and the value of using tamper-proof seals, command disable devices and PAL technology to prevent the theft or unauthorised use of nuclear weapons. Ultimately the strained relations between the United States and some nuclear proliferants may preclude the proffering of much assistance, whether on a formal or informal basis, and US administrations are unlikely to proffer assistance to new proliferants beyond the realms of safety and security.[36]

Accidents, theft, and unauthorised usage could also occur in connection with chemical and biological weapons. Once again the superpowers had to cope with the safety and security aspects of these weapons, incurring intense criticism when highly conspicuous accidents happened, notably the death of some 6,000 sheep from the inadvertent spraying of VX near the Dugway Proving Ground, Utah (13 March 1968), the leakage of VX from a container on the US base at Okinawa (summer 1969), and the accidental release of anthrax from a BW facility at Sverdlovsk (April 1979).[37] Although the United States has developed considerable expertise in the relevant areas of safety and containment, it could hardly share the appropriate technology and procedures (other than in the destruction and disposal of toxic weapons). Having renounced its own CBW capabilities, it could not flaunt its own export controls, domestic legislation (such as the Chemical and Biological Weapons Control and Warfare Elimination Act of 1991 and the Iran-Iraq Arms Nonproliferation Act of 1992), and its commitments under the biological and chemical weapons treaties.[38] In any case proliferants are unlikely to seek assistance for these weapons lest this reveal the nature and extent of their clandestine programmes. If more fearful of an American attack than of the effects of an accident, they may prefer to compromise on the safety of personnel and local residents rather than install conspicuous safety and containment facilities.

Stemming the proliferation of weapons of mass destruction poses a more immediate and complex challenge to the United States. The Clinton administration has reiterated this theme throughout its period in office. In San Francisco on 26 February 1999, the President claimed that 'fighting that threat ['the use of weapons of mass destruction by an outlaw nation or a terrorist group'] has become a central priority of American foreign policy', while on 8 March 1999 General Henry 'Hugh' Shelton, chairman of the Joint Chiefs of Staff, warned a conference on 'NATO at 50' that WMD and their means of delivery are 'arguably the most significant Article 5 threat we collectively face'.[39] This continuing concern reflects the fact that chemical and biological weapons in particular remain comparatively cheap, technologically straightforward, and potentially usable whether as instruments of terror, or on the battlefield, or as strategic weapons. They complicate US foreign policy inasmuch as many of the countries identified as seeking these weapons are located in inherently unstable regions. A few proliferants are long-established democracies (and hardly fit the criteria of "rogue" regimes), others are politically unstable, and some have histories of recent aggression or rulers that harbour hegemonic ambitions. As few states openly acknowledge their WMD capabilities, preferring to retain them in "opaque" forms or as "virtual" capabilities, this complicates the quest for regional stability.

Like Woolsey, Major-General Burns argued that these weapons were destabilising in themselves and could enhance 'opportunities for adventurism and miscalculation'.[40] The latter is possibly more likely than the former (despite the much-vaunted fears of pre-emptive attacks during the Cold War, the only major incident was Israel's bombing of the Osiraq nuclear reactor). Although an adversary might be deterred from deliberate pre-emption by the risks of failure or of external intervention, if one or other side feared pre-emption, and had vulnerable WMD assets, they might launch at the first (and possibly mistaken) indication of an attack.[41]

Fortunately there are relatively few examples of NBC weapons being used in combat but their mere existence, coupled with ballistic or cruise missiles and high-performance aircraft, could affect the willingness of the United States or a US-led coalition to intervene in certain regions. At the very least, these weapons would increase the difficulty of reassuring allies or friends in the zones of conflict, and they could complicate the task of securing coalition support in regions where neither the United States nor its coalition partners had any strong national interests. The potential risks to intervention forces could weaken domestic and international support for the proposed operation, especially if the prospective adversary had not emulated the brazen and foolhardy behaviour of Saddam Hussein. Paralysis need not follow, especially if US leadership is resolute, the cause is widely perceived as legitimate, and NATO allies have met the targets set by the alliance's 'WMD Initiative' (see Chapter 7) at national level. Prospective coalition partners need not have a uniform doctrine (as their NBC defences may be organised quite differently), but they will require a broad understanding of the problems posed by weapons of mass destruction, particularly by biological weapons. They will also need to be aware of any differing doctrinal priorities within the coalition and of how they could coordinate their activities effectively. As the crisis could occur in East Asia, it would seem prudent to expand the NATO-wide discussions to include representatives from Australia, Japan, the Republic of Korea and New Zealand.[42] Nevertheless, joining these coalitions will remain a matter of choice, and the political leaders concerned will have the daunting task of weighing the consequences of either entering a conflict in which weapons of mass destruction are already being used or where they might be used.

Less drastic will be the requirements and credibility of any desire to project power or to proffer an extended deterrent by the United States. The former has often involved the despatch of naval forces with a high visibility, and in some regions, this could mean surface ships sailing within range of anti-ship cruise missiles or, conceivably, downwind of a chemical or biological attack. Once again the proliferation of advanced military capabilities, whether carrying conventional or unconventional ordnance, could increase the risks to forward-deployed forces. It could also complicate the task of reassuring allies or clients in zones of conflict,[43] although General Sundarji has perceptively noted that in the 1990s

> Any U.S. offer of a nuclear umbrella to a non-nuclear country has greater credibility, for the United States can be bolder now, with no fear of retaliation on the continental United States by the other global power.[44]

Belatedly the Clinton administration recognised the potential threat to US forward-deployed and allied forces from pre-emptive or retaliatory missile strikes, involving conventional or NBC warheads. By doubling expenditure on ballistic missile defences, the administration reflected concerns about the potential nuclear and missile capabilities of North Korea and probably China (following the revelations of its espionage at Los Alamos and other weapons laboratories),[45] and demonstrated that it wished to preserve the credibility of US commitments to overseas allies. Were those commitments to be called into question, the Pentagon has reasonably concluded that other 'states may seek unilateral alternatives to ensure their security, thus stimulating proliferation'.[46]

Arms control and to a lesser extent export controls remain pivotal in the international efforts to meet the challenge of proliferation. Neither are panaceas, and their limitations, even utter irrelevance in some cases, were exposed by the embarrassing revelations of the 1990s. Those states who responded to these events (and the new opportunities of the post-Cold War era) by trying to bolster existing regimes, and establish new conventions, sought to reinforce international norms, broaden their base of support, and increase the costs for prospective proliferators. They doubtless realised that export controls, if unable to stem the diffusion of technology, could at least delay the process and facilitate trade within the multilateral cartels, and that arms control, if unable to guarantee detection of all illicit activity, could confirm compliant behaviour and provide the basis for collective action against those who brazenly violated the treaties. Whether these multilateral regimes will strengthen the 'web of deterrence' remains to be seen, especially after the difficulties of UNSCOM and the way in which its integrity was compromised. The regimes will remain in place but they will represent only part of the political, economic and military measures that might be invoked to deter those who are intent on the acquisition, transfer, use, or threatened use of weapons of mass destruction.

Militarily the challenges posed by CBW to US and allied forces extend beyond the development, production and procurement of improved protective equipment. Even in this area there are important gaps to be filled – the deployment of timely and accurate detection systems, a wider range of approved vaccines, more rapid diagnostic techniques, and less burdensome methods of decontamination. As resources are finite (and far less than they were during the height of the Cold War) priorities have to be imposed in research, development and acquisition programmes. Balances need to be struck between working to counter the effects of traditional agents and examining ways of countering the challenge of novel or modified agents,[47] and between improving existing pieces of kit and pursuing entirely new technological possibilities. Just as important, if not more so, is to sustain levels of CB awareness in matters of training, operational planning and doctrine. Understandably this awareness, so prominent during the Gulf War, appeared to diminish thereafter as senior officers retired, the armed forces contracted, and the remaining personnel found themselves stretched in fulfilling a diverse array of missions, often without any semblance of a chemical or biological threat. If this trend has been partially arrested in the US forces, it probably reflects the forward deployment of forces in regions such as the Middle East and East Asia, where they face continuing NBC threats, heightened anxiety about NBC terrorism within the United States, and the galvanising effects of periodic Congressional inquiries and GAO reports. It remains to be seen whether the DGP can infuse a broader level of interest in NBC defensive requirements, readiness and training throughout NATO as a whole.

Underpinning the military predicament is the difficulty of gathering accurate intelligence on the CBW programmes of proliferant states. US intelligence agencies have encountered difficulties in monitoring these activities: they completely missed the preparations for the nuclear tests at the Pokhran test site on May 1998, despite monitoring that site for years, and they seriously underestimated the scope and extent of the Iraqi WMD programme. The Directors of the CIA have also regularly testified to the much greater difficulties involved in gathering accurate intelligence on CBW activities in small, easily concealed facilities without distinct "signatures" than on nuclear research and development (where the US had a conspicuous success in detecting the North Korean programme).[48] Doubtless these practical difficulties have been compounded by the switch of focus from the elaborate methodology created to monitor and estimate the probable directions of Soviet behaviour during the Cold War. Intelligence agencies now have to grapple with more diverse challenges including, amongst others, understanding the dimensions of the terrorist threat, the possible leakage of nuclear and other advanced arms from the former Soviet Union, the pace at which ballistic missiles and weapons of mass destruction might spread, the demands of crisis-management in South Asia, and the possible impact of any regional initiatives by China.

The nature and utility of intelligence gleaned on WMD matters compounds the difficulty of taking diplomatic or military action. The major successes in uncovering BW programmes have come from defectors, emphasising the value of human intelligence (HUMINT), but all forms of HUMINT activities have to compete for scarce resources with the costly investment in national technical means of gathering intelligence. It may also be much more difficult to use the information gathered by espionage without compromising the sources and methods employed. Timing is critical as the best time to act against a WMD programme is during the early stages of its development, when economic sanctions, tightened export controls, more intrusive international inspections, political pressure and even pre-emptive military action can have most effect. However, David Kay shrewdly observed that it is peculiarly difficult at the early stages to 'draw compelling conclusions' about the aims of covert weapons programmes, and that

> The intelligence world at the best of times is characterized by uncertain data and sources and methods for acquiring such data that are difficult to share even with friends. If effective collective action is to be taken to halt further nuclear proliferation, policymakers – and not just intelligence professionals – must address the need to produce better, more sharable intelligence on states with suspected nuclear ambitions.[49]

In view of the controversies that erupted after the cruise missile attack on the al-Shifa factory (see Chapter 6), this recommendation, proffered some two years earlier, could not have been more prescient.

Intelligence is also in the forefront of efforts to counter the threat from terrorists, armed with weapons of mass destruction. While intelligence successes in counter-terrorism, pre-empting terrorist attacks, necessarily receive less publicity than any failures, those failures rightly earned censure, especially when the consequences could have been extremely grave (as they could have been in the case of Aum Shinrikyo). A new form of terrorist organisation – partly religious, partly criminal – with transnational links, vast resources, and the wherewithal in scientific expertise and high-quality equipment to exploit its deeply-rooted interest in chemical and biological warfare, Aum posed a new challenge to intelligence officials. As terrorism has moved beyond its traditional paradigm of political terrorist activity, and Aum and others have demonstrated a willingness to flout taboos – even ineffectively – against the use of chemical and biological weapons, all manner of sects, cults, militias and extremist groups will have to be studied to learn more about their ideologies, motivations and likely patterns of behaviour. Whenever groups are thought to have transnational links, or to pose a threat to foreign citizens or overseas military bases, information ought to be shared, if possible, by the intelligence agencies of the relevant countries.

President Clinton has said that of all the new terrorist threats the one that 'keeps me awake at night' is an attack with biological weapons. He thought that this was 'highly likely to happen sometime in the next few years' and maintained that a biological attack, unlike a chemical attack which would be finite in its area coverage, could spread: 'it would be kind of like the gift that keeps on giving'.[50] If his administration is to be commended for raising public awareness about this prospect, and for investing resources and organisational effort in addressing its many dimensions, much remains to be done particularly in the initial response and consequence management phases. As a perfect nationwide defence is impossible, some threat analysis, as the GAO recommended, would give more focus to the planning. Concentrating upon the targets of highest risk, such as government buildings, and enclosed public spaces, such as lobbies, airports and subways, would seem more sensible than planning for "worst case" scenarios.[51] Establishing this priority would only be feasible, if assurances could be given that rapid-response teams could react promptly and efficiently to attacks elsewhere.

Whatever targets came under attack, it would obviously help if the "first responders" had devices that could rapidly and accurately detect and identify the toxic or infectious agents and track the agent cloud to determine safe and contaminated areas. Thereafter the responders and their specialist support would have to cope with the ramifications of public order (preventing flight from the contaminated area in the event of a BW attack), medical treatment (rapid provision of post-attack prophylaxis, for which the development of new antidotes and therapeutic drugs would be a prerequisite), public health (decontaminating people, buildings and equipment), and public information (to minimise panic and confusion). Any contingency planning should not underestimate the sheer terror that could be caused by the dissemination of invisible, odourless and tasteless agents against a population lacking any immunity or physical protection. Quite apart from the need to cope with public hysteria and overwhelming demands upon the provision of health care, counselling would have to be available for survivors, emergency workers and medical personnel. The psychological stresses that could be caused by the sight of large numbers of people, including children, falling ill or dying amidst a setting that otherwise seemed perfectly normal could be considerable.[52]

Planning to counter the challenge posed by weapons of mass destruction, particularly in the terrorist mode, is complicated by the fact that it will only become a conspicuous phenomenon when a terrorist attack is mounted. Awareness can be raised initially, emergency workers trained, and operational procedures developed, but sustaining these preparations once the federally funded programme is over, and an attack has still not occurred, could prove extremely difficult. Technology will doubtless evolve, and probably expand the scope of any terrorist challenge, while new capabilities, equipment, and medical resources will emerge with which to confront it. So there will be a requirement for updating the initial training, reviewing operational procedures, and ensuring that the latest information is fully disseminated.[53] The need to develop these procedures could not be more urgent, as the more often that the United States, either alone or with NATO allies, launches punitive aerial strikes against other states, so the United States, its allies, and its overseas bases are increasingly likely to become the targets of revenge attacks by embattled regimes or their embittered supporters. Even if conventional ordnance remains the main instrument of terrorism, the United States and its allies have to be prepared for an attack with weapons of mass destruction.

If the Clinton administration has responded to the potential challenge posed by NBC terrorism, and has built on Congressional initiatives, to launch a policy that should be consolidated in the next century, its foreign policy has been less impressive. All too often a gap has occurred between rhetoric and practice, with nonproliferation – despite its purported priority – being regularly subordinated to constructive engagement with China and Russia or trade liberalisation. The administration has oscillated over employing economic sanctions as an instrument of policy in support of nonproliferation (as favoured by many 'single-issue constituencies' and often supported in Congress as a means of expressing American outrage without risking American lives). Having initially supported the imposition of sanctions against numerous states and foreign companies, the administration became increasingly reluctant to restrict its freedom of manoeuvre. Forced by Saddam's resilience to rely on sanctions against Iraq, where the policy had international backing, the administration found that it was impractical against North Korea and that it failed to deter either India or Pakistan.[54] In arms control the administration gave precedence to nuclear matters to the detriment of the CWC ratification debate and the negotiations on strengthening the BTWC. While extending the NPT and concluding the CTBT negotiations were tempting diplomatic priorities, biological weapons – the cheapest and most discreetly produced of the weapons of mass destruction, with a potential for immense area coverage and technological refinement – remain a challenge that has to be met. Although the BTWC needs some verification provisions, an intrusive inspection regime in and of itself may not suffice. UNSCOM, despite its many procedural advantages, never fully uncovered Iraq's BW programme, although this hardly warranted the subsequent misuse of its inspection procedures. More direct dealings with the states concerned may be required, but preferably not after crises or near-crises have erupted. Whereas the Clinton administration responded pragmatically, preparing attractive economic and security 'packages' that would wean the Ukraine off its inherited nuclear arsenal and compose the short-term crisis in North Korea, this approach failed miserably in dealing with Pakistan.

If this record of inconsistency testifies to an erratic foreign policy that lurched from issue to issue and tackled crises as and when they arose, it also confirms the inherent difficulty of responding to the challenges of proliferation which tend to erupt episodically. Once proliferation is under way, it is difficult to detect and identify with precision, particularly if biological weapons are involved, and even more difficult to arrest. Upholding and strengthening international norms may serve as a basis of policy, but diplomatic, economic and military instruments may have to be employed too, whether the aim is to deter, frustrate, or encourage a reversal of policy. During the 1990s some states have abandoned their WMD programmes, if usually after a change of government and the adoption of new domestic and foreign policies, but these new regimes have often required external assurances about their security, status, and access to trade and technology. In dealing with more determined proliferants, US and allied governments may have to look beyond the weapons and try to address the security, status and political aspirations of the regimes themselves. In some cases these aspirations may not be easily met, and certainly could not be met if they involved a sacrifice of the legitimate interests of allies or clients. So the United States and its allies may have to contain some regimes and retain well-equipped and organised military forces able to counter any challenge and operate, if necessary, in contaminated conditions. However, they cannot rely unduly on their conventional military forces – not even the precision of contemporary air power. Unless continuing efforts are made to address the causes of proliferation, these weapons or the capacities to produce them are likely to accumulate, posing risks and challenges both regionally and in some cases globally.

Notes

1 Weapons of Mass Destruction: The Cold War Context

1 'Transcript of President's Address to a Joint Session of the House and Senate', *The New York Times*, 10 February 1989, p. A18.

2 W.H. Webster, Hearing on *Nuclear and Missile Proliferation* before the Committee on Governmental Affairs United States Senate, 101st Congress, first session, 18 May 1989, p. 9; see also Webster, D. Goldberg and B.J. Erlick, Hearings on *Global Spread of Chemical and Biological Weapons* before the Committee on Governmental Affairs and its Permanent Subcommittee on Investigations United States Senate, 101st Congress, first session (9 February 1989), pp. 10–42.

3 E.M. Spiers, *Chemical and Biological Weapons: A Study of Proliferation* (London: Macmillan, 1994), pp. 107–29; A. Devroy and R. Jeffrey Smith, 'US, Russia Pledge New Partnership', *The Washington Post*, 2 February 1992, p. A26; R. Ekéus and D.A. Kay, Hearings on *Global Proliferation of Weapons of Mass Destruction* before the Permanent Subcommittee on Investigations of the Committee on Governmental Affairs United States Senate, 104th Congress, second session, Part 2 (20 March 1996), pp. 90–110.

4 'In Clinton's Words: U.N. Cannot Become Engaged in Every World Conflict', *The New York Times*, 28 September 1993, p. A16.

5 R. Gates, Hearing on *Weapons Proliferation in the New World Order* before the Committee on Governmental Affairs United States Senate, 102nd Congress, second session (15 January 1992), p. 6; R. James Woolsey, Hearing on *Proliferation Threats of the 1990's* before the Committee on Governmental Affairs United States Senate, 103rd Congress, first session (24 February 1993), p. 9; J.M. Deutch, Hearing on *Current and Projected National Security Threats to the United States and its Interests Abroad* before the Select Committee on Intelligence of the United States Senate, 104th Congress, second session (22 February 1996), p. 8.

6 O[ffice of] T[echnology] A[ssessment], *Proliferation of Weapons of Mass Destruction* (Washington, DC: OTA, 1993), p. 11.

7 J.M. Deutch, 'The New Nuclear Threat', *Foreign Affairs*, vol. 71, no. 4 (1992), pp. 120–34; J.F. Sopko, 'The Changing Proliferation Threat', *Foreign Policy*, No. 105 (1996/97), pp. 3–20.

8 OTA, *Proliferation of Weapons of Mass Destruction* and *Technologies Underlying Weapons of Mass Destruction: Assessing the Risks* (Washington, DC: OTA, 1993).

9 *Nuclear Weapons: Report of the Secretary-General of the United Nations* (London: Frances Pinter, 1981), pp. 8–9; L. Martin, *Arms and Strategy* (London: Weidenfeld and Nicolson, 1973), pp. 11–12.

10 *Nuclear Weapons: Report*, pp. 10, 23–5; Deutch, 'The New Nuclear Threat', pp. 122–3; OTA, *Technologies Underlying Weapons of Mass Destruction*, p. 168; Kay, Hearings on *Global Proliferation*, part 2, p. 105.

11 *Nuclear Weapons: Report*, pp. 54–69, 199; L.W. McNaught, *Nuclear Weapons & Their Effects* (London: Brassey's, 1984), pp. 28–32; R[oyal] U[nited] S[ervices] I[nstitute] for Defence Studies], *Nuclear Attack: Civil Defence* (London: Brassey's, 1982), pp. 37–8, 99–121.

12 L.A. Dunn, 'Containing Nuclear Proliferation', *Adelphi Papers 263* (1991), p. 16.

13 OTA, *Proliferation of Weapons of Mass Destruction*, p. 53.

14 *Report of the Secretary-General on Chemical and Bacteriological (Biological) Weapons and the Effects of their Possible Use*, hereafter referred to as the *Report of the Secretary-General on CB Weapons*, U[nited] N[ations] General Assembly, A/7575 (New York, 1 July 1969), p. 6.

15 *Report of the Specialists Appointed by the Secretary-General to investigate allegations by the Islamic Republic of Iran concerning the use of chemical weapons*, S/16433 (26 March 1984), pp. 11–12; P. Dunn, 'The Chemical War: Journey to Iran', *Nuclear, Biological and Chemical Defense and Technology International*, vol. 1, no. 1 (April 1986), pp. 28–35.

16 *Report of the Secretary-General on CB Weapons*, p. 57, and S. Fetter, 'Ballistic Missiles and Weapons of Mass Destruction: What Is the Threat? What Should Be Done?' *International Security*, vol. 16, no. 1 (1991), pp. 5–42.

17 G.S. Pearson, 'Prospects for Chemical and Biological Arms Control: The Web of Deterrence', *The Washington Quarterly*, vol. 16, no. 2 (1993), pp. 145–62; G. Thatcher, 'Poison on the Wind: The New Threat of Chemical and Biological Weapons. Part 3: Tailor-made Toxins', *The Christian Science Monitor*, 2–8 January 1989, pp. B31–B42.

18 *Report of the Secretary-General on CB Weapons*, p. 6.

19 Col. A.G. Vicary and Wing Commander J. Wilson, 'Nuclear, Biological and Chemical Defence', *Journal of the RUSI*, vol. 126, no. 4 (December 1981), pp. 7–12.

20 G.S. Pearson, 'Biological Weapons: Their Nature and Arms Control' in E. Karsh, M.S. Navias and P. Sabin (eds), *Non-Conventional-Weapons Proliferation in the Middle East: Tackling the Spread of Nuclear, Chemical and Biological Capabilities* (Oxford: Clarendon Press, 1993), pp. 99–133.

21 Pearson, 'Prospects for Chemical and Biological Arms Control: The Web of Deterrence', p. 147.

22 *Report of the Secretary-General on CB Weapons*, pp. 4 and 8.

23 Pearson, 'Biological Weapons: Their Nature and Arms Control', pp. 112–14; Erlick, Hearings on *Global Spread*, pp. 32, 237, 240; M. Dando, *Biological Warfare in the 21st Century: Biotechnology and the Proliferation of Biological Weapons* (London: Brassey's, 1994), p. 8.

24 OTA, *Proliferation of Weapons of Mass Destruction*, p. 54.

25 Webster, Hearings on *Global Spread*, p. 10.

26 Brig. J. Hemsley, 'The Soviet Bio-Chemical Threat: The Real Issue', *The RUSI Journal*, vol. 133, no. 1 (1988), pp. 15–22; G.S. Pearson, 'Chemical and Biological Defence: An Essential National Security Requirement', *The RUSI Journal*, vol. 140, no. 4 (1995), pp. 20–7; *Nuclear Weapons: Report*, pp. 69–72.

27 Pearson, 'Chemical and Biological Defence', pp. 21–3, 25; W. Seth Carus, 'The Proliferation of Biological Weapons' in B. Roberts (ed.), *Biological Weapons: Weapons of the Future?* (Washington, DC: The Center for Strategic and International Studies, 1993), pp. 19–27; *Report of the Secretary-General on CB Weapons*, pp. 44 and 57.

28 N.B. Williams and D. Williams, 'Iraq, 4 Allies Urge Mideast Nuclear, Chemical Arms Ban', *Los Angeles Times*, 6 April 1990, p. A6; G. Kemp, 'Regional Security, Arms Control, and the End of the Cold War' in S.J. Brown and K.M. Schraub (eds), *Resolving Third World Conflict: Challenges for a New Era* (Washington, DC: Institute of Peace Press, 1992), pp. 121–50.

29 Maj.-Gen. R.G. Wooten, 'Protecting the Force: The 21st-Century Chemical Corps', *Military Review*, vol. 76 (1996), pp. 75–9.

30 L. Beaton, *Must the Bomb Spread?* (London: Penguin, 1966), p. 128.

31 M. Reiss, *Without the Bomb: The Politics of Nuclear Nonproliferation* (New York: Columbia University Press, 1988), pp. 37–77; J. Simpson, 'Trends in Nuclear Proliferation and Supply Side Controls' in J.-F. Rioux (ed.), *Limiting the Proliferation of Weapons: The Role of Supply-Side Strategies* (Ottawa: Carleton University Press, 1992), pp. 11–24.

32 E.L.M. Burns, 'The Nonproliferation Treaty: Its Negotiation and Prospects', *International Organization*, vol. 23, no. 4 (1969), pp. 788–807.

33 I. Smart, 'Non-Proliferation Treaty: Status and Prospects' in A.W. Marks (ed.), *NPT: Paradoxes and Problems* (Washington, DC: Arms Control Association, 1975), pp. 19–30 and appendix 2.

34 A. Myrdal, *The Game of Disarmament: How the United States and Russia Run the Arms Race* (Manchester: Manchester University Press, 1977), pp. 169–73.

35 M.J. Brenner, *Nuclear Power and Non-Proliferation: The remaking of U.S. Policy* (Cambridge: Cambridge University Press, 1981), appendices G and I.

36 P.L. Leventhal, 'Nuclear Export Controls: Can We Plug the Leaks?' in Rioux, *Limiting the Proliferation of Weapons*, pp. 39–53; see also D. Fischer, 'The London Club and the Zangger Committee: How Effective?' in K.C. Bailey and R. Rudney (eds), *Proliferation and Export Controls* (Lanham: University Press of America, 1993), pp. 39–48, and, on U.S. policies towards Pakistan, K.C. Bailey, *Doomsday Weapons in the Hands of Many: The Arms Control Challenge of the '90s* (Champaign: University of Illinois Press, 1991), pp. 40–9.

37 S[tockholm] I[nternational] P[eace] R[esearch] I[nstitute], *SIPRI Yearbook 1989: World Armaments and Disarmament* (Oxford: O[xford] U[niversity] P[ress], 1989), p. 478.

38 Simpson, 'Trends in Nuclear Proliferation' in Rioux, *Limiting the Proliferation of Weapons*, pp. 13–14.

39 B. Mayorsky, 'The Evolving International Consensus on Nuclear Non-Proliferation' in E.H. Arnett (ed.), *New Technologies for Security & Arms Control: Threats & Promise* (Washington, DC: A[merican] A[ssociation for the] A[dvancement of] S[cience], 1989), pp. 85–9.

40 J. Goldblat, *Nuclear Non-Proliferation: A Guide to the Debate* (London: Taylor & Francis, 1985), p. 30.

41 Special Issue on 'Opaque Nuclear Proliferation: Methodological and Policy Implications', *The Journal of Strategic Studies*, vol. 13, no. 3 (1990).

42 Webster, Hearing on *Nuclear and Missile Proliferation*, p. 11.

43 Dunn, 'Containing Nuclear Proliferation', pp. 6–11; J.W. de Villiers, R. Jardine, M. Reiss, 'Why South Africa Gave Up the Bomb', *Foreign Affairs*, vol. 72, no. 5 (1993), pp. 98–109; L. Spector, 'Nuclear Proliferation in the Middle East: The Next Chapter Begins' in Karsh, Navias and Sabin, *Non-Conventional-Weapons Proliferation in the Middle East*, pp. 135–59; D. Albright and T. Zamora, 'India, Pakistan's nuclear forces: all the pieces in place',

The Bulletin of the Atomic Scientists, vol. 45, no. 5 (1989), pp. 20–6; US D[efense] I[ntelligence] A[gency], *North Korea: The Foundations for Military Strength* (Washington, DC: October 1991), p. 60.

44 Office of the Secretary of Defense, *Proliferation: Threat and Response* (Washington, DC: November 1997), hereafter *Proliferation 1997*, p. 44.

45 J. Erickson, 'The Soviet Union's Growing Arsenal of Chemical Warfare', *Strategic Review*, vol. 7, no. 4 (1979), pp. 63–71.

46 US Dep[artmen]t of State, *Chemical Warfare in Southeast Asia and Afghanistan: Report to the Congress from Secretary of State Alexander M. Haig, Jr.*, 22 March 1982, Special Report no. 98, pp. 6, 10, 13–17; *Chemical Warfare in Southeast Asia and Afghanistan: An Update Report from Secretary of State George P. Shultz*, November 1982, Special Report no. 104, pp. 5–10; U.S. Dept. of State, *Chemical Weapons Use in Southeast Asia and Afghanistan* (Washington, DC: Bureau of Public Affairs, Current Policy no. 553, 21 February 1984), pp. 1–2.

47 D. Oberdorfer, 'Chemical Arms Curbs Are Sought', *The Washington Post*, 9 September 1985, pp. A1, A6; J. Anderson, 'The Growing Chemical Club', *The Washington Post*, 26 August 1984, p. C7.

48 D. Gasbarri, Hearings on *Department of Defense Authorization for Appropriations for Fiscal Year 1985* before the Committee on Armed Services United States Senate, 98th Congress, second session, 26 April 1984, p. 3627.

49 T.J. Welch, Hearings on *Department of Defense Authorization for Appropriations for Fiscal Year 1986*, before the Committee on Armed Services United States Senate, 99th Congress, first session, 28 February 1985, p. 1540.

50 Webster, Hearings on *Global Spread*, p. 10; M. Dowd, 'End the Scourge of Chemical Arms, Bush says at U.N.', *The New York Times*, 26 September 1989, pp. A1, A16.

51 Webster, Hearings on *Threat Assessment; Military Strategy; and Operational Requirements* before the Committee on Armed Services United States Senate, 101st Congress, second session (23 January 1990), pp. 60–1.

52 S.J. Lundin, J.P. Perry Robinson and R. Trapp, 'Chemical and biological warfare: developments in 1987' in *SIPRI Yearbook 1988: World Armaments and Disarmament* (Oxford: OUP, 1988), pp. 101–2; M. Richardson, 'Australia Holding Chemical Arms Talks', *International Herald Tribune*, 13–14 August 1988, p. 2.

53 G.M. Burck and C.C. Floweree, *International Handbook on Chemical Weapons Proliferation* (New York: Greenwood Press, 1991), ch. 3.

54 J. Perry Robinson, 'Chemical Weapons Proliferation: The Problem in Perspective' in T. Findlay (ed.), *Chemical Weapons & Missile Proliferation: With Implications for the Asia/Pacific Region* (Boulder, CO: Lynne Rienner, 1991), pp. 19–35.

55 L.R. Ember, 'Worldwide Spread of Chemical Arms Receiving Increased Attention', *C[hemical] & E[ngineering] N[ews]*, 14 April 1986, pp. 8–16.

56 Rear Adm. W.O. Studeman, Hearings on *National Defense Authorization Act for Fiscal Year 1989 – H.R. 4264 and Oversight of Previously Authorized Programs* before the Committee on Armed Service House of Representatives, Seapower and Strategic and Critical Materials Subcommittee Title 1, 100th Congress, second session (1 March 1988), p. 40; Dr T. Welch, Hearings on *National Defense Authorization Act for Fiscal Year 1989 – H.R. 4264 and Oversight of Previously Authorized Programs* before the Committee on Armed

Services, House of Representatives, 100th Congress, second session (9 March 1988), p. 120.

57 R. Jeffrey Smith, 'Agency Gets Last Word on Poison Gas', *The Washington Post*, 13 December 1989, p. A23.

58 Webster, Hearings on *Global Spread*, pp. 15–16.

59 Spiers, *Chemical and Biological Weapons*, p. 21; L.K. Altman, 'Poison Gas Attacks: Why a Diagnosis Is So Difficult', *The New York Times*, 18 September 1988, p. 14.

60 Lundin, Perry Robinson and Trapp, 'Chemical and biological warfare: developments in 1987', p. 103.

61 H. Allen Holmes, Hearings on *Global Spread*, p. 114; see also J. Perry Robinson, 'The Australia Group: A Description and Assessment' in H.G. Brauch, H.J. Van Der Graaf, J. Grin and W.A. Smit (eds), *Controlling the Development and Spread of Military Technology: Lessons from the past and challenges for the 1990s* (Amsterdam: VU University Press, 1992), pp. 157–75.

62 S. Hazarika, 'India Says It Sold Iran a Chemical Used in Poison Gas', *The New York Times*, 1 July 1989, pp. 1 and 4; T.C. Wiegele, *The Clandestine Building of Libya's Chemical Weapons Factory: A Study in International Collusion* (Carbondale: Southern Illinois University Press, 1992).

63 G. Thatcher, 'Their secret task is to halt spread of chemical weapons', *The Christian Science Monitor*, 2–8 January 1989, pp. B16–B17; see also B. Morel, 'How Effective is the Australia Group?' in Bailey and Rudney, *Proliferation and Export Controls*, pp. 57–64.

64 Dr T.J. Welch, Hearing on *Biological Warfare Testing* before the Subcommittee on Arms Control International Security and Science of the Committee on Foreign Affairs and the Subcommittee on Energy and Environment of the Committee on Interior and Insular Affairs and the Subcommittee on Military Installations and Facilities of the Committee on Armed Services House of Representatives, 100th Congress, second session (3 May 1988), p. 55.

65 Studeman, Hearings on *H.R. 4264*, p. 40; S. Engelberg, 'Iraq Said To Study Biological Arms', *The New York Times*, 18 January 1989, p. A7; T. Shanker, 'West Underwrites Third World's Chemical Arms', *Chicago Tribune*, 3 April 1989, pp. 1 and 6; Webster, Erlick, J. Hinds, Allen Holmes and Dr. B. Richardson, Hearings on *Global Spread*, pp. 10, 33, 174, 367 and 457.

66 J.B. Tucker, 'Lessons of Iraq's Biological Warfare Programme', *Arms Control*, vol. 14, no. 3 (1993), pp. 229–71.

67 *Report of the Chemical Warfare Review Commission* (Washington, DC; USGPO, June 1985), pp. 69–71; Hearing on *The Sverdlovsk Incident: Soviet Compliance with the Biological Weapons Convention?* before the Subcommittee on Oversight of the Permanent Select Committee on Intelligence House of Representatives, 96th Congress, second session (29 May 1980); J. Anderson, 'Upgrading Germ-Warfare Intelligence', 'Soviets Push Biological-Weapons Work', and 'CIA Pinpoints Soviet Germ Warfare Unit', *The Washington Post*, 30 November 1984, p. E7, 4 December 1984, p. B15 and 1 March 1985, p. B12.

68 *Report of the Chemical Warfare Review Commission*, pp. 67 and 70.

69 L. Cole, 'Sverdlovsk, Yellow Rain, and Novel Soviet Bioweapons: Allegations and Responses' and R. Falk and S. Wright, 'Preventing a Biological Arms Race: New Initiatives' in S. Wright (ed.), *Preventing a Biological Arms Race*

(Cambridge, MA: MIT Press, 1990), pp. 199–219 and 330–51; H. Strauss and J. King, 'The fallacy of defensive biological weapon programmes' in E. Geissler (ed.), *Biological and Toxin Weapons Today* (Oxford: OUP, 1986), pp. 66–73.

70 G. Carter, *Porton Down 75 Years of Chemical and Biological Research* (London: HMSO, 1992), pp. 76–9; on US funding, see Wright, 'Evolution of Biological Warfare Policy: 1945–1990' in Wright, *Preventing a Biological Arms Race*, pp. 26–68 and on the effects of the BTWC, see F. Gaffney, Hearings on *Chemical Weapons Convention (Treaty Doc. 103–21)* before the Committee on Foreign Relations United States Senate, 103rd Congress, second session (9 June 1994), p. 123; J. Hinds, Hearings on *Global Spread*, p. 176.

71 Goldberg, Erlick and M.S. Meselson, Hearings on *Global Spread*, pp. 37, 41, 499.

72 Meselson, Hearings on *Global Spread*, p. 208.

73 Hinds, Richardson, and Col. D.L. Huxsoll, Hearings on *Global Spread*, pp. 175, 178, 463, 484.

74 J.R. Harvey, 'Missiles and Advanced Strike Aircraft Comparing Military Effectiveness', *International Security*, vol. 17, no. 2 (1992), pp. 41–83; Senator J. McCain, 'Proliferation in the 1990s: Implications for US Policy and Force Planning', *Strategic Review*, vol. 17, no. 3 (1989), pp. 9–20.

75 Webster, Hearing on *Nuclear and Missile Proliferation*, pp. 11–12; T.L. McNaugher, 'Ballistic Missiles and Chemical Weapons: The Legacy of the Iran–Iraq War', *International Security*, vol. 15, no. 2 (1990), pp. 5–34; W. Seth Carus, *Ballistic Missiles in Modern Conflict* (New York: Praeger, 1991), p. 3; J.E. Nolan, *Trappings of Power: Ballistic Missiles in the Third World* (Washington, DC: Brookings Institution, 1991), p. 64.

76 I[nternational] I[nstitute for] S[trategic] S[tudies], *Strategic Survey 1988–1989* (London: Brassey's, 1989), p. 15; see also A. Karp, 'Ballistic missile proliferation' in SIPRI, *SIPRI Yearbook 1990: World Armaments and Disarmament* (Oxford: OUP, 1990), pp. 369–91.

77 Estimates of '$3.2 billion to develop the Condor missile and build 400 of them, or about $8 million per missile'. W. Seth Carus, Hearing on *Ballistic and Cruise Missile Proliferation in the Third World* before the Subcommittee on Defense Industry and Technology of the Committee on Armed Services United States Senate, 101st Congress, first session (2 May 1989), p. 52.

78 J.E. Nolan, 'Third World Ballistic Missiles', *Scientific American*, vol. 263 (1990), pp. 16–22; W. Seth Carus, *Ballistic Missiles*, pp. 18–26; M. Navias, 'Ballistic Missile Proliferation in the Third World', *Adelphi Papers 252* (1990), pp. 15–19.

79 J.E. Hinds, Hearing on *Ballistic and Cruise Missile Proliferation*, p. 18.

80 J.E. Nolan, 'Conventional Arms Proliferation: The Case of Ballistic Missiles' in Arnett, N*ew Technologies for Security and Arms Control Threats and Promises*, pp. 239–52.

81 J. Baker with T.M. Defrank, *The Politics of Diplomacy* (New York: Putnam's, 1995), p. 589; see also Webster, Hearing on *Nuclear and Missile Proliferation*, p. 13; Fetter, 'Ballistic Missiles and Weapons of Mass Destruction', p. 35; IISS, *Strategic Survey 1988–1989*, p. 23; K.C. Bailey, 'Can Missile Proliferation Be Reversed?' *Orbis*, vol. 35, no. 1 (1991), pp. 5–14.

82 A. Mack, 'Beyond MTCR: Additional Response to the Missile Proliferation Problem' in Findlay, *Chemical Weapons and Missile Proliferation*, pp. 123–31.

83 'Al-Qadhdhafi Wants Long-Range Arab "Missile"', *F[oreign] B[roadcast] I[nformation] S[ervice] – N[ear] E[ast and] S[outh Asia] – 90-078*, 23 April 1990, p. 8.

84 M.A. Heller, 'Coping with Missile Proliferation in the Middle East', *Orbis*, vol. 35, no. 1 (1991), pp. 15–28.

2 WMD Crises and Revelations in the 1990s

1 The Commission on Integrated Long-Term Strategy, *Discriminate Deterrence* (January 1988), pp. 9–10.

2 Gates, Hearing on *Weapons Proliferation in the New World Order*, p. 7; R. James Woolsey, Hearings on *U.S. Security Policy Toward Rogue Regimes* before the Subcommittee on International Security International Organizations and Human Rights of the Committee on Foreign Affairs House of Representatives, 103rd Congress, first session, 28 July 1993, p. 11; see also B. Roberts, 'Between Panic and Complacency: Calibrating the Chemical and Biological Warfare Problem' in S.E. Johnson (ed.), *The Niche Threat: Deterring the Use of Chemical and Biological Weapons* (Washington, DC: National Defense University Press, 1997), pp. 9–41.

3 Gates, Hearings on *Weapons Proliferation in the New World Order*, p. 7; Woolsey, Hearings on *U.S. Security Policy Toward Rogue Regimes*, p. 10.

4 W.S. Cohen, *Report of the Quadrennial Defense Review* (Washington, DC: D[epartment] o[f] D[efense], May 1997), pp. II 2–II 3.

5 Woolsey, Hearings on *U.S. Security Policy Toward Rogue Regimes*, p. 9; Deutch, Hearing on *Current and Projected National Security Threats*, p. 9.

6 Cohen, *Report of the Quadrennial Defense Review*, p. II 3; Wooten, 'Protecting the Force', p. 75.

7 Senator J. Lieberman, Hearing on *Proliferation Threats of the 1990's*, p. 7.

8 A.B. Carter, Hearings on *Nominations before the Senate Armed Services Committee, First Session, 103D Congress*, before the Committee on Armed Services United States Senate, 103rd Congress, first session (28 April 1993), p. 777; see also J.M. Broder and S. Meisler, 'Terrifying Pursuit of Nuclear Arms', *Los Angeles Times*, 19 January 1992, pp. A1, A4–A5; Woolsey, Hearing on *Proliferation Threats of the 1990's*, p. 16; Z.S. Davis, 'U.S. Counter-proliferation Doctrine: Issues for Congress', *Congressional Research Service Report for Congress*, 94-734 ENR (21 September 1994), pp. CRS-3–CRS-10.

9 Gen. H. Norman Schwarzkopf, with P. Petre, *The Autobiography: It Doesn't Take a Hero* (New York: Bantam Press, 1992), p. 300.

10 Adm. E. Zumvalt, Hearing on *Proliferation and Regional Security in the 1990's* before the Committee on Governmental Affairs United States Senate, 101st Congress, second session (9 October 1990), p. 23; R. Jeffrey Smith, 'Relying on Chemical Arms', *The Washington Post*, 10 August 1990, pp. A25, A27; Spiers, *Chemical and Biological Weapons*, pp. 110–13.

11 Col. T.N. Dupuy, Hearings on *Crisis in the Persian Gulf: Sanctions, Diplomacy and War* before the Committee on Armed Services House of Representatives, 101st Congress, second session (13 December 1990), p. 329.

12 J.J. Fialka, 'Allies May Already Have Survived Iraq's Top Chemical Weapon: Fear', *The Wall Street Journal*, 1 October 1990, p. B16; R. Jeffrey Smith, 'US Warns of Retaliation if Iraq Uses Poison Gas', *The Washington Post*, 9 August 1990, pp. A31, A38; F. Reed, 'Chemical Combat Caveats', *The Washington Times*, 13 November 1990, p. G3.

13 Dr B. Richardson, Hearings on *Department of Defense Authorization for Appropriations for Fiscal Years 1992 and 1993* before the Committee on Armed Services, United States Senate,102nd Congress, first session (13 June 1991), p. 753.

14 Gen. Sir Peter de la Billière, *Storm Command: A Personal Account of the Gulf War* (London: HarperCollins, 1992), pp. 98, 174; DoD, *Conduct of the Persian Gulf War Final Report to Congress* (Washington, DC, April 1992), pp. Q-2, Q-5, Q-8; and G.S. Pearson and written evidence in H[ouse] of C[ommons] Defence Committee, Fifth Report, *Implementation of Lessons Learned from Operation Granby*, 43, session 1993–94 (25 May 1994), pp. 29, 52.

15 DoD, *Conduct of the Persian Gulf War*, pp. G-26, Q-2, Q-7, Q-8.

16 Gen. H.N. Schwarzkopf, Hearings on *Operation Desert Shield/Desert Storm* before the Committee on Armed Services United States Senate, 102nd Congress, first session (12 June 1991), p. 349 and *It Doesn't Take a Hero*, p. 439.

17 Baker, *The Politics of Diplomacy*, p. 359; for other US threats, see R. Cheney quoted in DoD, *Conduct of the Persian Gulf War*, p. Q-2 and 'Text of Letter from Bush to Hussein', *The New York Times*, 13 January 1991, p. L9.

18 Ekéus, Hearings on *Global Proliferation*, Part 2, p. 92.

19 *Ibid.*

20 T.A. Postol, 'Lessons of the Gulf War Experience with Patriot', *International Security*, vol. 16, no. 3 (1991–2), pp. 119–71; J. Record, *Hollow Victory: A Contrary View of the Gulf War* (London: Brassey's, 1993), p. 146; [U.S.] G[eneral] A[ccounting] O[ffice], *Patriot Missile Defense Software Problem Led to System Failure at Dhahran, Saudi Arabia* (Washington, DC: GAO/IMTEC-92–96, February 1992), pp. 1, 7–8.

21 'Experts Puzzled Why Saddam Didn't Use Chemical Arsenal', *The Jerusalem Post*, 1 March 1991, p. 2; T.M. Prociv, Hearings on *National Defense Authorization Act for Fiscal Year 1997 – H.R. 3230 and Oversight of Previously Authorized Programs* before the Committee on National Security House of Representatives, 104th Congress, second session (12 March 1996), p. 197.

22 Schwarzkopf, Hearings on *Operation Desert Shield/Desert Storm*, p. 334.

23 *Ibid.*, p. 347.

24 Gen. C.L. Powell, Hearings on *National Defense Authorization Act for Fiscal Year 1994 – H.R. 2401 and Oversight of Previously Authorised Programs* before the Committee on Armed Services, House of Representatives, 103rd Congress, first session (30 March 1993), p. 112.

25 'Proclaiming Victory, Bush Seeks Wider Mideast Peace', *The New York Times*, 7 March 1991, p. A9.

26 A. Friedman and L. Barber, 'U.S. finds Iraq still has N-capacity', *Financial Times*, 13 June 1991, p. 1; M.R. Gordon, 'Pentagon Begins Effort to Combat More Lethal Arms in Third World', *The New York Times*, 8 December 1993, p. A15.

27 Compare 'Briefing by Powell: A Data-Filled Showcase', *The New York Times*, 24 January 1991, p. A11 with M. Evans, 'General reveals secrets of war', *The Times*, 25 March 1991, p. 11 and A.J. Mauroni, *Chemical–Biological*

Defense U.S. Military Policies and Decisions in the Gulf War (Westport, CT: Praeger, 1998), pp. 94–5.

28 *Gulf War Air Power Survey*, 5 vols (Washington, DC: US G[overnment] P[rinting] O[ffice], 1993), vol. 2, p. 340; on the SCUD/Patriot propaganda claims, see P.M. Taylor, *War and the Media Propaganda and Persuasion in the Gulf War* (Manchester: Manchester University Press, 1992), pp. 70–3.

29 Kay, Hearings on *Global Proliferation*, Part 2, p. 105; D.T. Kuehl, 'Thunder and Storm: Strategic Air Operations in the Gulf War' in W. Head and E.H. Tilford (eds), *The Eagle in the Desert: Looking Back on US Involvement in the Persian Gulf War* (Westport, CT: Praeger, 1996), p. 120; 'Excerpts From Briefing at Pentagon by Cheney and Powell', *The New York Times*, 24 January 1991, p. A11.

30 IISS, *Strategic Survey 1997/98* (London: OUP, 1998), pp. 55–66.

31 DoD, *Conduct of the Persian Gulf War*, p. 207.

32 R.F. Lehman, II and S.J. Ledogar, Hearing on *Status of 1990 Bilateral Chemical Weapons Agreement and Multilateral Negotiation on Chemical Weapons Ban* before the Committee on Foreign Relations United States Senate, 102nd Congress, first session (22 May 1991), pp. 17–18.

33 Deutch, Hearing on *Current and Projected National Security Threats*, pp. 8–9.

34 Dr W.B. Shuler, Hearings on *Department of Defense Authorization for Appropriations for Fiscal Year 1996 and the Future Years Defense Program, Part 5* before the Committee on Armed Services, United States Senate, 104th Congress, first session (30 March 1995), p. 189; G.L. Schulte, 'Responding to proliferation: NATO's role', *NATO Review*, vol. 43, no. 4 (1995), pp. 15–19; JPRS Report, 'Proliferation Issues: Russian Federation: Foreign Intelligence Service Report' in Hearing on *Proliferation Threats of the 1990s*, pp. 67–108; US A[rms] C[ontrol and] D[isarmament] A[gency], *Threat Control Through Arms Control Annual Report to Congress* (Washington, DC: ACDA, 1995), p. 25.

35 G.P. Shultz, *Turmoil and Triumph: My Years as Secretary Of State* (New York: Charles Scribner's Sons, 1993), pp. 240–3; Baker, *The Politics of Diplomacy*, pp. 268–9.

36 K. Bailey, Hearings on *Military Implications of The Chemical Weapons Convention (CWC)*, before the Committee on Armed Services United States Senate, 103rd Congress, second session (18 August 1994), p. 124.

37 V. Karpov, 'Soviet Assurances on Toxic Weapons', *The Times*, 18 February 1989, p. 11; S. Whyte, 'Military Glasnost and Force Comparisons', *I[nternational] D[efense] R[eview]*, vol. 22, no. 5 (1989), pp. 559–66; R.G. Harrison and R.G. Joseph, Hearings on *Department of Defense Authorization for Appropriations for Fiscal Years 1990 and 1991* before the Committee on Armed Services United States Senate, 101st Congress, first session (8 June 1989), pp. 235–6.

38 OTA, *Technologies Underlying Weapons of Mass Destruction*, p. 101; A. Devroy and R. Jeffrey Smith, 'U.S., Russia Pledge New Partnership', pp. A1 and A26.

39 F. von Hippel, 'Russian Whistleblower Faces Jail', *The Bulletin of the Atomic Scientists*, vol. 49, no. 2 (1993), pp. 7–8; M.R. Gordon, 'Russia Hides Effort to Develop Deadly Poison Gas, U.S. Says', *The New York Times*, 23 June 1994, p. A3; W. Englund, 'Ex-Soviet scientist says Gorbachev's regime created new nerve gas in '91', *The Baltimore Sun*, 16 September 1992, p. 3A.

40 Curt Weldon, *Hearings on National Defense Authorization Act for Fiscal Year 1997: H.R. 3230*, p. 193.

41   Woolsey, Hearings on *Chemical Weapons Convention*, p. 164; see also Pearson, 'Chemical and Biological Defence', p. 22.
42   Woolsey, Hearings on *Chemical Weapons Convention*, pp. 164–5; DIA report quoted by Senator J. Glenn, Hearings on *Military Implications of The Chemical Weapons Convention*, pp. 46–7.
43   Office of the Secretary of Defense, *Proliferation: Threat and Response* (Washington, DC: April 1996), hereafter *Proliferation 1996*, pp. 32, 34 and DoD, *Proliferation 1997*, pp. 44–6, 48.
44   DoD, *Proliferation 1997*, p. 46; see also L. Ember, 'Russia's arms treaty compliance faulted', *C&EN*, vol. 73 (16 January 1995), p. 23; and A.J. Venter, 'The invisible threat: what does Russia have up its biological warfare sleeve?' *Jane's IDR*, vol. 31, no. 9 (1998), pp. 25–8.
45   R. Bartholomew, Statement in Hearings on *Assisting the Build-Down of the Former Soviet Military Establishment* before the Committee on Armed Services, United States Senate, 102nd Congress, second session (5 February 1992), pp. 13–19; S.E. Miller, 'Western diplomacy and the Soviet nuclear legacy', *Survival*, vol. 34, no. 3 (1992), pp. 3–27; 'Congress Clears Aid Bill In Late Reversal of Sentiment', *Congressional Quarterly Weekly Report*, Vol. 49, no. 48 (30 November 1991), p. 3536.
46   R. Gates, Statement in *Preventing Chaos in the Former Soviet Union The Debate on Providing Aid*, Report of the Committee on Armed Services, House of Representatives, 102nd Congress, second session (17 January 1992), pp. 172, 180, 183–4; K. Bradsher, 'Noting Soviet Eclipse, Baker Sees Arms Risks', *The New York Times*, 9 December 1991, p. A8.
47   R. Gates, Hearing on *H.R. 4803, The Non-Proliferation of Weapons of Mass Destruction and Regulatory Improvement Act of 1992* before the Committee on Banking, Finance and Urban Affairs House of Representatives, 102nd Congress, second session (8 May 1992), p. 12.
48   Miller, 'Western diplomacy', pp. 11–14; T.L. Friedman, 'Hurdles, Big and Small, for Baker's Trip'; 'Russia Asks Baker for Recognition of Independence'; and 'US to Delay Post Soviet Recognition', *The New York Times*, 14; 16; and 20 December, 1991, pp. 6; A1, A14; and A10; and Baker's speech in *Preventing Chaos in the Former Soviet Union*, pp. 223–37.
49   Under START 1 the former Soviet Union must reduce its strategic nuclear force to 1,600 launchers with 6,000 accountable warheads and only 1,540 warheads on 154 heavy ICBMs. Under the Lisbon Protocol, Russia, Ukraine, Belarus and Kazakhstan agreed to assume the responsibilities of the former Soviet Union. Under START 2, if ratified, the US and Russia would reduce their accountable warheads to between 3,000 and 3,500 by 31 December 2007. For more detailed summaries of these agreements, see IISS, *Military Balance 1991–1992* (London: Brassey's, 1991), pp. 216–20 and *The Military Balance 1993–1994* (London: Brassey's, 1993), pp. 230–1.
50   DoD, *Proliferation 1996*, pp. 30–1.
51   W.C. Potter, 'Proliferation Determinants in the Commonwealth of Independent States' in W. Thomas Wander and E.H. Arnett (eds), *The Proliferation of Advanced Weaponry: Technology, Motivations, and Responses* (Washington, DC: AAAS, 1992), pp. 147–63.
52   S. Talbott, Hearing on *U.S. Policy Toward the New Independent States* before the Committee on Foreign Affairs House of Representatives, 103rd Congress,

second session (25 January 1994), pp. 5, 76; G.C. Duffy and J.F. Collins, Hearings on *Rewrite of the Foreign Assistance Act of 1961 and Fiscal Year 1995 Foreign Assistance Request (Part 2)* before the Subcommittee on Europe and the Middle East of the Committee on Foreign Affairs House of Representatives, 103rd Congress, second session (24 March 1994), pp. 54–5, 311, 386–7; see also IISS, *Strategic Survey 1993–1994*, pp. 51–3.

53 S.D. Sagan, 'The Causes of Nuclear Proliferation', *Current History*, vol. 96, no. 609 (1997), pp. 151–56; see also M. Reiss, *Bridled Ambition: Why Countries Constrain Their Nuclear Capabilities* (Washington, DC: Woodrow Wilson Center Press, 1995), pp. 90–129 and J.C. Baker, 'Non-Proliferation Incentives for Russia and Ukraine', *Adelphi Papers 309* (1997).

54 DoD, *Proliferation 1997*, pp. 41–3; Deutch, 'The Threat of Nuclear Diversion' in Hearings on *Global Proliferation*, Part 2, p. 313.

55 R. Gates, Hearings on *Weapons Proliferation in the New World Order*, pp. 7–8; written answer in Hearing on *Proliferation Threats of the 1990's*, p. 144; J. Deutch, 'The Threat of Nuclear Diversion', in Hearings on *Global Proliferation*, Part 2, pp. 302–23; DoD, *Proliferation 1997*, p. 43.

56 GAO, 'Nuclear Non Proliferation: U.S. Efforts to Help Newly Independent States Improve Their Nuclear Material Controls' (GAO-T-NSIAD/RCED-96-118, 13 March 1996), W.C. Potter, 'Nuclear Leakage from the Post-Soviet States', 13 March 1996 and Deutch, 'The Threat of Nuclear Diversion' in Hearings on *Global Proliferation*, Part 2, pp. 187–93; 198–229; and 305–6, 309, 313; IISS, *Strategic Survey 1994–1995* (London: OUP, 1995), pp. 17–25.

57 C. Krauthammer, 'North Korea's Coming Bomb', *The Washington Post*, 5 November 1993, p. A27; see also S.J. Solarz, 'Next of Kim', *The New Republic*, 8 August 1994, pp. 23–7.

58 M.J. Mazarr, *North Korea and the Bomb: A Case Study in Nonproliferation* (New York: St Martin's Press, 1995); P. Bracken, 'Nuclear Weapons and State Survival in North Korea', *Survival*, vol. 35, no. 3 (1993), pp. 137–53; A. Mack, 'The Nuclear Crisis in the Korean peninsula', *Asian Survey*, vol. 33, no. 4 (1993), pp. 339–59; Reiss, *Bridled Ambition*, pp. 231–319.

59 D.E. Sanger, 'Nuclear Activity by North Koreans Worries the US', *The New York Times*, 10 November 1991, p. 1; A. Mack, 'North Korea and the Bomb', *Foreign Policy*, no. 83 (1991), pp. 87–104.

60 R. Gates, Hearings on *The Future of U.S. Foreign Policy in the Post-Cold War Era* before the Committee on Foreign Affairs House of Representatives, 102nd Congress, second session (25 February 1992), pp. 207–8.

61 'Meet the Press', FBIS-EAS-93-214, 8 November 1993, p. 29.

62 R. Galluci and W. Slocombe, Hearings on *National Defense Authorization Act for Fiscal Year 1995 – S. 2182 (H.R. 4301) and Oversight of Previously Authorized Programs* before the Committee on Armed Services House of Representatives, 103rd Congress, second session (24 March 1994), p. 995; D. Albright, 'How Much Plutonium Does North Korea Have?', *The Bulletin of the Atomic Scientists*, vol. 50, no. 5 (1994), pp. 46–53.

63 M.R. Gordon, 'Pentagon Begins Effort to Combat More Lethal Arms in Third World', *The New York Times*, 8 December 1993, p. A15; on the advocacy of military strikes, see, B. Scowcroft and A. Kanter, 'Korea: Time For Action', *The Washington Post*, 15 June 1994, p. A2, but on the problems of them, see Solarz, 'Next of Kim', pp. 26–7.

64   D.E. Sanger, 'Missile Tested by North Koreans', *The New York Times*, 13 June 1993, p. L7; on the problems of sanctions, see, Solarz, 'Next of Kim', p. 26 and W.J. Perry, Hearing on *Security Implications of the Nuclear Non-Proliferation Agreement with North Korea* before the Committee on Armed Services United States Senate, 104th Congress, first session (26 January 1995), p. 9.

65   R. Marcus and R. Jeffrey Smith, 'North Korea Confirms Freeze; U.S. Agrees to Resume Talks', *The Washington Post*, 23 June 1994, pp. A1 and A25; C. Krauthammer, 'Peace in Our Time', *The Washington Post*, 24 June 1994, p. A27; L.V. Sigal, 'Jimmy Carter Makes a Deal', *The Bulletin of the Atomic Scientists*, vol. 54, no. 1 (1998), pp. 40–6.

66   W. Drozdiak, 'N. Korea, U.S. Sign Broad Pact', *The Washington Post*, 22 October 1994, pp. A1 and A26.

67   G. Milhollin, Hearing on *Security Implications of the Nuclear Non-Proliferation Agreement with North Korea*, p. 59; see also Senator J. McCain, *ibid.*, pp. 5–7; 'The Content of the Korea Accord', *The Washington Post*, 21 October 1994, p. A24; C. Krauthammer, 'Romancing the Thugs', *Time*, 7 November 1994, p. 90; R.V. Allen and D.M. Plunk, 'To Strengthen the Deal With North Korea', *The Washington Post*, 9 November 1994, p. A19; W. Safire, 'Clinton's Concessions', *The New York Times*, 24 October 1994, p. A17.

68   W.J. Perry, Hearing on *Security Implications of the Nuclear Non-Proliferation Agreement with North Korea*, pp. 8–13, 87–8.

69   R. Jeffrey Smith, 'U.S. Accord With North Korea May Open Country to Change', *The Washington Post*, 23 October 1994, p. A36; M.Y. (Michael) Park, ' "Lure" North Korea', *Foreign Policy*, no. 97 (1994–5), pp. 97–105.

70   R. Galluci, Hearings on *National Defense Authorization Act for Fiscal Year 1995*, p. 1012.

71   M. Thompson, 'Well, Maybe a Nuke or Two', *Time*, 11 April 1994, p. 58.

72   M.J. Mazarr, 'Going Just a Little Nuclear', *International Security*, vol. 20, no. 2 (1995), pp. 92–122.

73   R. Jeffrey Smith, 'N. Korea and the Bomb: High-Tech Hide-and-Seek', *The Washington Post*, 27 April 1993, pp. A1 and A11.

74   McCain, Hearing on *Security Implications of the Nuclear Non-Proliferation Agreement with North Korea*, p. 35; G. Gerardi and J. Bermudez, Jr, 'An Analysis of North Korean Ballistic Missile Testing' and J.S. Bermudez, Jr, 'Inside North Korea's CW infrastructure', *J[ane's] I[ntelligence] R[eview]*, vol. 7, no. 4 (1995), pp. 184–90 and vol. 8, no. 8 (1996), pp. 378–82; DoD, *Proliferation 1997*, pp. 5–8.

75   Lt-Gen. J.R. Clapper to Senator D. DeConcini, 22 March 1994, in Hearing on *Security Implications of the Nuclear Non-Proliferation Agreement with North Korea*, pp. 48–9; see also Deutch, 'The Threat of Nuclear Diversion', *Hearings on Global Proliferation*, Part 2, p. 308 and DoD, *Proliferation 1997*, pp. 4–5.

76   Memorandum by Ambassador Rolf Ekéus, 'Iraq's Biological Weapons Programme: UNSCOM's Experience', presented to the Fourth Review Conference of the States Parties to the Biological and Toxin Weapons Convention, 20 November 1996, pp. 1–2; F[oreign &] C[ommonwealth] O[ffice], 'The Work of the United Nations Special Commission in Iraq', Background Brief (London, January 1997), p. 1; Note by the Secretary-General, UN Security

Council, S/1995/1038 (17 December 1995), paras. 22–3, 27–8, 31; IISS, *Strategic Survey 1997/98*, pp. 64–66.

77 SIPRI, Fact sheet, *Iraq: The UNSCOM Experience* (October 1998); U[nited] S[tates] I[nformation] S[ervice], 'Iraqi Weapons of Mass Destruction Programs' (13 February 1998).

78 D. Albright and M. Hibbs, 'Iraq's Bomb: Blueprints and Artifacts' and D. Albright and R. Kelley, 'Has Iraq Come Clean at Last?' *The Bulletin of the Atomic Scientists*, vol. 48, no. 1 (1992), pp. 30–1, 33–40 and vol. 51, no. 6 (1995), pp. 53–64; R. Gates, Hearing on *H.R. 4803*, p. 20; Kay, Hearings on *Global Proliferation*, Part 2, pp. 324–32; Deutch, 'The New Nuclear Threat', p. 121; OTA, *Technologies Underlying Weapons of Mass Destruction*, pp. 168–9.

79 H. Porteus, 'Grappling with the BW Genie', *IDR*, vol. 28, no. 3 (1995), pp. 32–4; B. Richardson, 'The Threat of Chemical and Biological Proliferation' in Bailey and Rudney, *Proliferation and Export Controls*, p. 16.

80 B. Roberts, 'Between Panic and Complacency' in Johnson, *The Niche Threat*, p. 14.

81 'Iraqi CBW Armament and the UN Special Commission', *Chemical Weapons Convention Bulletin*, hereafter referred to as *CBWCB*, no. 13 (September 1991), p. 21; A.H. Cordesman, 'Iraq and Weapons of Mass Destruction', *Congressional Record: Senate*, 8 April 1992, pp. S5062–76.

82 G. Robertson, *Parliamentary Debates*, vol. 305, 9 February 1998, cols. 3 and 6.

83 R.A. Zilinskas, 'Iraq's Biological Weapons The Past as Future?' *JAMA*, vol. 278, no. 5 (6 August 1997), pp. 418–24; Note by the Secretary-General, UN Security Council, S/1995/864 (11 October 1995), p. 24.

84 Notes by the Secretary-General, UN Security Council, S/1995/864 (11 October 1995), p. 18 and S/1995/1038 (17 December 1995), paras. 52–3; S/1997/774 (6 October 1997), paras 62–3; S/1998/920 (6 October 1998), para. 29 (b); and Letter dated 26 October from the Executive Chairman of the Special Commission, S/1998/995.

85 Ekéus, Hearings on *Global Proliferation*, Part 2, pp. 101–2.

86 'News Chronology', *CBWCB*, no. 42 (December 1998), p. 33; Kay, Hearings on *Global Proliferation*, Part 2, pp. 324–32; IISS, *Strategic Survey 1997/98*, p. 58; J. Barry, 'Unearthing the Truth', *Newsweek*, 2 March 1988, pp. 20–1.

87 Note by the Secretary-General, UN Security Council, S/1997/774 (6 October 1997), pp. 19–20; Letter dated 8 April 1998 from the Executive Chairman of the Special Commission, UN Security Council, S/1998/308 (8 April 1998), p. 11.

88 Note by the Secretary-General, UN Security Council, S/23165 (25 October 1991), p. 6; R. Scarborough and B. Gertz, 'U.N. May Destroy the Hardware, But Iraqi Nuclear Workers Remain', *The Washington Times*, 16 November 1991, p. A3; Tucker, 'Lessons of Iraq's Biological Warfare Programme', pp. 257–8.

89 Ekéus, 'Iraq's Biological Weapons Programme', pp. 3–5; M. Leitenberg, 'Biological Weapons Arms Control', *Contemporary Security Policy*, vol. 17, no. 1 (1996), pp. 1–79; FCO, 'The Work of the United Nations Special Commission in Iraq', p. 5; A.J. Venter, 'UNSCOM Odyssey: The Search for Saddam's Biological Arsenal', *JIR*, vol. 10, no. 3 (1998), pp. 16–21.

90 J. Walker in R. Ranger (ed.), 'The Devil's Brews 1: Chemical and Biological Weapons and Their Delivery Systems', *Bailrigg Memorandum 16* (Lancaster University: Centre for Defence and International Security Studies, 1996),

pp. 14 and 16; G.S. Pearson, 'The Complementary Role of Environmental and Security Biological Control Regimes in the 21st Century', *JAMA*, vol. 278, no. 5 (6 August 1997), pp. 369–72.

91 A. Levran, *Israeli Strategy After Desert Storm* (London: Frank Cass, 1997), p. 51; Capt. H. Lee Buchanan, 'Poor Man's A-Bomb?' *Proceedings of the US Naval Institute*, vol. 123, no. 4 (1997), pp. 83–6; F. Gaffney, Hearings on *Chemical Weapons Convention*, p. 144.

92 R.P. Kadlec, A.P. Zelicoff and A.M. Vrtis, 'Biological Weapons Control Prospects and Implications for the Future', *JAMA*, vol. 278, no. 5 (6 August 1997), pp. 351–6.

93 S. Black, 'The UN Special Commission and CBW Verification', *CBWCB*, no. 32 (June 1996), pp. 1, 7–8; see also K.C. Bailey, 'Responding to the Threat of Biological Weapons', *Security Dialogue*, vol. 26, no. 4 (1995), pp. 383–97; Kay, Hearings on *Global Proliferation*, Part 2, p. 120.

94 On Iraqi co-operation, see K. Bailey, Hearings on *Chemical Weapons Convention*, p. 128.

95 H. Blix, 'Verification of Nuclear Nonproliferation: The Lesson of Iraq', *The Washington Quarterly*, vol. 15, no. 4 (1992), pp. 57–65.

96 Ekéus, 'Iraq's Biological Weapons Programme', p. 6.

97 P. Lewis, 'U.S. Won't Discuss Embargo Terms With Iraq', *The New York Times*, 28 November 1993, p. 16.

98 FCO, 'The Work of the United Nations Special Commission in Iraq', pp. 5–6; USIS, 'Iraqi Weapons of Mass Destruction Programs', pp. 1, 3–4; M. Colvin, 'Saddam Hides Secret Arsenal', *The Sunday Times*, 16 November 1997, p. 24.

99 Leitenberg, 'Biological Weapons Arms Control', p. 26; Ekéus, 'Iraq's Biological Weapons Programme', pp. 6–8; see also Zilinskas, 'Iraq's Biological Weapons The Past as Future?', p. 423.

3 Political Leadership and Nonproliferation

1 M. Dowd and T.L. Friedman, 'The Fabulous Bush & Baker Boys', *The New York Times*, 6 May 1990, pp. 34, 36, 58, 62, 64, 67; Charles-Philippe David, 'Who was the Real George Bush? Foreign Policy Decision-Making Under the Bush Administration', *Diplomacy & Statecraft*, vol. 7, no. 1 (1996), pp. 197–220.

2 President Bush, 'Toward a New World Order', 11 September 1990 (US Dept of State, *Bureau of Public Affairs*, Current Policy Brief No. 1298).

3 President Bush, 'The UN: World Parliament of Peace', 1 October 1990 (US Dept of State, *Bureau of Public Affairs*, Current Policy Brief No. 1303).

4 'Proclaiming Victory, Bush Seeks Wider Mideast Peace', p. A9; 'President Bush: Remarks at Maxwell Air Force Base War College in Montgomery, Alabama, 13 April 1991', and R. Gates, 'American Leadership in a New World Order', address to the American Newspaper Publisher's Association, Vancouver, British Columbia, 7 May 1991 in USIS, 'The New World Order: An Analysis and Document Collection', 29 July 1991.

5 C. Krauthammer, 'The Unipolar Moment', *Foreign Affairs, America and the World 1990/91*, vol. 70, no. 1 (1991), pp. 23–33.

6 D. Gergen, 'America's Missed Opportunities', *Foreign Affairs, America and the World 1991/92*, vol. 71, no. 1 (1992), pp. 1–19.

7   *Ibid.*, p. 3; see also S. Talbott, 'Post-Victory Blues', *Foreign Affairs, America and the World 1991/92*, vol. 71, no. 1 (1992), pp. 53–69.

8   Baker, *The Politics of Diplomacy*, p. 336.

9   L. Freedman, 'The Gulf War and the New World Order', *Survival*, vol. 33, no. 3 (1991), pp. 195–209; D. Hiro, *Desert Shield to Desert Storm* (London: Paladin, 1992), p. 446; J. Pimlott, 'International Ramifications' in J. Pimlott and S. Badsey (eds), *The Gulf War Assessed* (London: Arms and Armour Press, 1992), pp. 193–217.

10 J.S. Nye, Jr, 'What New World Order?' *Foreign Affairs*, vol. 71, no. 2 (1992), pp. 83–96.

11 B. Scowcroft, 'Who Can Harness History? Only the U.S.', *The New York Times*, 2 July 1993, p. A15; E. Kier and J. Mercer, 'Setting Precedents in Anarchy: Military Intervention and Weapons of Mass Destruction', *International Security*, vol. 20, no. 4 (1996), pp. 77–106.

12 Baker, *The Politics of Diplomacy*, p. 151; Spiers, *Chemical and Biological Weapons*, ch. 5.

13 'In Clinton's Words: U.N. Cannot Become Engaged in Every World Conflict', p. A16.

14 R.D. Shuey, S.R. Bowman and Z.S. Davis, 'Proliferation Control Regimes: Background and Status', CRS Report for Congress, 97-343F (10 March 1997), p. CRS-20; DoD, *Proliferation 1997*, pp. 61–2; Deutch, 'The Threat of Nuclear Diversion' and C.B. Curtis, Statement in Hearings on *Global Proliferation*, Part 2, pp. 314–15 and 448–58.

15 'In Clinton's Words: U.N. Cannot Become Engaged in Every World Conflict', p. A16; J.R. Bolton, 'Wrong Turn in Somalia', *Foreign Affairs*, vol. 73, no. 1 (1994), pp. 56–66.

16 Cohen, *Report of the Quadrennial Defense Review*, pp. III-1; see also W.J. Perry, 'Defense in an Age of Hope', *Foreign Affairs*, vol. 75, no. 6 (1996), pp. 64–79 and Schulte, 'Responding to Proliferation: NATO's role', pp. 15–19.

17 S. Talbott, 'Democracy and the National Interest', *Foreign Affairs*, vol. 75, no. 6 (1996), pp. 47–63; for a critique of Clinton's foreign policy, see M. Mandelbaum, 'Foreign Policy as Social Work', *Foreign Affairs*, vol. 75, no. 1 (1996), pp. 16–32.

18 L.E. Davis, Hearing on *Review of the Clinton Administration Nonproliferation Policy* before the Committee on International Relations House of Representatives, 104th Congress, second session (19 June 1996), pp. 47–8.

19 Shuey, Bowman and Davis, 'Proliferation Control Regimes', p. CRS-49.

20 Reiss, *Bridled Ambition*, p. 32; J.W. de Villiers, R. Jardine, and M. Reiss, 'Why South Africa Gave Up the Bomb', pp. 98–109; W. Bowen and A. Koch, 'Non-Proliferation Is Embraced by Brazil', *JIR*, vol. 8, no. 6 (1996), pp. 283–7; V. Gamba-Stonehouse, 'Argentina and Brazil' in R.C. Karp (ed.), *Security with Nuclear Weapons?* (Oxford: OUP, 1991), pp. 229–57.

21 R.L. Rothstein, 'Democracy, Conflict and Development in the Third World', *The Washington Quarterly*, vol. 14, no. 2 (1991), pp. 43–63.

22 C. Lockwood and R. Bedi, 'Sanctions on India after new N-tests', *The Daily Telegraph*, 14 May 1998, p. 1; A.L. Kazmin and Q. Peel, 'Explosion of Self-esteem', *Financial Times*, 13 May 1998, p. 25.

23 D. Bereuter, Hearings on *US Security Policy Toward Rogue Regimes*, p. 3.

24   T. Lantos, Hearings on *US Security Policy Toward Rogue Regimes*, p. 2; see also Kay, Hearings on *Global Proliferation*, Part 2, p. 116 and Shuey, Bowman and Davis, 'Proliferation Control Regimes', p. CRS-17.
25   Levran, *Israeli Strategy After Desert Storm*, pp. 76–8; Lantos, Hearing on *US Security Policy Toward Rogue Regimes*, p. 40.
26   R. Einhorn, *Compilation of Hearings on National Security Issues* before the Subcommittee on International Security, Proliferation, and Federal Services of the Committee on Governmental Affairs United States Senate, 105th Congress, second session (April 1998), p. 295; B. Gertz, 'Clinton's veto blocks sanctions on Russia', *The Washington Times*, 24 June 1998, pp. A1 and A16.
27   Einhorn, *Compilation of Hearings*, pp. 288–90; R. Wright, 'Russia Warned on Helping Iran Missile Program', *Los Angeles Times*, 12 February 1997, pp. A1 and A6; B. Gertz, 'Russia, China Aid Iran's Missile Program', *The Washington Times*, 10 September 1997, pp. A1 and A11; M.R. Gordon, 'Despite Bomb Tests, Russia Is Selling 2 Nuclear Plants to India', *The New York Times*, 23 June 1998, p. A9.
28   J. Mann, 'China Said to Sell Pakistan Dangerous New Missiles', *Los Angeles Times*, 4 December 1992, pp. A1 and A18; G. Milhollin and M. Dennison, 'China's Cynical Calculation' and E. Sciolino, 'C.I.A. Report Says Chinese Sent Iran Arms Components', *The New York Times*, 24 April 1995, p. A17 and 22 June 1995, pp. A1 and A6; B. Gertz, 'Albright Concedes Concern Over China–Iran Transfers', *The Washington Times*, 24 January 1997, p. A6; R. Jeffrey Smith, 'CIA Report Calls China and Russia Key Suppliers of Most Destructive Arms Technology', *The Washington Post*, 2 July 1997, p. A24.
29   Milhollin, Hearing on *Global Proliferation*, part 2, pp. 111, 336; Einhorn, *Compilation of Hearings*, pp. 221–4; R. Jeffrey Smith, 'U.S. Relents On Chinese Sanctions', *The Washington Post*, 11 May 1996, pp. A1 and A24.
30   G. Milhollin, *Compilation of Hearings*, p. 248.
31   R.H. Speier, *Compilation of Hearings*, p. 313.
32   R. Cook and T. Blair, *Parliamentary Debates*, vol. 312, 14 and 20 May 1998, cols. 516 and 955; G. Hasnain and A. Bose, 'Pakistan Warns of Nuclear Retaliation', *The Sunday Times*, 17 May 1998, p. 21.
33   T.W. Lippman, 'Russia to Sell India 2 reactors, Drawing Criticism from U.S.', *The Washington Post*, 23 June 1998, p. A14; B. Gertz, 'Clinton's Veto Blocks Sanctions on Russia', *The Washington Times*, 24 June 1998, pp. A1, A16.
34   Webster, Hearings on *Global Spread*, p. 18.
35   Gen. J.M. Shalikashvili, 'Posture Statement' in Hearings on *National Defense Authorisation Act for Fiscal Year 1996 – H.R. 1530 and Oversight of Previously Authorized Programs* before the Committee on National Security House of Representatives, 104th Congress, first session (8 February 1995), pp. 58–62.
36   Lt-Gen. J.R. Clapper, Hearing on *Worldwide Intelligence Review* before the Select Committee on Intelligence United States Senate, 104th Congress, first session (10 January 1995), p. 36.
37   Kay, Hearings on *Global Proliferation*, Part 2, pp. 121–2.
38   P. Sawhney, 'A Force in Waiting: India's Defense Organization Sets Its Sights on the Future', *Jane's IDR*, vol. 31, no. 6 (1998), pp. 29–31.

39 'Former Army Chief on "Aggressive Nuclear Policy"', *FBIS-NES-92-199*, 14 October 1992, p. 47.

40 Johnson, *The Niche Threat*, pp. 4–5; P.J. Garrity, 'Implications of the Persian Gulf War for Regional Powers', *The Washington Quarterly*, vol. 16, no. 3 (1993), pp. 153–70.

41 B. Roberts, 'From Nonproliferation to Antiproliferation', *International Security*, vol. 18, no. 1 (1993), pp. 139–73.

42 Quoted in Garrity, 'Implications of the Persian Gulf War for Regional Powers', p. 156.

43 *Ibid.*, p. 157.

44 *Ibid.*, p. 158.

45 H.D. Sokolski, 'Nonapocalyptic Proliferation: A New Strategic Threat?' *The Washington Quarterly*, vol. 17, no. 2 (1994), pp. 115–27 and 'Fighting Proliferation with Intelligence', *Orbis*, vol. 38, no. 2 (1994), pp. 245–60.

46 The last five French tests were held from 5 September 1995 to 27 January 1996 and the last two Chinese on 8 June and 29 July 1996. 'Nuclear testing in the 1990s', *International Herald Tribune*, 12 May 1998, p. 1.

47 'India's Statement About the Tests', *International Herald Tribune*, 12 May 1998, p. 4; B. Maddox, 'Rebuff exposes new limits of American power', *The Times*, 14 May 1998, p. 17; R. Jeffrey Smith, 'CIA Missed Signs Of India's Tests, U.S. Officials Say', *The Washington Post*, 13 May 1998, pp. A1, A25; A. Faulkner, 'CTBT: Towards Its Entry into Force', *Disarmament*, vol. 20, no. 1 (1997), pp. 26–40.

48 H. Gordon, 'Treaty Killed by Failure of Surveillance', *The Daily Telegraph*, 13 May 1998, p. 4.

49 M. Binyon and R. Whymant, 'Japan Cuts Aid while Britain Protests', *The Times*, 14 May 1998, p. 17; R. Cook, *Parliamentary Debates*, vol. 312, 14 May 1998, cols. 515, 518.

50 M. Campbell and J. Burke, 'Pakistan Calls Clinton's Bluff', *The Sunday Times*, 31 May 1998, p. 21.

51 A. Rashid, 'N-blasts put Pakistan in Arms Race', *The Daily Telegraph*, 29 May 1998, pp. 1–2.

52 S.D. Drell, 'Reasons to Ratify, Not to Stall', *The New York Times*, 2 June 1998, p. A27; J. Isaacs, 'Senate: Test Ban Prospects Shaken', *The Bulletin of the Atomic Scientists*, vol. 54, no. 4 (1998), pp. 40–1.

53 R. Bedi, 'Premier Vows that Defence of India Is "Safeguarded"', *The Daily Telegraph*, 29 May 1998, p. 19; Campbell and Burke, 'Pakistan Calls Clinton's Bluff'.

54 T. Rhodes, 'Senators Outraged by "Colossal Failure" of CIA to Give Warning', *The Times*, 14 May 1998, p. 17; see also T. Weiner, 'U.S. Suspects India Prepares To Conduct Nuclear Test', *The New York Times*, 15 December 1995, p. A9.

55 'Secretary's Remarks to Stimson Center', 10 June 1998 (US Department of State, 10 June 1998), p. 3.

56 UN Security Council Resolution 1172 (6 June 1998); B. Schweid, 'India, Pakistan Cut Off by G-8', *The Washington Times*, 13 June 1998, p. A1.

57 F. Heisbourg, 'The Prospects for Nuclear Stability between India and Pakistan' and B. Chellaney, 'After the Tests: India's Options', *Survival*, vol. 40, no. 4 (1998/99), pp. 77–92 and 93–111.

4   Military Utility of Weapons of Mass Destruction

1   J.W. Anderson and K. Khan, 'Pakistan Again Explodes Bomb', *The Washington Post*, 31 May 1998, pp. A1 and A23; 'Secretary's Remarks to Stimson Center', p. 3.

2   W.B. Slocombe, *Compilation of Hearings*, pp. 20–4; M[inistry] o[f] D[efence], *The Strategic Defence Review*, Cm 3999 (London: The Stationery Office, 1998), p. 17.

3   M.R. Narayan Swamy, 'Indian Lashes West for "Hypocrisy" of Anti-nuclear Stance', *The Washington Times*, 21 May 1998, p. A17.

4   E.N. Luttwak, 'An Emerging Postnuclear Era?', *The Washington Quarterly*, vol. 11, no. 1 (1988), pp. 5–15; M. Reiss, 'Conclusion: Nuclear Proliferation after the Cold War' in M. Reiss and R.S. Litwak (eds), *Nuclear Proliferation after the Cold War* (Washington, DC: The Woodrow Wilson Center Press, 1994), pp. 335–50.

5   C. Richards, 'Major Blunders on Nuclear Plans', *The Independent*, 9 January 1991, p. 11; 'L'entretien télévisé du président de la République: "Cette épreuve cruelle de vérité aura lieu. Il faut que les français préparent leur esprit"', *Le Monde*, 9 February 1991, pp. 8–9; Baker, *The Politics of Diplomacy*, p. 359.

6   OTA, *Proliferation of Weapons of Mass Destruction*, p. 7.

7   G. Weaver and J. David Glaes, *Inviting Disaster: How Weapons of Mass Destruction Undermine U.S. Strategy For Projecting Military Power* (McLean, Virginia: AMCODA Press, 1997), pp. 28–9 and 45–50.

8   Harvey, 'Missiles and Advanced Strike Aircraft', p. 68; J.H. Kahan, 'Deterrence and Warfighting in an NBC Environment' in Johnson, *The Niche Threat*, p. 57.

9   Fetter, 'Ballistic Missiles and Weapons of Mass Destruction', p. 29.

10   Slocombe, *Compilation of Hearings*, pp. 22–4; see also 'Former Army Chief on "Aggressive Nuclear Policy"' and K.J. Cooper, 'Leader Says India Has A "Credible" Deterrent', *The Washington Post*, 17 June 1998, p. A21.

11   Harvey, 'Missiles and Advanced Strike Aircraft', pp. 67–8.

12   W.E. Burrows and R. Windrem, *Critical Mass: the Dangerous Race for Superpowers in a Fragmenting World* (New York: Simon & Schuster, 1994), p. 496.

13   DoD, *Proliferation 1996*, p. A-5.

14   OTA, *Technologies Underlying Weapons of Mass Destruction*, p. 97; Pearson, 'Chemical and Biological Defence', p. 24; Buchanan, 'Poor Man's A-Bomb?', p. 84; Tucker, 'Lessons of Iraq's Biological Warfare Programme', p. 234.

15   Proteus, 'Grappling with the BW Genie', p. 34; IISS, *Strategic Survey 1996/7* (London: OUP, 1997), p. 36.

16   OTA, *Technologies Underlying Weapons of Mass Destruction*, pp. 97–8; IISS, *Strategic Survey 1996/7*, p. 36.

17   OTA, *Proliferation of Weapons of Mass Destruction*, pp. 52 and 61.

18   R. Preston, 'Annals of Warfare: The Bioweaponeers', *New Yorker*, 9 March 1998, pp. 52–65.

19   T. Weiner, 'Soviet Defector Warns of Biological Weapons', *The New York Times*, 25 February 1998, pp. A1 and A8.

20   V.A. Utgoff, 'The Biotechnology Revolution and Its Potential Military Implications' in Roberts, *Biological Weapons: Weapons of the Future?*, p. 31; see also IISS, *Strategic Survey 1996/7*, p. 37.

21 Roberts, 'Between Panic and Complacency' in Johnson, *The Niche Threat*, pp. 19, 21–2; Dando, *Biological Warfare*, p. 13; R. Danzig and P.B. Berkowsky, 'Why Should We Be Concerned About Biological Warfare?', *JAMA*, vol. 278, no. 5 (1997), pp. 431–2.

22 Lt-Gen. P.M. Hughes, Hearing on *Current and Projected National Security Threats to the United States* before the Select Committee on Intelligence of the United States Senate, 105th Congress, first session (5 February 1997), p. 13; see also Cohen, *Report of the Quadrennial Defense Review*, pp. II 2, VII 12.

23 Bailey, 'Responding to the Threat of Biological Weapons', p. 383; R.K. Betts, 'What Will It Take to Deter the United States?' *Parameters*, vol. 25, no. 4 (1995–96), pp. 70–9; Gen. C.G. Krulak, Hearings on *Department of Defense Authorization for Appropriations for Fiscal Year 1997 and the Future Years Defense Program* before the Committee on Armed Services, United States Senate, 104th Congress, second session (15 March 1996), p. 13.

24 Roberts, 'Between Panic and Complacency' in Johnson, *The Niche Threat*, pp. 22–3.

25 Lt-Col. G.W. Carpenter et al., 'Biological Warfare A Historical Perspective', *JAMA*, vol. 278, no. 5 (1997), pp. 412–17; B. Roberts and G.S. Pearson, 'Bursting the Biological Bubble: How Prepared Are We for Biowar?' *Jane's IDR*, vol. 31, no. 4 (1998), pp. 21–4.

26 UN Security Council, 'Note by the Secretary-General', S/1995/864, 11 October 1995, p. 25.

27 S. Whitby and P. Rogers, 'Anti-crop Biological Warfare: Implications of the Iraqi and US Programs', *Defense Analysis*, vol. 13, no. 3 (1997), pp. 303–18; J.B. Tucker, 'The Biological Weapons Threat', *Current History*, vol. 96, no. 609 (1997), pp. 167–72; G.B. Carter, 'Biological Warfare and Biological Defence in the United Kingdom 1940–1979', *RUSI Journal*, vol. 137, no. 6 (1992), pp. 67–74.

28 R. Novick and S. Shulman, 'New Forms of Biological Warfare?' in Wright, *Preventing a Biological Arms Race*, pp. 103–19; S. Murphy, A. Hay and S. Rose, *No Fire No Thunder: The Threat of Chemical and Biological Weapons* (London: Pluto Press, 1984), p. 67.

29 Col. R.J. Larsen and Lt-Col. R.P. Kadlec, 'Biological Warfare: A Silent Threat to America's Defense Transportation System', *Strategic Review*, vol. 26, no. 2 (1998), pp. 5–10.

30 J.G. Roos, 'Chem-Bio Defense Agency Will Tackle "Last Major Threat to a Deployed Force"', *Armed Forces Journal International*, December 1992, p. 10; see also Maj. G.B. Knudson, 'Operation Desert Shield: Medical Aspects of Weapons of Mass Destruction', *Military Medicine*, vol. 156 (1991), pp. 267–71; Vicary and Wilson, 'Nuclear Biological and Chemical Defence', p. 7; and Zilinskas, 'Iraq's Biological Weapons: The Past as Future?', pp. 418–24.

31 Knudson, 'Operation Desert Shield: Medical Aspects of Weapons of Mass Destruction', p. 268; Vice Admiral R.F. Dunn, ' "Gas Attack, This Is No Drill!" ', *Proceedings of the US Naval Institute*, vol. 123, no. 5 (1997), pp. 64–6; Roberts, 'Between Panic and Complacency' in Johnson, *Niche Threat*, p. 21.

32 J.D. Douglass, Jr, 'The Expanding Threat of Chemical–Biological Warfare: A Case of U.S. Tunnel-Vision', *Strategic Review*, vol. 14, no. 4 (1986), pp. 37–46.

33 Hence the rhetorical question: 'Would we nuke an adversary for giving us the flu?' in Larsen and Kadlec, 'Biological Warfare: A Silent Threat', p. 8;

A.J. Venter, 'Poisoned Chalice Poses Problems: The Terrorist Threat to the World's Water', *Jane's IDR*, vol. 32, no. 1 (1999), pp. 57–61.

34   Gen. C.G. Krulak, Hearings on *Department of Defense Authorization for Appropriations for Fiscal Year 1998 and the Future Years Defense Program* before the Committee on Armed Services United States Senate, 105th Congress, first session (26 February 1997), p. 358.

35   United States of America, 'Technological Developments of Relevance to the Biological and Toxin Weapons Convention', paper submitted to the Second Review Conference of the Biological and Toxin Weapons Convention (1986), pp. 1 and 6; see also J. Finder, 'Biological Warfare, Genetic Engineering, and the Treaty That Failed', *The Washington Quarterly*, vol. 9, no. 2 (1986), pp. 5–14.

36   Venter, 'Poisoned Chalice Poses Problems', p. 59.

37   USA, 'Technological Developments of Relevance to the Biological and Toxin Weapons Convention', p. 2; OTA, *Technologies Underlying Weapons of Mass Destruction*, p. 116; Canada, *Novel Toxins and Bioregulators: The Emerging Scientific and Technological Issues Relating to Verification and the Biological and Toxin Weapons Convention* (Ottawa, September 1991), p. 47.

38   Canada, *Novel Toxins and Bioregulators*, p. 46; USA, 'Technological Developments of Relevance to the Biological and Toxin Weapon Convention', p. 3.

39   OTA, *Technologies Underlying Weapons of Mass Destruction*, p. 115; Dando, *Biological Warfare*, p. 156.

40   B. Starr, 'Bio Agents Could Target Ethnic Groups, Says CIA', *J[ane's] D[efence] W[eekly]*, vol. 27 (25 June 1997), p. 6.

41   DoD, *Proliferation 1996*, p. A-4; B. Starr, 'US DoD Reveals Horrific Future of Biological Wars', *JDW*, vol. 28 (13 August 1997), p. 6.

42   'Interview', *JDW*, vol. 28 (13 August 1997), p. 32; on race-specific agents, see A. Conadera, 'Biological Weapons and Third World Targets', *Science for the People*, vol. 13, no. 4 (1981), pp. 16–20; M. Dando, '"Discriminating" bio-weapons could target ethnic groups', *Jane's IDR*, vol. 30, no. 3 (1997), pp. 77–8.

43   DoD, *Proliferation 1997*, pp. 82–3.

44   Preston, 'Annals of Warfare: The Bioweaponeers', p. 64; see also Weiner, 'Soviet Defector Warns of Biological Weapons', pp. A1 and A8; K. Alibek, 'Russia's Deadly Expertise', *The New York Times*, 27 March 1998, p. A19.

45   Preston, 'Annals of Warfare: The Bioweaponeers', p. 64; Alibek, 'Russia's Deadly Expertise', p. A19; J. Miller and W.J. Broad, 'Germ Weapons: In Soviet Past Or in the New Russia's Future?' *The New York Times*, 28 December 1998, pp. A1 and A11.

46   Tucker, 'The Biological Weapons Threat', p. 168; Buchanan, 'Poor Man's A-Bomb', p. 84; Pearson, 'Chemical and Biological Defence', p. 26.

47   V. Sidel, 'Weapons of Mass Destruction: The Greatest Threat to Public Health', *JAMA*, vol. 262, no. 5 (1989), pp. 680–2.

48   DoD, *Conduct of the Persian Gulf War*, p. Q-2; Schwarzkopf, Hearings on *Operation Desert Shield/Desert Storm*, pp. 334, 347 and *It Doesn't Take a Hero*, p. 439.

49   Wooten, 'Protecting the Force', p. 76.

50   Gen. J.M. Shalikashvili, Hearings on *Military Implications of the Chemical Weapons Convention*, p. 41.

51 Fetter, 'Ballistic Missiles and Weapons of Mass Destruction', pp. 18–19.

52 B. Roberts, 'Chemical Disarmament and International Security', *Adelphi Papers 267* (1992), p. 79; V. Utgoff, *The Challenge of Chemical Weapons* (London: Macmillan, 1990), pp. 240–1 and OTA, *Weapons of Mass Destruction*, p. 60.

53 Roberts, 'Chemical Disarmament and International Security', p. 79; Fetter, 'Ballistic Missiles and Weapons of Mass Destruction', p. 19.

54 A.H. Cordesman, *Weapons of Mass Destruction in the Middle East* (London: Brassey's, 1991), p. 92.

55 E.M. Spiers, *Chemical Weaponry: A Continuing Challenge* (London: Macmillan, 1989), pp. 156–7; OTA, *Weapons of Mass Destruction*, p. 9.

56 Pearson, 'Chemical and Biological Defence', p. 23.

57 OTA, *Weapons of Mass Destruction*, pp. 52, 59–60.

58 Shalikashvili, Hearings on *Chemical Weapons Convention*, p. 157.

59 JPRS Report, 'Proliferation Issues Russian Federation', in Hearing on *Proliferation Threats of the 1990's*, p. 85.

60 Dunn, ' "Gas Attack, This Is No Drill!" ', p. 65.

61 Lt-Gen. K. Burke, Dr R.L. Wagner and Maj-Gen. N.J. Fulwyler, Hearings on *Department of Defense Authorization for Appropriations for Fiscal Year 1983* before the Committee on Armed Services United States Senate, 97th Congress, second session (15 March 1982), pp. 4764, 4787, 4794, 4797; see also Gen. F.J. Kroesen et al., *Chemical Warfare Study: Summary Report*, IDA Paper P-1820 (Bethesda, MD: Institute for Defense Analyses, February 1985), p. 6.

62 Gaffney, Hearings on *Military Implications of the Chemical Weapons Convention*, p. 115.

63 Weaver and Glaes, *Inviting Disaster*, pp. 22–7.

64 *Ibid.*, pp. 39–45.

65 *Ibid.*, p. 50; J. Krause, 'Proliferation Risks and their Strategic Relevance: What Role for NATO?' *Survival*, vol. 37, no. 2 (1995), pp. 135–48.

5 NBC Terrorism

1 J. Annells and J. Adams, 'Did Terrorists Kill with Deadly Nerve Gas Test?' *The Sunday Times*, 19 March 1995, p. 15.

2 'News Chronology', *CBWCB*, no. 28 (June 1995), pp. 21–5, 32–3; G. Robinson, 'Nerve Gas Solvent Found as Police Swoop on Sect'; 'Panic grips Tokyo after Threat of More Gas Attacks'; and 'Japan cult leader has terminal illness', *The Times*, 23 March 1995, p. 10; 25 March 1995, p. 9; and 17 April 1995, p. 9. See also D.E. Kaplan and A. Marshall, *The Cult at the End of the World* (London: Hutchinson, 1996).

3 R. Guest, 'Cult Germ War Claim as Police Find Bacteria', *The Daily Telegraph*, 29 March 1995, p. 13; K.B. Olson, Hearings on *Global Proliferation*, Part 1, p. 106. For a detailed analysis of the BW attacks, see W.J. Broad, 'How Japan Germ Terror Alerted World', *The New York Times*, 26 May 1998, pp. A1, A10.

4 Sen. R. Lugar, Hearings on *Global Proliferation*, Part 2, pp. 69–70; J.B. Tucker, 'Chemical/Biological Terrorism: Coping with a New Threat', *Politics and the Life Sciences*, vol. 15, no. 2 (1996), pp. 167–83.

5 J.B. Tucker, 'Policy Approaches to Chemical and Biological Terrorism' in B. Roberts (ed.), *Terrorism with C[hemical and] B[iological] Weapons* (Alexandria, VA; Chemical and Biological Arms Control Institute, 1997), p. 95.

6 Webster, Hearings on *Chemical and Biological Weapons Threat: The Urgent Need for Remedies* before the Committee on Foreign Relations United States Senate, 101st Congress, first session (1 March 1989), p. 42; M. Meselson, Hearing on the *Biological Weapons Act of 1989; Inter-American Convention on International Commercial Arbitration* before the Subcommittee on Immigration, Refugees, and International Law of the Committee on the Judiciary, House of Representatives, 101st Congress, second session (1 May 1990), p. 51; J. Anderson, 'Chemical Arms In Terrorism Feared by CIA', *The Washington Post*, 27 August 1984, p. C14.

7 Webster, Hearings on *Global Spread*, pp. 11, 14–15; J.E. Stern, 'Will Terrorists Turn to Poison?' *Orbis*, vol. 37, no. 3 (1993), pp. 393–410.

8 J.D. Douglass and N.C. Livingstone, *America the Vulnerable: The Threat of Chemical/Biological Warfare* (Lexington, MA: Heath, 1987).

9 B. Starr, 'NBC Terrorists a "Most Nightmarish Concern"', *JDW*, vol. 22 (10 December 1994), p. 10.

10 US Dept of State, *Patterns of Global Terrorism 1996* (Washington, DC: 1997), pp. 1, 3–4, 12, 15, 17 and appendix D.

11 B. Hoffman, 'Low-intensity Conflict: Terrorism and Guerilla Warfare in the Coming Decades' in L. Howard (ed.), *Terrorism: Roots. Impact. Responses* (New York: Praeger, 1992), pp. 139–54.

12 Deutch, Hearing on *Current and Projected National Security Threats*, p. 10.

13 H.J. McGeorge, 'Chemical and Biological Terrorism: Analyzing The Problem', *The ASA Newsletter*, no. 42 (16 June 1994), pp. 1, 12–13; Stern, 'Will Terrorists Turn to Poison?', pp. 395–6; R. Purver, *Chemical and Biological Terrorism: The Threat According to the Open Literature* (Ottawa: Canadian Security Intelligence Service, June 1995), pp. 31–40, 80–90.

14 B. Hoffman, 'Responding to Terrorism Across the Technological Spectrum', *Terrorism and Political Violence*, vol. 6 (1993), pp. 366–90; J.E. Stern, 'Weapons of Mass Impact: A Growing and Worrisome Danger', *Politics and the Life Sciences*, vol. 15, no. 2 (1996), pp. 222–5; 'The Preachers of Apocalypse', *Newsweek*, 3 April 1995, pp. 14–15.

15 J.B. Tucker, 'Chemical/Biological Terrorism: Coping with a New Threat', pp. 169–70; *Countering the Chemical and Biological Weapons Threat in the Post-Soviet World*, report of the special inquiry into the chemical and biological threat of the Committee on Armed Services House of Representatives, 102nd Congress, second session (23 February 1993), p. 26.

16 G.C. Oehler, Hearings on *DoD Authorization for Appropriations for Fiscal Year 1997* (27 March 1996), p. 212.

17 K. Kellen, 'The Potential for Nuclear Terrorism: A Discussion' and appendix in P. Leventhal and Y. Alexander (eds), *Preventing Nuclear Terrorism: The Report of the International Task Force on Prevention of Nuclear Terrorism* (Lexington, MA: Lexington Books, 1987), pp. 104–45; A. Loehmer, 'The Nuclear Dimension' in P. Wilkinson (ed.), *Technology and Terrorism* (London: Frank Cass, 1993), pp. 48–69.

18 G. Allison, Hearings on *Global Proliferation*, Part 2, p. 22.

19 Oehler, Hearings on *DoD Authorization for Appropriations for 1997*, p. 212; Leventhal and Alexander, *Preventing Nuclear Terrorism*, p. 9; B.M. Jenkins, 'Will Terrorists Go Nuclear?' *Orbis*, vol. 29, no. 3 (1985), pp. 507–15.
20 Compare S.A. Mullen with Deutch, Hearings on *Global Proliferation*, Part 2, pp. 31–4, 311–12.
21 Deutch, Hearings on *Global Proliferation*, Part 2, p. 312.
22 *Ibid.*, p. 309.
23 Jenkins, 'Will Terrorists Go Nuclear?' pp. 514–15.
24 Deutch, Hearings on *Global Proliferation*, Part 2, p. 75; see also O.B. Revell, Hearings on *High-Tech Terrorism* before the Subcommittee on Technology and the Law of the Committee on the Judiciary United States Senate, 100th Congress, second session (19 May 1988), p. 21.
25 Kaplan and Marshall, *The Cult*, pp. 270, 273, 290, 322, 324; Sopko, Hearings on *Global Proliferation*, Part 1, pp. 21–2.
26 Kaplan and Marshall, *The Cult*, pp. 155, 184–5.
27 Written answer, Hearings on *Current and Projected National Security Threats* (5 February 1997), p. 129.
28 A.E. Smithson, Hearings on *Global Proliferation*, Part 1, pp. 156–66; Stern, 'Will Terrorists Turn to Poison?' pp. 394–5, 400–1.
29 L. Paul Bremer III, R.H. Kupperman and Revell, Hearings on *High-Tech Terrorism*, pp. 40, 54, 132.
30 B. Starr, 'Nightmare in the Making', *JDW*, vol. 23 (23 June 1995), p. 23.
31 Kaplan and Marshall, *The Cult*, pp. 232, 265; Oehler, Hearings on *DoD Authorization for Appropriations for 1997*, p. 213; E. Hurwitz, 'Terrorists and Chemical/Biological Weapons', *Naval War College Review*, vol. 35, no. 3 (1982), pp. 36–40.
32 Kaplan and Marshall, *The Cult*, pp. 163–4, 190, 241, 270; Sopko and Olson, Hearings on *Global Proliferation*, Part 1, pp. 21, 24, 60, 105–6.
33 Col H. Stringer, *Deterring Chemical Warfare: US Policy Options for the 1990s* (Cambridge, MA: Institute for Foreign Policy Analysis, 1986), p. 39.
34 Kaplan and Marshall, *The Cult*, pp. 337–9.
35 Stern, 'Will Terrorists Turn to Poison?', pp. 395–6.
36 'Transcript of President's Address to a Joint Session of the House and Senate', p. A18; 'News Chronology', *CBWCB*, no. 28 (June 1995), p. 34.
37 Kupperman, Hearings on *High-Tech Terrorism*, p. 54; Lt Col E.M. Eitzen, Hearings on *Global Proliferation*, Part 1, p. 117; Nelan, 'The Price of Fanaticism', *Time*, 3 April 1995, pp. 40–1; *Countering the Chemical and Biological Weapons Threat*, p. 26; OTA, *Technology against Terrorism: Structuring Security* (Washington, DC: OTA, January 1992), p. 37.
38 Kaplan and Marshall, *The Cult*, pp. 68–9, 189, 291–2; Sopko and Leitenberg, Hearings on *Global Proliferation*, Part 1, pp. 63 and 338; Broad, 'How Japan Germ Terror Alerted World', p. A10.
39 M. Leitenberg, Hearings on *Global Proliferation*, Part 1, pp. 338–9; see also R. Zilinskas, 'Aum Shinrikyo's Chemical/Biological Terrorism as a Paradigm?' *Politics and the Life Sciences*, vol. 15, no. 2 (1996), pp. 237–9.
40 K. Lowe, 'Analyzing Technical Constraints on Bio-Terrorism: Are They Still Important?' in Roberts, *Terrorism with CB Weapons*, pp. 53–64.

41 OTA, *Technology against Terrorism*, p. 37; J.D. Simon, 'Biological Terrorism Preparing to Meet the Threat', *JAMA*, vol. 278, no. 5 (1997), pp. 428–30.

42 W. Patrick III, 'Biological Terrorism and Aerosol Dissemination', *Politics and the Life Sciences*, vol. 15, no. 2 (1996), pp. 208–10; see also Broad, 'How Japan Germ Terror Alerted World', p. A10.

43 Eitzen, Hearings on *Global Proliferation*, Part 1, pp. 118–19; see also M. Meselson, Hearings on *Biological Weapons Act of 1989*, p. 51 and R.H. Kupperman and D.M. Smith, 'Coping with Biological Terrorism' in Roberts, *Biological Weapons*, pp. 35–46.

44 G.S. Pearson, 'Chemical/Biological Terrorism: How Serious a Risk?' *Politics and the Life Sciences*, vol. 15, no. 2 (1996), pp. 210–12.

45 Broad, 'How Japan Germ Terror Alerted World', p. A10.

46 Olson, Eitzen and J. Sopko, Hearings on *Global Proliferation*, Parts 1 and 3, pp. 105, 119 and 7; OTA, *Technology against Terrorism*, p. 40; Simon, 'Biological Terrorism', p. 429; Zilinskas, 'Aum Shinrikyo's Chemical/Biological Terrorism as a Paradigm?' p. 239; T. Atlas, 'U.S. officials fear terrorists soon may move beyond bombs', *Chicago Tribune*, 11 July 1996, p. 6; J. Heinz Jackson, 'When Terrorists Turn to Chemical Weapons', *JIR*, vol. 4, no. 11 (1992), p. 520.

47 J.F. Pilat, 'Prospects for NBC Terrorism After Tokyo' in Roberts, *Terrorism with CB Weapons*, p. 10; Pearson, 'Chemical/Biological Terrorism: How Serious a Risk?' p. 210.

48 Jenkins, 'Will Terrorists Go Nuclear?' p. 514; R. Clutterbuck, 'Trends in Terrorist Weaponry' in Wilkinson, *Technology and Terrorism*, pp. 130–9; Bremer, Hearings on *High-Tech Terrorism*, p. 34.

49 Wilkinson, *Technology and Terrorism*, p. 4.

50 Jenkins, 'Will Terrorists Go Nuclear?', p. 511; see also A. Fainberg, 'Debating Policy Priorities and Implications' in Roberts, *Terrorism with CB Weapons*, p. 78; Tucker, 'Chemical/Biological Terrorism: Coping with a New Threat', pp. 168–9; Leitenberg, Hearings on *Global Proliferation*, Part 1, p. 339; Kaplan and Marshall, *The Cult*, p. 295.

51 E. Sprinzak, 'Terrorism, Real and Imagined', *The Washington Post*, 19 August 1998, p. A21; OTA, *Technology Against Terrorism*, p. 39.

52 Olson, Hearings on *Global Proliferation*, Part 1, pp. 104–9; Stern, 'Weapons of Mass Impact: A Growing and Worrisome Danger', *Politics and the Life Sciences*, vol. 15, no. 2 (1996), pp. 222–5; Leventhal and Alexander, *Preventing Nuclear Terrorism*, p. 8.

53 Sopko, Staff statement in Hearings on *Global Proliferation*, Part 1, p. 47; see also Kaplan and Marshall, *The Cult*, pp. 362–3.

54 J.B. Tucker, 'Policy Approaches to Chemical and Biological Terrorism' in Roberts, *Terrorism with CB Weapons*, p. 102; see also Leitenberg, Hearings on *Global Proliferation*, Part 1, p. 173; J. Gee, 'CBW Terrorism and the Chemical Weapons Convention', *Politics and the Life Sciences*, vol. 15, no. 2 (1996), pp. 203–4; G.S. Pearson, 'Forbidden, not forgotten', *Jane's IDR*, vol. 30, no. 3 (1997), pp. 27–9.

55 G.C. Oehler, Hearings on *Global Proliferation*, Part 1, pp. 283–4.

56 G.J. Tenet, Hearings on *Current and Projected National Security Threats* (5 February 1997), p. 51.

57 Maj-Gen. W.F. Burns, Hearings on *Global Spread*, p. 107.

58 S. Moglewer, 'International Safeguards and Nuclear Terrorism' in Leventhal and Alexander, *Preventing Nuclear Terrorism*, pp. 248–58; Loehmer, 'The Nuclear Dimension', pp. 61–2.

59 R.K. Betts, 'The New Threat of Mass Destruction', *Foreign Affairs*, vol. 77, no. 1 (1998), pp. 26–41; see also R. Latter, 'Nuclear Weapons in the Twenty-First Century', *Wilton Park Papers 128* (April 1998), pp. 28–9.

60 Memorandum by Ambassador Rolf Ekéus, 'Iraq's Biological Weapons Programme', p. 3; see also R.P. Kadlec, 'Biological Weapons Control Prospects and Implications for the Future', *JAMA*, vol. 278, no. 5 (1997), pp. 351–6; A.P. Zelicoff, 'Preparing for Biological Terrorism: First Do No Harm', *Politics and the Life Sciences*, vol. 15, no. 2 (1996), pp. 235–6.

61 Sopko, Olson, Oehler and Sen Cohen, Hearings on *Global Proliferation*, Part 1, pp. 82, 106–7, 111, 273–4, 276, 279; R. Jeffrey Smith and C. Suplee, 'Nations [SIC]Unready to Thwart Mass Poisoning, Experts Say', *The Washington Post*, 21 March 1995, p. A12; L.K. Altman, 'Plans Drawn To Help Fight Poison Attack', *The New York Times*, 26 March 1995, p. 9; Broad, 'How Japan Germ Terror Alerted World', p. A10.

62 Roberts, *Terrorism with CB Weapons*; Tucker, 'Chemical/Biological Terrorism: Coping with a New Threat' and commentaries in *Politics and the Life Sciences*, vol. 15, no. 2 (1996); B. Roberts and M. Moodie, *Combating NBC Terrorism: An Agenda for Enhancing International Cooperation* (Livermore, CA: Center for Global Security Research, n.d.).

63 E.M. Spiers, *Chemical Warfare* (London: Macmillan, 1985), p. 71.

64 W. Webster, Hearings on *Threats to U.S. National Security* before the Committee on National Security House of Representatives, 105th Congress, first session (13 February 1997), p. 23.

65 Roberts and Moodie, *Combating NBC Terrorism*, pp. 28–30; 'A Case of Mistaken Identity?' *The Economist*, 29 August 1998, pp. 53–4.

66 GAO, *Combating Terrorism: Federal Agencies' Efforts to Implement National Policy and Strategy*, hereafter *Combating Terrorism* (Washington, DC: GAO/NSIAD-97-254, September 1997), pp. 3, 46–7; C[ounter] P[roliferation] R[eview] C[ommittee], *Report on Activities and Programs for Countering Proliferation and NBC Terrorism*, hereafter referred to as the *Counter-proliferation Report* (May 1998), p. 8-4.

67 R.A. Falkenrath, 'Confronting Nuclear, Biological and Chemical Terrorism', *Survival*, vol. 40, no. 3 (1998), pp. 43–65.

68 W.J. Broad and J. Miller, 'Germ Defense Plan in Peril As Its Flaws Are Revealed', *The New York Times*, 7 August 1998, pp. A1 and A16.

69 GAO, *Combating Terrorism*, pp. 21, 30–2, 70–2.

70 R. Halloran, 'Changing Tide of Terror Puts U.S. at Risk', *The Washington Times*, 14 September 1998, p. A13.

71 GAO, *Combating Terrorism*, and *Combating Terrorism: Status of DoD Efforts to Protect Its Forces Overseas* (Washington, DC: GAO/NSIAD-97-207, 21 July 1997), hereafter referred to as *Combating Terrorism 1997*.

72 Judith Miller, 'Nation Lacks Plan to Deter Terrorism, Study Says', *The New York Times*, 6 September 1998, p. 30; E. Sprinzak, 'The Great Superterrorism Scare', *Foreign Policy*, no. 112 (1998), pp. 110–23; G. Seigle, 'A Chemical Weapons Dress Rehearsal', *The Washington Post*, 11 October 1998, p. C8; GAO, *Combating Terrorism: Opportunities to Improve Domestic Preparedness*

Program Focus and Efficiency (Washington, DC: GAO/NSIAD-99-3, November 1998) hereafter referred to as *Combating Terrorism 1998*, p. 39.

73 B. Graham, 'AntiTerrorism Plans Termed Inadequate: FBI Chosen to Lead Coordinated Effort' and V. Loeb, 'U.S. Targeting Terrorism With More Funds: Embassy Bombings Prompt Agencies to Spend More on Prevention, Preparedness', *The Washington Post*, 3 October 1998, p. A9 and 2 February 1999, p. A4; J. Miller and W.J. Broad, 'Clinton Describes Terrorism Threat for 21st Century', *The New York Times*, 22 January 1999, pp. A1 and A12.

74 GAO, *Combating Terrorism*, pp. 4–5, 27–30; CPRC, *Counterproliferation Report*, p. 8-5.

75 GAO, *Combating Terrorism*, pp. 33–4, 38.

76 Kupperman and Smith, 'Coping with Biological Terrorism', pp. 44–6; E.M. Spiers, 'Chemical and Biological Terrorism', *Brassey's Defence Yearbook 1996* (London: Brassey's, 1996), pp. 254–72; M.E. Gates, 'The Nuclear Emergency Search Team' in Leventhal and Alexander, *Preventing Nuclear Terrorism*, pp. 397–402.

77 US Department of Health and Human Services, 'Department of Health and Human Services Health and Medical Services Support Plan for the Federal Response to Acts of Chemical/Biological (C/B) Terrorism' (Washington, DC: 21 June 1996).

78 GAO, *Combating Terrorism 1997*, pp. 45–6, 48.

79 *Ibid.*, pp. 56–8, 60–9; CPRC, *Counterproliferation Report*, pp. 8-2, 8-5–8-8; F.J. Cilluffo and T.I. Herlihy, 'First Responders to a Sneak Attack', *The Washington Post*, 26 June 1998, p. A28; S.C. Fehr, 'Major Disaster Drill Planned for D.C. Area', *The Washington Post*, 2 July 1998, p. A12.

80 GAO, *Combating Terrorism 1998*, pp. 2–3, 7, 17, 19–22.

81 B. Graham, 'Clinton to Order Reserves of Germ War Antidotes', *The Washington Post*, 21 May 1998, pp. A1 and A19; Broad and Miller, 'Germ Defense Plan in Peril as its Flaws Are Revealed', p. A12.

82 B. Graham, 'U.S. Gearing up against Germ War Threat', *The Washington Post*, 14 December 1997, pp. A1 and A16; P. Richter, 'U.S. Germ War Defenses Porous, Officials Warn', *Los Angeles Times*, 26 December 1997, pp. A1 and A20; T. Masland, 'America Goes on Guard', *Newsweek*, 31 August 1998, p. 31; D. MacKenzie, 'Bioarmaggedon', *New Scientist*, vol. 159 (19 September 1998), pp. 42–6; on UK provisions, see MoD, *Defending Against the Threat from Biological and Chemical Weapons* (London, 1999), pp. 17–18.

6 Multilateral Control Regimes: Their Role and Impact

1 Shuey, Bowman, and Davis, 'Proliferation Control Regimes', p. 1.

2 Kay, Hearings on *Global Proliferation*, Part 2, p. 107.

3 Ekéus and Kay, Hearings on *Global Proliferation*, Part 2, pp. 93–4, 108; K.C. Bailey and G. Milhollin, Hearings on *H.R. 4803*, pp. 53 and 57–8; W. Schneider, Jr, *Compilation of Hearings*, p. 379.

4 G. Perkovich, 'Nuclear Proliferation', *Foreign Policy*, no. 112 (1998), pp. 12–23.

5 J. Simpson, 'The Nuclear Non-proliferation Regime after the NPT Review and Extension Conference' in SIPRI, *SIPRI Yearbook 1996: Armaments,*

Disarmament and International Security (Oxford: OUP, 1996), pp. 561–89; *SIPRI Yearbook 1998: Armaments and Disarmament and International Security* (Oxford: OUP, 1998), p. 584; L.A. Dunn, 'The Nuclear Non-Proliferation Treaty: Issues of Compliance and Implementation', *P[rogramme for] P[romoting] N[uclear] N[on-Proliferation]*, issue review, no. 9 (February 1997), pp. 1–8.

6   J. Gee, 'Implementing the CWC: The First Year', *The Arena*, no. 8 (July 1998), pp. 1–7.

7   Huang Yu, 'The CWC: Verification in Action', *CBWCB*, no. 41 (September 1998), pp. 1–3.

8   Pearson, 'Prospects for Chemical and Biological Arms Control', p. 157; Ambassador T. Tóth, 'A Window of Opportunity for the BWC Ad Hoc Group', *CBWCB*, no. 37 (September 1997), pp. 1–5.

9   Shuey, Bowman, and Davis, 'Proliferation Control Regimes', pp. CRS-5–6, 22–3, 31–2; I. Anthony and T. Stock, 'Multilateral Military-Related Export Control Measures', in *SIPRI Yearbook 1996*, pp. 537–51; J.E. Nolan, 'Preventive Approaches: The MTCR Regime' in W.H. Lewis and S.E. Johnson (eds), *Weapons of Mass Destruction: New Perspectives in Counterproliferation* (Washington, DC: National Defense University Press, 1995), pp. 193–206.

10   K. Sullivan, 'N. Korea Admits Selling Missiles', *The Washington Post*, 17 June 1998, pp. A1 and A21; 'Need a Biological War? Labs Sell Anthrax Germs by Mail Order', *The Sunday Times*, 22 November 1998, pp. 1 and 8.

11   D. Fischer, 'The London Club and the Zangger Committee: How Effective?', in Bailey and Rudney, *Proliferation and Export Controls*, pp. 39–48.

12   Slocombe, *Compilation of Hearings*, p. 7; see also A. Sands, 'The Impact of New Technologies on Nuclear Weapons Proliferation' in Reiss and Litwak, *Nuclear Proliferation after the Cold War*, pp. 259–74.

13   J.R. Redick, J.C. Carasales and P.S. Wrobel, 'Nuclear Rapprochement: Argentina, Brazil, and the Nonproliferation Regime', *The Washington Quarterly*, vol. 18, no. 1 (1994), pp. 107–22.

14   B. Chellaney, 'An Indian Critique of U.S. Export Controls', *Orbis*, vol. 38, no. 3 (1994), pp. 439–56; K. Subrahmanyam, 'Export Controls and the North–South Controversy', *The Washington Quarterly*, vol. 16, no. 2 (1993), pp. 135–44; Shuey, Bowman, Davis, 'Proliferation Control Regimes', pp. CRS-6, 27, 33.

15   W. Rope, Hearings on *H.R. 4803*, p. 29; W.A. Reinsch, *Compilation of Hearings*, p. 342.

16   Compare I. Kristol, 'Forget Arms Control', *The New York Times*, 12 September 1989, p. A25 with B. Roberts, 'Arms Control and the End of the Cold War', *The Washington Quarterly*, vol. 15, no. 4 (1992), pp. 39–56.

17   Redick et al., 'Nuclear Rapprochement', p. 115; Gee, 'Implementing the CWC', p. 2.

18   E. Harris, Hearing on *Proliferation and Arms Control in the 1990's* before the Subcommittee on Arms Control, International Security and Science of the Committee on Foreign Affairs House of Representatives, 102nd Congress, second session (3 March 1992), pp. 49–52; 'News Chronology', *CBWCB*, no. 41 (September 1998), p. 21.

19   R. Johnson, 'The In-Comprehensive Test Ban', *The Bulletin of the Atomic Scientists*, vol. 52, no. 6 (1996), pp. 30–5; L. Weiss, 'The Nuclear Nonproliferation Treaty: Strengths and Gaps' in H. Sokolski (ed.), *Fighting*

Proliferation: New Concerns for the Nineties (Maxwell Air Force Base, AL: Air University Press, 1996), pp. 31–55.

20 J.E. Nolan, Hearings on *Proliferation and Arms Control in the 1990's*, p. 28; Kay, 'Preventive Approaches', p. 183; J. Simpson and E. Bailey, 'The 1998 PrepCom for the 2000 NPT Review Conference: Issues and Options', *PPNN Issue Review*, no. 14 (April 1998), pp. 1–8.

21 Kay, Hearings on *Global Proliferation*, Part 2, p. 107; IISS, *Strategic Survey 1997/98*, pp. 68–9; *PPNN Newsbrief*, no. 43 (3rd quarter 1998), p. 7.

22 D.A. Kay, 'Preventive Approaches: Expectations and Limitations for Inspections' in Lewis and Johnson, *Weapons of Mass Destruction*, pp. 181–92; Simpson and Bailey, 'The 1998 PrepCom for the 2000 NPT Review Conference', p. 8.

23 Shuey, Bowman, and Davis, 'Proliferation Control Regimes', p. CRS-4.

24 D. Feakes, 'Developments in the Organization for the Prohibition of Chemical Weapons', *CBWCB*, no. 40 (June 1998), pp. 5–13 and no. 41 (September 1998), pp. 6–15.

25 Dunn, 'The Nuclear Non-Proliferation Treaty', p. 3; J.C. Davis and D.A. Kay, 'Iraq's Secret Nuclear Weapons Program', *Physics Today*, vol. 45, no. 7 (1992), pp. 21–7; A. Sands, 'The Impact of New Technologies on Nuclear Weapons Proliferation', pp. 259–74.

26 DIA, *Soviet Biological Warfare Threat*, DST-1610F-057-86 (Washington, DC: 1986), pp. 2–3.

27 USA, 'Technological Developments of Relevance to the Biological and Toxin Weapons Convention', pp. 3–4.

28 D. Huxsoll, C.D. Parrott, and W.C. Patrick III, 'Medicine in Defense Against Biological Warfare', *JAMA*, vol. 262, no. 5 (1989), pp. 677–9.

29 'Soviets Violate Ban on Biological Warfare', *The Army Chemical Journal*, vol. 3, no. 1 (1987), pp. 42–3.

30 Webster, Hearings on *Global Spread*, p. 13; L. Hansen quoted in L. Ember, 'CMA's Olson Unravels Intricacies of Verifying a Chemical Arms Treaty', *C&EN*, vol. 67, no. 17 (1989), pp. 7–12; A. Rathmell, 'Chemical Weapons in the Middle East: Lessons from Iraq', *JIR*, vol. 7, no. 12 (1995), pp. 556–60.

31 Ember, 'CMA's Olson Unravels Intricacies', pp. 7, 10; U[nited] K[ingdom], 'Verification of the Chemical Weapons Convention: Practice Challenge Inspections at Civil Chemical Plants', CD/CW/WP.341 (5 June 1991), p. 4; G.M. Burck and C.C. Floweree, *International Handbook*, pp. 583–611.

32 UK, 'Verification of the Chemical Weapons Convention', pp. 4–6; R.G. Sutherland, 'Thiodyglycol' in S.J. Lundin (ed.), *Verification of Dual-use Chemicals under the Chemical Weapons Convention: The Case of Thiodiglycol*, SIPRI Chemical & Biological Warfare Studies, no. 13 (Oxford: OUP, 1991), pp. 24–43.

33 Richardson, 'The Threat of Chemical and Biological Proliferation', in Bailey and Rudney, *Proliferation and Export Controls*, p. 16.

34 Ember, 'CMA's Olson Unravels Intricacies', p. 7.

35 JPRS Report, 'Proliferation Issue: Russian Federation' in Hearing on *Proliferation Threats of the 1990's*, p. 85.

36 E. Harris and W. Seth Carus, Hearings on *Global Spread*, pp. 65–6.

37 Z. Davis, Hearing on *National Security Implications of Lowered Export Controls on Dual-Use Technologies and U.S. Defense Capabilities* before the Committee

on Armed Services, United States Senate, 104th Congress, first session, 11 May 1995, pp. 17–18; R. Einhorn and R.H. Speier, *Compilation of Hearings*, pp. 289, 314, 316–18; *The Proliferation Primer*, A Majority Report of the Subcommittee on International Security, Proliferation, and Federal Services, Committee on Governmental Affairs United States Senate (January 1998), pp. 17–29.

38   Shuey, Bowman, and Davis, 'Proliferation Control Regimes', p. CRS-26.

39   Deutch, Hearing on *Current and Projected National Security Threats* (22 February 1996), p. 41; see also K. Bailey, 'Nonproliferation Export Controls: Problems and Alternatives' in Bailey and Rudney, *Proliferation and Export Controls*, pp. 49–55; K.B. Payne, 'Post-Cold War Deterrence and Missile Defense', *Orbis*, vol. 39, no. 2 (1995), pp. 201–23.

40   M.S. Meselson, Hearings on *Chemical and Biological Weapons Threat*, p. 199; K. Bailey, Hearing on *H.R. 4803*, pp. 53, 58.

41   M.B. Wallerstein, Hearing on *National Security Implications of Lowered Export Controls*, pp. 42–3.

42   Bailey, 'Nonproliferation Export Controls: Problems and Alternatives' in Bailey and Rudney, *Proliferation and Export Controls*, pp. 52–3.

43   M. Moodie and B. Roberts, 'Rethinking Export Controls on Dual-Use Materials and Technologies: From Trade Restrictions to Trade Enabling' in Hearings on *Global Proliferation*, Part 1, pp. 194, 196–200; Reinsch, *Compilation of Hearings*, p. 342.

44   G. Milhollin, Hearings on *Iran and Proliferation: Is the U.S. Doing Enough? The Arming of Iran: Who Is Responsible?* before the subcommittee on Near Eastern and South Asian Affairs of the Committee on Foreign Relations United States Senate, 105th Congress, first session (6 May 1997), pp. 49–50, 62.

45   Einhorn and Milhollin, Hearings on *Iran and Proliferation*, pp. 15–16, 26, 45–6, 48–50, 59.

46   Kay, Hearings on *Global Proliferation*, Part 2, pp. 108–09.

47   K.C. Bailey, *The UNSCOM Inspections in Iraq Lessons for On-Site Inspection* (Boulder, CO: Westview Press, 1995), pp. 15–30.

48   'Memorandum of Ambassador Rolf Ekéus', pp. 8–11.

49   Kay, 'Preventive Approaches', pp. 188–89; Bailey, *The UN Inspections*, pp. 30–5.

50   R. Wright, 'U.N. Inspections in Iraq Deemed Badly Crippled', *Los Angeles Times*, 23 February 1998, pp. A1 and A9; SIPRI Fact sheet, *Iraq: The UNSCOM Experience*.

51   Letter dated 25 February 1998 from the Secretary-General, S/1998/166; SIPRI Fact sheet, *Iraq: The UNSCOM Experience*; IISS, *Strategic Survey 1997/98*, p. 64.

52   J. Miller, 'American Inspector on Iraq Quits, Accusing U.N. and U.S. of Cave-In', *The New York Times*, 27 August 1998, pp. A1 and A6; see also B. Gellman, 'U.S. Sought to Prevent Iraqi Arms Inspections', *The Washington Post*, 14 August 1998, pp. A1 and A29; C. Evans, 'Arms Team Forced to Let Saddam off Hook', *The Sunday Times*, 25 October 1998, p. 24.

53   Note by the Secretary-General, S/1998/920 (6 October 1998), paras. 39–40, 75.

54   Letter dated 15 December 1998 from the Secretary-General addressed to the President of the Security Council, S/1998/1172; T. Weiner, 'U.S. Spied on Iraq under U.N. Cover, Officials Now Say' and 'U.S. Used U.N. Team to

Place Spy Device in Iraq, Aides Say', *The New York Times*, 7 and 8 January 1999, pp. A1 and A6, A1 and A8; M. Hirsh, G.L. Vistica and G. Beals, 'The Strains Are Showing', *Newsweek*, 18 January 1999, pp. 42–3; BBC Panorama, 'The Weapons Inspectors', 22 March 1999.

55 W. Seth Carus, Hearings on *Iran and Proliferation*, pp. 71–2.

56 *Congressional Record-Senate*, 24 April 1997, p. S3574; A.E. Smithson, 'Playing Politics with the Chemical Weapons Convention', *Current History*, vol. 96, no. 609 (1997), pp. 162–6.

57 A. Hoeber and Woolsey, Hearings on the *Chemical Weapons Convention*, pp. 93 and 163; Roberts, 'Between Panic and Complacency' in Johnson, *The Niche Threat*, p. 37.

58 W.B. Slocombe and M. Moodie, Hearings on the *Chemical Weapons Convention*, pp. 53 and 103; Maj-Gen. J.R. Landry and J.M. Deutch, Hearings on *Military Implications of the Chemical Weapons Convention*, pp. 22–3, 35.

59 Deutch, Hearings on the *Military Implications of the Chemical Weapons Convention*, p. 31; J.D. Holum and Woolsey, Hearings on the *Chemical Weapons Convention*, pp. 159 and 162; G.J. Tenet, Hearing on *Current and Projected National Security Threats* (5 February 1997), pp. 38, 40.

60 Moodie, Hearings on the *Chemical Weapons Convention*, p. 104; Gaffney, Hearings on the *Military Implications of the Chemical Weapons Convention*, p. 136.

61 O. Thraenert, 'Biological Weapons and the Problems of Nonproliferation', *Aussen Politik*, vol. 48, no. 2 (1997), pp. 148–57; *SIPRI Yearbook 1998*, pp. 470–4.

62 Tenet, Hearing on *Current and Projected National Security Threats* (5 February 1997), p. 35; see also Bailey, 'Responding to the Threat of Biological Weapons', pp. 383–97.

63 Pearson, 'Prospects for Chemical and Biological Arms Control', pp. 157–61; R. Latter, 'Preventing the Proliferation of Biological Weapons', *Wilton Park Papers 109* (October 1995), p. 2.

64 Kadlec et al., 'Biological Weapons Control', pp. 354–6; Bailey, 'Responding to the Threat of Biological Weapons', pp. 387–9; M. Isabelle Chevrier, 'The Threat That Won't Disperse', *The Washington Post*, 21 December 1997, pp. C1–C2.

65 J. Hoagland, 'A Foreign Policy That Asks, "Can't We All Just Get Along?"', *The Washington Post*, 30 October 1997, p. A23.

66 Einhorn, *Compilation of Hearings*, pp. 219, 227, 234–5, 289–94.

67 Wallerstein, Hearing on *National Security Implications*, p. 3; Reinsch, *Compilation of Hearings*, p. 342.

68 Z. Davis, Hearing on *National Security Implications*, pp. 20–1, 53; Milhollin, Hearings on *Iran and Proliferation*, p. 63; Schneider, *Compilation of Hearings*, p. 375; B. Gertz, 'Chinese Delivery', *National Review* (1 June 1998), pp. 43–5.

69 Schneider, *Compilation of Hearings*, p. 376; see also P.W. Rodman, 'Chinese Puzzle', *National Review* (1 June 1998), pp. 45–6.

70 M. Kettle, 'The Enemy Within', *The Guardian*, 10 March 1999, pp. 2–3.

71 Davis, Hearing on *National Security Implications*, pp. 19, 53; Milhollin and Seth Carus, Hearings on *Iran and Proliferation*, pp. 46, 50, 55, 65; R. Jeffrey Smith, 'Iran's Missile technology Linked to China, Report Says', *The Washington Post*, 17 June 1995, p. A14; J. Mintz, 'Signs of Chinese Arms Sale

Dismissed, Ex-Official Says', *The Washington Post*, 12 June 1998, p. A20; Sen. T. Cochran and Schneider, *Compilation of Hearings*, pp. 334, 351, 380.

72 P. Baker and H. Dewar, 'Clinton-Lott Connection Emerges in Treaty Fight', *The Washington Post*, 26 April 1997, pp. A1 and A12; L. Ember, 'U.S. inaction could harm chemical arms accord', *C&EN*, vol. 76 (28 September 1998), p. 22.

73 Johnson, 'The In-Comprehensive Test Ban', p. 34; DIA written answer, Hearing on *Current and Projected National Security Threats* (5 February 1997), p. 87; Drell, 'Reasons to Ratify Not to Stall', p. A27.

74 Dunn, 'The Nuclear Non-Proliferation Treaty', p. 4.

75 D. MacKenzie, 'Questions First, Bombs Later', *New Scientist*, vol. 159 (19 September 1998), p. 51; S. Lee Myers and T. Weiner, 'Possible Benign Use Is Seen for Chemical at Factory in Sudan' and 'U.S. Notes Gaps in Data About Drug Plant but Defends Attack; Sudan Envoy Is Angry', *The New York Times*, 27 August 1998, pp. A1 and A8 and 3 September 1998, p. A6; 'Punish and Be Damned', *The Economist*, 29 August 1998, p. 16.

76 T. Weiner, 'Pentagon and C.I.A. Defend Sudan Missile Attack', *The New York Times*, 2 September 1998, p. A5.

77 T. Weiner and J. Risen, 'Decision to Strike Factory in Sudan Based on Surmise', *The New York Times*, 21 September 1998, pp. A1 and A8; 'News Chronology', *CBWCB*, no. 42 (December 1998), pp. 27, 30–1; 'Punish and Be Damned', *The Economist*, 29 August 1998, p. 16.

7 Counterproliferation

1 Gordon, 'Pentagon Begins Effort to Combat More Lethal Arms in Third World', p. A15.

2 M.B. Wallerstein, 'Concepts to Capabilities: The First Year of Counterproliferation' in Lewis and Johnson, *Weapons of Mass Destruction*, pp. 17–25.

3 Gen. J.M. Shalikashvili, Hearings on *DoD Authorization for Appropriations for Fiscal Year 1998*, p. 23 and W.S. Cohen, Hearings on the *Quadrennial Defense Review* before the Committee on Armed Services United States Senate, 105th Congress, first session (20 May 1997), p. 12; IISS, *Military Balance 1998/99* (London: OUP, 1998), p. 33.

4 MoD, *The Strategic Defence Review*, pp. 13–16.

5 Shalikashvili, Hearings on *DoD Authorization for Appropriations for Fiscal Year 1998*, p. 24.

6 Shalikashvili and Cohen, Hearings on *Quadrennial Defense Review*, pp. 20–1, 64, 83, 90; see also *Quadrennial Defense Review*, section VII, pp. 3–5.

7 Cohen, Hearings on *Quadrennial Defense Review*, pp. 63–4, 88; *Report of the Quadrennial Defense Review*, sections II, p. 2 and III, pp. 5–6.

8 The other bodies were the Senior Politico-Military Group on Proliferation and the Joint Committee on Proliferation, see A.B. Carter and D.B. Omand, 'Countering the Proliferation Risks: Adapting the Alliance to the New Security Environment', *NATO Review*, vol. 44, no. 5 (1996), pp. 10–15.

9 *Ibid.*; R. Joseph, 'Proliferation, Counter-Proliferation and NATO', *Survival*, vol. 38, no. 1 (1996), pp. 111–30; Schulte, 'Responding to Proliferation: NATO's Role', p. 18.

10　'The Alliance's New Strategic Concept', *NATO Review*, vol. 39, no. 6 (1991), pp. 25–32.

11　Slocombe, *Compilation of Hearings*, p. 7.

12　*Ibid.*, p. 8.

13　D. Omand, 'Nuclear Deterrence in a Changing World: The View from a UK Perspective', *RUSI Journal*, vol. 141, no. 3 (1996), pp. 15–22.

14　Bailey, 'Responding to the Threat of Biological Weapons', pp. 390–1; Roberts, 'Between Panic and Complacency', in Johnson, *The Niche Threat*, p. 35.

15　Deutch and Gen. Shalikashvili, Hearings on the *Military Implications of the Chemical Weapons Convention*, pp. 34, 39, 43.

16　Shalikashvili, Hearings on the *Chemical Weapons Convention*, p. 172; see also Holum, *ibid.*, p. 9.

17　For useful analyses of this literature, see IISS, *Strategic Survey 1997/98*, pp. 45–54 and R.G. Joseph and J.F. Reichart, 'The Case for Nuclear Deterrence Today', *Orbis*, vol. 42, no. 1 (1998), pp. 7–19.

18　P. Bedard and G. Constantine, 'U.S. Vows No Nuke Attacks against Non-nuclear Nations', *The Washington Times*, 6 April 1995, p. A3; Simpson, 'The Nuclear Non-proliferation Regime after the NPT Review and Extension Conference', pp. 584–5.

19　The Canberra Commission on the Elimination of Nuclear Weapons, 'The Nuclear Weapon Debate' (Canberra: Department of Foreign Affairs and Trade, Australia, 1996), Part 1, p. 4; The H.L. Stimson Center, *An Evolving US Nuclear Posture, Second Report of the Steering Committee Project on Eliminating Weapons of Mass Destruction* (Washington, DC, December 1995), pp. 7, 15–16; P.H. Nitze, 'A Conventional Approach', *Proceedings of U.S. Naval Institute*, vol. 120, no. 5 (1994), pp. 46–9; National Academy of Sciences, *The Future of U.S. Nuclear Weapons Policy* (Washington, DC: National Academy Press, 1997), pp. 74–5.

20　Nitze, 'A Conventional Approach', p. 48; Gen. A.J. Goodpaster, *Compilation of Hearings*, p. 32; Stimson Center, *An Evolving US Nuclear Posture*, pp. 14–15, 28.

21　Gaffney and Bailey, Hearings on the *Military Implications of the Chemical Weapons Convention*, pp. 114 and 124–5; D. Gompert, K. Watman, and D. Wilkening, 'Nuclear First Use Revisited', *Survival*, vol. 37, no. 3 (1995), pp. 27–44.

22　M. Moodie, *Chemical and Biological Weapons: Will Deterrence Work?* (Alexandria, VA: Chemical and Biological Arms Control Institute, 1998), p. 47.

23　*Ibid.*, p. 50; V.A. Utgoff, *Nuclear Weapons and the Deterrence of Biological and Chemical Warfare* (Washington, DC: Henry L. Stimson Center, Occasional Paper No. 36, 1997), pp. 7–8; W. Slocombe, 'Is There Still a Role for Nuclear Deterrence?', *NATO Review*, vol. 45, no. 6 (1997), pp. 23–6.

24　Moodie, *Chemical and Biological Weapons: Will Deterrence Work?*, pp. 18, 21; K. Payne, 'Deterring Weapons of Mass Destruction' in Johnson, *The Niche Threat*, pp. 73–4.

25　Kahan, 'Deterrence and Warfighting in an NBC Environment' in Johnson, *The Niche Threat*, pp. 48–9.

26　D. Oberdorfer, 'Missed Signals In the Middle East', *The Washington Post Magazine*, 17 March 1991, p. 39.

27 Payne, 'Deterring Weapons of Mass Destruction' in Johnson, *The Niche Threat*, pp. 84–5; see also Moodie, *Chemical and Biological Weapons: Will Deterrence Work?*, pp. 19–25, 44–6.

28 Gordon, 'Pentagon Begins Effort to Combat More Lethal Arms in Third World', p. A15; C. Williams, 'DOD's Counterproliferation Initiative: A Critical Assessment' in Sokolski, *Fighting Proliferation*, pp. 249–56; M. Klare, *Rogue States and Nuclear Outlaws [America's Search for a New Foreign Policy]* (New York: Hill and Wang, 1995), pp. 198–203.

29 Williams, 'DOD's Counterproliferation Initiative', p. 255; Kahan, 'Deterrence and Warfighting in an NBC Environment' in Johnson, *The Niche Threat*, p. 66; Lt. Cdr A. McColl, 'Is Counterproliferation Compatible with Non-proliferation?', *AIRPOWER Journal*, vol. 9, no. 1 (1997), pp. 99–109.

30 A. Carter, Hearings on *Department of Defense Authorization for Appropriations for Fiscal Year 1995 and the Future Years Defense Program* before the Committee on Armed Services, US Senate, 104th Congress, first session (28 April 1994), p. 199.

31 McColl, 'Is Counterproliferation Compatible?', p. 104; G. William Heiser and Dr W.B. Schuler, Hearings on *Department of Defense Authorization for Appropriations for Fiscal year 1996 and the Future Years Defense Program* before the Committee on Armed Services, US Senate, 104th Congress, second session (30 March 1995), pp. 162–8; CPRC, *Counterproliferation Report*, pp. 1-5–1-7.

32 DoD, *Proliferation 1997*, pp. 61–3.

33 CPRC, *Counterproliferation Report*, pp. 5-5–5-7.

34 L.D. Kozaryn, '98450. New Defense Threat Reduction Agency Takes the Lead', 21 July 1998 and J. Garamone, '98582. Threat Reduction Agency Stands Up', 2 October 1998, http://www.dtic.mil/afps/news/archive.html.

35 J.E. Nolan, 'Proliferation and International Security: An Overview' in Wander and Arnett, *The Proliferation of Advanced Weaponry*, pp. 5–11; Kahan, 'Deterrence and Warfighting' in Johnson, *The Niche Threat*, p. 52; Klare, *Rogue States and Nuclear Outlaws*, pp. 200–01; H. Müller, 'Options for Nonproliferation Security Policy' in Bailey and Rudney, *Proliferation and Export Controls*, pp. 69–78.

36 DoD, *Conduct of the Persian Gulf War*, p. 207; 'US Air Force to Test anti-CBW warheads', *Jane's IDR*, vol. 28, no. 6 (1995), p. 16; CPRC, *Counterproliferation Report*, p. 5-26.

37 DoD, *Proliferation 1997*, pp. 73–4; Gordon, 'Pentagon Begins Effort to Combat More Lethal Arms in Third World', p. A15; M. Evans, 'Weaponry deadlier than in Gulf War', *The Times*, 17 December 1998, p. 3; CPRC, *Counter-proliferation Report*, pp. 5-24–5-28; Gen. E.E. Habiger, Hearings on *DoD Authorization for Appropriations for Fiscal Year 1998* (13 March 1997), p. 726.

38 M. Hewish and J. Janssen Lok, 'Stopping the Scud Threat: Engaging Theater Ballistic Missiles on the Ground', *Jane's IDR*, vol. 30, no. 6 (1997), pp. 40–7.

39 CPRC, *Counterproliferation Report*, pp. 5-26–5-28.

40 M. Hastings, 'Bombing: It Looks Tough But What Does It Really Achieve?' *Evening Standard*, 18 December 1998, pp. 8–9.

41 'Russia and China Condemn Air Action against Saddam'; H. Gordon, 'Clinton Is Accused of "Crying Wolf"'; and 'Gulf General Joins Attack on Air Raids', *The Daily Telegraph*, 18 December 1998, pp. 2, 5; and 21 December 1998, p. 1.

42 J. Swain, 'Saddam Prospers in Rubble of Baghdad', *The Sunday Times*, 27 December 1998, p. 17; L.D. Kozaryn, 'Once Should Be Enough, Says Desert Fox Commander', 21 December 1998, http://www.defenselink.mil/news/Dec 1998/n1221 1998 9812214.html; S. Lee Myers, 'Jets Said to Avoid Poison Gas Sites', *The New York Times*, 18 December 1998, pp. A1 and A25; MoD, *Defending Against the Threat*, p. 7.

43 P. Stone, 'Desert Fox Target Climbs Past 75 Iraqi Sites', 18 December 1998, http://www.defenselink.mil/news/Dec1998/n1218 1998 9812182.html.

44 Swain, 'Saddam Prospers in Rubble of Baghdad', p. 17.

45 J.M. Collins, Z.S. Davis, and S.R. Bowman, 'Nuclear, Biological and Chemical Weapons Proliferation: Potential Military Countermeasures', CRS Report for Congress, CRS 94-528 S (5 July 1994), p. 19; J.R. Lilley, *Compilation of Hearings*, p. 245.

46 Collins, Davis, and Bowman, 'Nuclear, Biological and Chemical Weapons Proliferation', p. 30; see also B.R. Schneider, *Future War and Counter-proliferation: U.S. Responses to NBC Proliferation Threats* (Westport, CT: Praeger, 1999), pp. 162–6.

47 Payne, 'Post-Cold War Deterrence and Missile Defense', pp. 219–20; Ranger, 'The Devil's Brews 1', pp. 30–1.

48 Lt-Gen. L.L. Lyles, Hearings on *National Defense Authorization Act for Fiscal Year 1998 – H.R. 1119 and Oversight of Previously Authorized Programs* before the Committee on National Security House of Representatives, 105th Congress, first session (6 March 1997), p. 309.

49 R.L. Pfaltzgraff, Hearings on *H.R. 1119* (7 May 1997), p. 444; Payne, 'Post-Cold War Deterrence and Missile Defense', pp. 219–21.

50 M. Hewish, 'Providing the Umbrella', *IDR*, vol. 28, no. 8 (1995), pp. 28–34; 'UK to join European TMD assessment', *Jane's IDR*, vol. 32, no. 2 (1998), p. 6.

51 P.G. Kaminski, Lyles and D.R. Tanks, Hearings on *H.R. 1119* (6 March 1997), pp. 209–10, 219, 222, 243, 272–80, 313, 316–17 and 7 May 1997, p. 456; GAO, *Ballistic Missile Defense: Improvements Needed In THAAD Acquisition Planning* (Washington DC: GAO/NSIAD-97-188, September 1997), p. 3.

52 Pfaltzgraff, Hearings on *H.R. 1119*, pp. 451, 456; Kahan, 'Deterrence and Warfighting in an NBC Environment', in Johnson, *The Niche Threat*, pp. 53–4; Hearing on *Ballistic Missile Defense: Responding to the Current Ballistic Missile Threat* before the Subcommittee on National Security, International Affairs, and Criminal Justice of the Committee on Government Reform and Oversight House of Representatives, 104th Congress, second session (30 May 1996); E. Becker, 'Missile Plan Puts U.S. in Quandary on China', *The New York Times*, 22 January 1999, p. A8.

53 DoD, *Conduct of the Persian Gulf War*, pp. viii, G-26, G-28, Q-2, Q-7, Q-11; T. Prociv and Maj. Gen. G.E. Friel, Hearings on *H.R. 3230*, pp. 155 and 170; Mauroni, *Chemical–Biological Defense*, pp. 132–41.

54 G.S. Pearson and written evidence, HoC Defence Committee, *Implementation of Lessons Learned from Operation Granby*, pp. x–xii, 27–9, 33–5, 50, 52–3.

55 Prociv, Hearings on *DoD Authorization for Appropriations for Fiscal Year 1997*, p. 243.

56 DoD Nuclear/Biological/Chemical (NBC) Defense, *Annual Report to Congress February 1998*, pp. A-3–A-9; Friel, Hearings on *National Defense Authorization Act for Fiscal Year 1997 – H.R. 3230*, pp. 166, 178–9.

57 Friel, Hearings on *National Defense Authorization Act for Fiscal Year 1997 – H.R. 3230*, p. 171; Prociv, Hearings on *DoD Authorization for Appropriations for Fiscal Year 1997*, pp. 289, 295; DoD NBC Defense, *Annual Report*, pp. A-15–A-18.

58 Roberts and Pearson, 'Bursting the Biological Bubble', pp. 21–4; M. Hewish, 'Surviving CBW Detection and Protection: What You Don't Know Can Kill You', *Jane's IDR*, vol. 30, no. 3 (1997), pp. 30–48; H of C Defence Committee, *Implementation of Lessons Learned from Operation Granby*, p. xi; C. Beal, 'An Invisible Enemy', IDR, vol. 28, no. 3 (1995), pp. 36–41.

59 DoD NBC Defense, *Annual Report*, pp. B-3–B-6, B-17–B-23; Hewish, 'Surviving CBW', p. 47.

60 *Ibid.*, p. 47.

61 Prociv, Hearings on *National Defense Authorization Act for Fiscal Year 1997 – H.R. 3230*, p. 155; DoD NBC Defense, *Annual Report*, pp. 2-18–2-19, 4-33–4-34, B-11–B-13; M. Hewish and J. Janssen Lok, 'Air Forces Face up to NBC Reality', *Jane's IDR*, vol. 31, no. 5 (1998), pp. 47–52.

62 Hewish, 'Surviving CBW', p. 48; Prociv and Friel, Hearings on *National Defense Authorization Act for Fiscal Year 1997 – H.R. 3230*, pp. 162–3, 176; Lt-Col R.S. Shelton, 'No Democracy Can Feel Secure', *Proceedings of US Naval Institute*, vol. 124, no. 8 (1998), pp. 39–44.

63 Hewish and Janssen Lok, 'Air Forces Face up to NBC Reality', pp. 49–51.

64 DoD NBC Defense, *Annual Report*, pp. 2-19–2-20; Prociv, Hearings on *National Defense Authorization Act for Fiscal Year 1997 – H.R. 3230*, p. 163; Hewish, 'Surviving CBW', p. 48.

65 Hewish, 'Surviving CBW', p. 45; Prociv, Hearings on *National Defense Authorization Act for Fiscal Year 1997 – H.R. 3230*, p. 160; DoD NBC Defense, *Annual Report*, pp. 3–8, D-5.

66 DoD, *Proliferation 1997*, p. 70; Prociv, Hearings on *DoD Authorization for Appropriations for Fiscal Year 1997*, p. 289; Graham, 'Clinton to Order Reserves of Germ Weapon Antidotes', p. A19.

67 M. Mendoza, ' "Immune Boosters" eyed as biological arms defense', *San Diego Union Tribune*, 26 November 1998, p. A41; B. Graham, 'Dose of Explanation Comes with Anthrax Shots: Pentagon Campaigns to Overcome Some Soldiers' Health Fears about Vaccine', *The Washington Post*, 30 October 1998, p. A3; GAO, *Chemical and Biological Defense: Observations on DOD's Plans To Protect U.S. Forces* (Washington DC: GAO/T-NSIAD-98-83, 17 March 1998), pp. 3–9.

68 M. Hewish, 'On Alert against the Bio Agents: Tactical Biological-Agent Detection Approaches Reality', *Jane's IDR*, vol. 31, no. 11 (1998), pp. 53–7; J. Stephenson, 'Pentagon-Funded Research Takes Aim at Agents of Biological Warfare', *JAMA*, vol. 278, no. 5 (1997), pp. 373–5.

69 S.R. Gourley, 'Ready or Not: Preparing for the Chemical Onslaught' and M. Wells, 'Informed Risk-taking: The UK's First Line of Defence', *Jane's IDR*, vol. 30, no. 3 (1997), pp. 63–7 and 68–9.

70 GAO, *Chemical and Biological Defense: Emphasis Remains Insufficient to Resolve Continuing Problems* (Washington, DC: GAO/T-NSIAD-96-123, 12 March 1996), pp. 2–9; 'New Foxes Enter Service', *IDR*, vol. 26, no. 5 (1993), p. 387.

71 Friel, Hearings on *National Defense Authorization Act for Fiscal Year 1997 – H.R. 3230*, p. 194.

72 DoD NBC Defense, *Annual Report*, pp. 5–30, E-5; Ali, Rodrigues, Moodie, *US Chemical–Biological Defense Guidebook*, p. 165; Cohen and Shalikashvili, Hearings on the *Quadrennial Defense Review*, pp. 26 and 89.

73 GAO, *Chemical and Biological Defense: Observations on DOD's Plans To Protect U.S. Forces*, p. 3.

74 Roberts and Pearson, 'Bursting the Biological Bubble', pp. 23–4.

8 Proliferation: Risks and Challenges

1 Roberts, 'From Nonproliferation to Antiproliferation', pp. 151–3.

2 Broad and Miller, 'Germ Defense Plan in Peril as Its Flaws Are Revealed', p. A16.

3 Nolan, *Trappings of Power*, pp. 1–13; J.J. Weltman, 'Managing Nuclear Multipolarity', *International Security*, vol. 6, no. 3 (1981/2), pp. 182–94.

4 S.T. Wezeman and P.D. Wezeman, 'Transfers of Major Conventional Weapons', in SIPRI, *SIPRI Yearbook 1998: World Armament and Disarmament* (Oxford: OUP, 1998), pp. 291–319; Roberts, 'From Nonproliferation to Antiproliferation', p. 145.

5 Woolsey, Hearings on *Proliferation Threats of the 1990's*, p. 15; Sokolski, 'Fighting Proliferation with Intelligence', pp. 248–9; D. Foxwell and M. Hewish, 'GPS: Is It Lulling the Military into a False Sense of Security?', *Jane's IDR*, vol. 31, no. 9 (1998), pp. 32–41.

6 G.M. Steinberg, 'Non-proliferation: Time for Regional Approaches?' *Orbis*, vol. 38, no. 3 (1994), pp. 409–23.

7 K.D. Waltz, 'More May Be Better' in S.D. Sagan and K.D. Waltz, *The Spread of Nuclear Weapons: A Debate* (New York: W.W. Norton, 1995), pp. 13, 15, 19–21, 23, 33, 39.

8 J. Mearsheimer, 'Back to the Future: Instability in Europe After the Cold War', *International Security*, vol. 15, no. 1 (1990), pp. 5–56; S. Van Evera, 'Why Europe Matters. Why the Third World Doesn't: American Grand Strategy After the Cold War', *The Journal of Strategic Studies*, vol. 13, no. 2 (1990), pp. 1–51; B.R. Posen, 'The Security Dilemma and Ethnic Conflict', *Survival*, vol. 35, no. 1 (1993), pp. 27–47; M. van Creveld, *Nuclear Proliferation and the Future of Conflict* (New York: Free Press, 1993), pp. 106–7, 115, 122–4.

9 Woolsey, Hearings on *Proliferation Threats of the 1990's*, p. 134.

10 J. Lewis Gaddis, 'The Long Peace: Elements of Stability in the Postwar International System', *International Security*, vol. 10, no. 4 (1986), pp. 99–142.

11 Roberts, 'From Nonproliferation to AntiProliferation', p. 159.

12 Heisbourg, 'The Prospects for Nuclear Stability between India and Pakistan', pp. 83–6; Fetter, 'Ballistic Missiles and Weapons of Mass Destruction', pp. 29–30; Bracken, 'Nuclear Weapons and State Survival in North Korea', pp. 142–5; S.D. Sagan to the Editors, 'Correspondence', *International Security*, vol. 22, no. 1 (1997), pp. 193–201.

13 S.E. Miller, 'The Case against a Ukrainian Nuclear Deterrent', *Foreign Affairs*, vol. 72, no. 3 (1993), pp. 67–80.

14 B.G. Blair, *The Logic of Accidental Nuclear War* (Washington, DC: The Brookings Institution, 1993), pp. 6–8, 19–20; S.D. Sagan, *The Limits of Safety: Organizations, Accidents, and Nuclear Weapons* (Princeton: Princeton University Press, 1993), pp. 264, 266–7.

15 Sagan, *The Limits of Safety*, p. 264; P.D. Feaver, 'Command and Control in Emerging Nuclear Nations', *International Security*, vol. 17, no. 3 (1992/3), pp. 160–87.

16 S. Fetter, 'Correspondence', *International Security*, vol. 21, no. 1 (1996), pp. 176–81.

17 Blair, *The Logic of Accidental Nuclear War*, p. 254.

18 D.J. Karl, 'Proliferation Pessimism and Emerging Nuclear Powers', *International Security*, vol. 21, no. 3 (1996/97), pp. 87–119.

19 General K. Sundarji, 'Leashing the Nuclear Menace', *Foreign Service Journal*, vol. 69 (1992), pp. 35–7; see also D.T. Hagerty, 'Nuclear Deterrence in South Asia: The 1990 Indo-Pakistani Crisis', *International Security*, vol. 20, no. 3 (1995/96), pp. 79–114.

20 R.S. Norris, A.S. Burrows, and R.W. Fieldhouse, *Nuclear Weapons Databook Volume V: British, French, and Chinese Nuclear Weapons* (Boulder, CO: Westview Press, 1994), p. 374; B. Naughton, 'The Third Front: Defence Industrialization in the Chinese Interior', *China Quarterly*, no. 115 (1988), pp. 351–86; D.A. Fulghum and J.M. Lenorovitz, 'Israeli Missile Base Hidden in Hill', *Aviation Week and Space Technology* (8 November 1993), p. 29; DIA, *North Korea*, pp. 36 and 41; de Villiers, Jardine, and Reiss, 'Why South Africa Gave up the Bomb', p. 100.

21 Karl, 'Proliferation Pessimism and Emerging Nuclear Powers', pp. 109–10; van Creveld, *Nuclear Proliferation and the Future of Conflict*, p. 123; K.N. Waltz, 'Waltz Responds to Sagan', in Sagan and Waltz, *The Spread of Nuclear Weapons*, p. 113; de Villiers, Jardine, and Reiss, 'Why South Africa Gave Up the Bomb', p. 100.

22 G. Milhollin, 'Building Saddam Hussein's Bomb', *The New York Times Magazine*, 8 March 1992, pp. 30, 32, 34, 36.

23 K.M. Bhimaya, 'Nuclear Deterrence in South Asia: Civil–Military Relations and Decision-Making', *Asian Survey*, vol. 34, no. 7 (1994), pp. 647–61.

24 Heisbourg, 'The Prospects for Nuclear Stability between India and Pakistan', p. 79.

25 D. Albright, 'The Shots Heard Round the World' and 'Pakistan: The Other Shoe Drops', *The Bulletin of the Atomic Scientists*, vol. 54, no. 4 (1998), pp. 20–5.

26 R. Bedi, 'India Defies China and US with New Missile Test' and A. Rashid, 'Pakistan answers India with missile test', *The Daily Telegraph*, 12 and 15 April 1999, pp. 12 and 21.

27 S.D. Sagan, 'More Will Be Worse' in Sagan and Waltz, *The Spread of Nuclear Weapons*, pp. 67–72; J. Wilson Lewis and Hua Di, 'China's Ballistic Missile Programs Technologies, Strategies, Goals', *International Security*, vol. 17, no. 2 (1992), pp. 5–40.

28 Sagan, *The Limits of Safety*, pp. 266–7; 'More Will Be Worse' and 'Sagan Responds to Waltz' in Sagan and Waltz, *The Spread of Nuclear Weapons*, pp. 56–66, 82 and 125–6.

29 Feaver, 'Command and Control in Emerging Nations', p. 162; Y. Evron, *Israel's Nuclear Dilemma* (London: Routledge, 1994), pp. 127–8.

30 Bhimaya, 'Nuclear Deterrence in South Asia', p. 652; de Villiers, Jardine, and Reiss, 'Why South Africa Gave up the Bomb', p. 100; Evron, *Israel's Nuclear Dilemma*, pp. 128–9.

31 Karl, 'Proliferation Pessimism and the Emerging Nuclear Powers', p. 117; S. Fetter, D.T. Hagerty, 'Correspondence: Nuclear Deterrence and the 1990 Indo-Pakistani Crisis', *International Security*, vol. 21, no. 1 (1996), pp. 176–85.

32 Karl, 'Proliferation Pessimism and the Emerging Nuclear Powers', p. 114; Feaver, 'Command and Control in Emerging Nations', pp. 182–7; Weltman, 'Managing Nuclear Multipolarity', p. 193.

33 Norris, Burrows, and Fieldhouse, *Nuclear Weapons Databook*, vol. V, pp. 43–53, 189–93.

34 S.E. Miller, 'Assistance to Newly Proliferating Nations', in R.D. Blackwill and A. Carnesale (eds), *New Nuclear Nations: Consequences for U.S. Policy* (New York: Council for Foreign Relations Press, 1993), pp. 97–131; S. Feldman, *Israeli Nuclear Deterrence: A Strategy for the 1980s* (New York: Columbia University Press, 1982), pp. 164–5; Feaver, 'Command and Control in Emerging Nations', pp. 184–5.

35 Dunn, 'Containing Nuclear Proliferation', p. 49; Miller, 'Assistance to Newly Proliferating Nations', pp. 103–4.

36 *Ibid.*, pp. 116–23.

37 R. Harris and J. Paxman, *A Higher Form of Killing: The Secret Story of Gas and Germ Warfare* (London: Chatto & Windus, 1982), pp. 216–17; DIA, *Soviet Biological Warfare Threat*, pp. 4–7; OTA, *Technologies Underlying Weapons of Mass Destruction*, p. 103.

38 GAO, *Arms Control U.S. and International Efforts to Ban Biological Weapons* (Washington, DC: GAO/NSIAD-93-113, December 1992), pp. 60–2; Shuey, Bowman and Davis, 'Proliferation Control Regimes: Background and Status', pp. CRS-23–CRS-24.

39 'Clinton Remarks on U.S. Foreign Policy' and 'Shelton on "The Trans-atlantic Commitment"', United States Information Service, 1 and 10 March 1999.

40 W. Burns, 'Proliferation, NATO, and the Common Interest' in Bailey and Rudney, *Proliferation and Export Controls*, pp. 65–8.

41 Fetter, 'Ballistic Missiles and Weapons of Mass Destruction', p. 29; see also Karl, 'Proliferation Pessimism and Emerging Nuclear Powers', pp. 96, 106–7; Hagerty, 'Nuclear Deterrence in South Asia', pp. 113–14.

42 Roberts and Pearson, 'Bursting the Biological Bubble', p. 24.

43 Roberts, 'Between Panic and Complacency', in Johnson, *The Niche Threat*, pp. 25–6.

44 Sundarji, 'Leashing the Nuclear Menace', p. 37.

45 Kettle, 'The Enemy Within', p. 3; J. Barry and G.L. Vistica, '"The Penetration Is Total"', *Newsweek*, 29 March 1999, pp. 20–1; J. Gerth and J. Risen, 'Intelligence Report Points to 2D China Nuclear Leak', *The New York Times*, 8 April 1999, pp. A1 and A10.

46 DoD, *Proliferation 1997*, p. 4.

47 Ali, Rodrigues, and Moodie, *US Chemical–Biological Defense Guidebook*, p. 316.

48 Deutch, Hearing on *Military Implications of the Chemical Weapons Convention*, p. 31; Tenet, Hearing on *Current and Projected National Security Threats*, pp. 38, 40.

49 Kay, Hearings on *Global Proliferation*, Part 2, pp. 331–2.

50 Miller and Broad, 'Clinton Describes Terrorism Threat for 21st Century', pp. A1 and A12.

51 Tucker, 'Policy Approaches to Chemical and Biological Terrorism', in Roberts, *Terrorism with CB Weapons*, p. 106; GAO, *Combating Terrorism 1998*, p. 3.
52 Simon, 'Biological Terrorism', pp. 429–30.
53 Ali, Rodrigues, and Moodie, *US Chemical–Biological Defense Guidebook*, p. 320.
54 B. Slavin, 'Sanctions May Be Losing Favor as Top Policy Weapon', *USA Today*, 25 June 1998, p. 10A.

Select Bibliography

As material for this book has drawn upon a wide array of sources, only some items will be listed here. For references to Parliamentary Debates, the Congressional Record, annual reports or yearbooks, correspondence in journals, official briefing papers and articles or speeches in newspapers, magazines, and on the World Wide Web, readers should consult the Notes.

Primary sources

1. REVIEW CONFERENCES OF STATES PARTIES TO THE BIOLOGICAL AND
TOXIN WEAPONS CONVENTION

Memorandum by Ambassador Rolf Ekéus, 'Iraq's Biological Weapons Programme: UNSCOM's Experience', 20 November 1996.
United States of America, 'Technological Developments of Relevance to the Biological and Toxin Weapons Convention', 1986.

2. UNITED KINGDOM REPORTS AND PUBLICATIONS

Ministry of Defence, *The Strategic Defence Review*, Cm 3999 (London: The Stationery Office, July 1998).
——. *Defending Against the Threat from Biological and Chemical Weapons* (London, 1999).

3. UNITED NATIONS REPORTS AND PUBLICATIONS

Nuclear Weapons: Report of the Secretary-General of the United Nations (London: Frances Pinter, 1981).
Report of the Secretary-General on Chemical and Bacteriological (Biological) Weapons and the Effects of their Possible Use, United Nations General Assembly, A/7575 (New York, 1 July 1969).
Report of the Specialists Appointed by the Secretary-General to Investigate Allegations by the Islamic Republic of Iran Concerning the Use of Chemical Weapons, S/16433 (26 March 1984).
Security Council, Resolution S/1998/1172 (6 June 1998).
UNSCOM Reports, S/23165 (25 October 1991); S/24829 (20 November 1992); S/1995/284 (10 April 1995); S/1995/864 (11 October 1995); S/1995/1038 (17 December 1995); S/1997/774 (6 October 1997); S/1998/308 (8 April 1998); S/1998/920 (6 October 1998); S/1998/995 (26 October 1998); S/1998/1172 (15 December 1998).

4. UNITED STATES REPORTS AND PUBLICATIONS

Cohen, W.S., *Report of the Quadrennial Defense Review* (Washington, DC: May 1997).

Counterproliferation Program Review Committee, *Report on Activities and Programs for Countering Proliferation and NBC Terrorism* (May 1998).

Defense Intelligence Agency, *North Korea: The Foundations for Military Strength* (Washington, DC: October 1991).

——, *Soviet Biological Warfare Threat*, DST-1610F-057-86 (Washington, DC, 1986).

Department of Defense, *Conduct of the Persian Gulf War Final Report to Congress* (Washington, DC, April 1992).

Department of Defense Nuclear/Biological/Chemical (NBC) Defense, *Annual Report to Congress February 1998.*

Department of Health and Human Services, 'Department of Health and Human Services Health and Medical Services Support Plan for the Federal Response to Acts of Chemical/Biological (C/B) Terrorism' (Washington, DC: 21 June 1996).

Department of State, *Chemical Warfare in Southeast Asia and Afghanistan: An Update Report from Secretary of State George P. Shultz*, Special Report no. 104, November 1982.

Department of State, *Chemical Warfare in Southeast Asia and Afghanistan: Report to Congress from Secretary of State Alexander M. Haig, Jr.*, Special Report no. 98, 22 March 1982.

Department of State, *Chemical Weapons Use in Southeast Asia and Afghanistan.* Washington, DC: Bureau of Public Affairs, Current Policy no. 553, 21 February 1984.

General Accounting Office, *Arms Control: U.S. and International Efforts to Ban Biological Weapons* (Washington, DC: GAO/NSIAD-93-113, December 1992).

——, *Ballistic Missile Defense: Improvements Needed in THAAD Acquisition Planning* (Washington, DC: GAO/NSIAD-97-188, September 1997).

——, *Chemical and Biological Defense: Emphasis Remains Insufficient to Resolve Continuing Problems* (Washington, DC: GAO/T-NSIAD-96-123, 12 March 1996).

——, *Chemical and Biological Defense: Observations on DOD's Plans to Protect U.S. Forces* (Washington, DC: GAO/T-NSIAD-98-83, 17 March 1998).

——, *Combating Terrorism: Federal Agencies' Efforts to Implement National Policy and Strategy* (Washington, DC: GAO/NSAID-97-254, September 1997).

——, *Combating Terrorism: Opportunities to Improve Domestic Preparedness Program Focus and Efficiency* (Washington, DC: GAO/NSAID-99-3, November 1998).

——, *Combating Terrorism: Status of DOD Efforts to Protect Its Forces Overseas* (Washington, DC: GAO/NSAID-97-207, July 1997).

——, *Patriot Missile Defense: Software Problem Led to System Failure at Dhahran, Saudi Arabia* (Washington, DC: GAO/IMTEC-92-96, February 1992).

Gulf War Air Power Survey, 5 vols. (Washington, DC: USGPO, 1993).

Office of Technology Assessment, *Proliferation of Weapons of Mass Destruction Assessing the Risks* (Washington, DC: OTA, 1993).

——, *Technology Against Terrorism: Structuring Security* (Washington, DC: OTA, January 1992).

——, *Technologies Underlying Weapons of Mass Destruction* (Washington, DC: OTA, 1993).

Office of the Secretary of Defense, *Proliferation: Threat and Response* (Washington, DC: April 1996)

——, *Proliferation: Threat and Response* (Washington, DC: November 1997).

Report of the Chemical Warfare Review Commission (Washington, DC: USGPO, June 1985).

The Commission On Integrated Long-Term Strategy, *Discriminate Deterrence* (January 1988).

United States Arms Control and Disarmament Agency, *Threat Control Through Arms Control Annual Report to Congress* (Washington, DC: ACDA, 1995).

5. CONGRESSIONAL HEARINGS AND REPORTS

This section will only refer to special sessions devoted to aspects of NBC and missile proliferation. For the hearings on nominations, the annual submissions of the Department of Defense, State Department, Intelligence Agencies and the Arms Control Impact statements, readers should consult the notes.

House of Representatives

Committee on Armed Services, *Biological Warfare Testing*, 100th Congress, second session, 3 May 1988.

——, *Countering the Chemical and Biological Weapons Threat in the Post-Soviet World*, report of special inquiry into the chemical and biological threat, 102nd Congress, second session, 23 February 1993.

——, *Crisis in the Persian Gulf: Sanctions, Diplomacy and War*, 101st Congress, second session, 4–6, 12–14, 17, 19–20 December 1990.

——, *Preventing Chaos in the Former Soviet Union The Debate on Providing Aid*, report, 102nd Congress, second session, 17 January 1992.

Committee on Banking, Finance and Urban Affairs, *H.R. 4803, The Non-Proliferation of Weapons of Mass Destruction and Regulatory Improvement Act of 1992*, 102nd Congress, second session, 8 May 1992.

Committee on Foreign Affairs, *Proliferation and Arms Control in the 1990's*, 102nd Congress, second session, 3 March 1992.

——, *U.S. Policy Toward the New Independent States*, 103rd Congress, second session, 25 January 1994.

——, *The Future of U.S. Foreign Policy in the Post-Cold War Era*, 102nd Congress, second session, 25 February 1992.

——, *U.S. Security Policy Toward Rogue Regimes*, 103rd Congress, first session, 28 July 1993.

Committee on International Relations, *Review of the Clinton Administration Nonproliferation Policy*, 104th Congress, second session, 19 June 1996.

Committee on the Judiciary, *Biological Weapons Act of 1989; Inter-American Convention on International Commercial Arbitration* before the Subcommittee on Immigration, Refugees, and International Law, 101st Congress, second session, 1 May 1990.

Committee on National Security, *Threats to U.S. National Security*, 105th Congress, first session, 13 February 1997.

Subcommittee on National Security, International Affairs, and Criminal Justice of the Committee on Government Reform and Oversight, *Ballistic Missile Defense: Responding to the Current Ballistic Missile Threat*, 104th Congress, second session, 30 May 1996.

Subcommittee on Oversight of the Permanent Select Committee on Intelligence, *The Sverdlovsk Incident: Soviet Compliance with the Biological Weapons Convention?* 96th Congress, second session, 29 May 1980.

Senate

Committee on Armed Services (Subcommittee on Defense Industry and Technology), *Ballistic and Cruise Missile Proliferation in the Third World*, 101st Congress, first session, 2 May 1989.

Committee on Armed Services, *Assisting the Build-Down of the Former Soviet Military Establishment*, 102nd Congress, second session, 5 February 1992.

——, *Military Implications of The Chemical Weapons Convention (CWC)*, 103rd Congress, second session, 18 August 1994.

——, *National Security Implications of Lowered Export Controls on Dual-Use Technologies and U.S. Defense Capabilities*, 104th Congress, first session, 11 May 1995.

——, *Operation Desert Shield/Desert Storm*, 102nd Congress, first session, 12 June 1991.

——, *Quadrennial Defense Review*, 105th Congress, first session, 20 May 1997.

——, *Security Implications of the Nuclear Non-Proliferation Agreement with North Korea*, 104th Congress, first session, 26 January 1995.

——, *Threat Assessment: Military Strategy; and Operational Requirements*, 101st Congress, second session, 23 January 1990.

Committee on Foreign Relations, *Chemical and Biological Weapons Threat: The Urgent Need for Remedies*, 101st Congress, first session, 1 March 1989.

——, *Chemical Weapons Convention (Treaty Doc. 103-21)*, 103rd Congress, second session, 9 June 1994.

——, *Iran and Proliferation: Is the U.S. Doing Enough? The Arming of Iran: Who is Responsible?* before the Subcommittee on Near Eastern and South Asian Affairs, 105th Congress, first session, 6 May 1997.

——, *Status of 1990 Bilateral Chemical Weapons Agreement and Multilateral Negotiation on Chemical Weapons Ban*, 102nd Congress, first session, 22 May 1991.

Committee on Governmental Affairs, *Compilation of Hearings on National Security Issues* by the Subcommittee on International Security, Proliferation, and Federal Services, 105th Congress, second session, April 1998.

——, *Global Spread of Chemical and Biological Weapons*, 101st Congress, first session, 9 February 1989.

——, *Nuclear and Missile Proliferation*, 101st Congress, first session, 18 May 1989.

——, *Proliferation and Regional Security in the 1990's*, 101st Congress, second session, 9 October 1990.

——, *Proliferation Threats of the 1990's*, 103rd Congress, first session, 24 February 1993.

——, *The Proliferation Primer*, A Majority Report of the Subcommittee on International Security, Proliferation and Federal Services (January 1998).

——, *Weapons Proliferation in the New World Order*, 102nd Congress, second session, 15 January 1992.

Committee on the Judiciary, *High-Tech Terrorism* before the Subcommittee on Technology and the Law, 100th Congress, second session, 19 May and 15 September 1988.

Permanent Subcommittee on Investigations of the Committee on Governmental Affairs, *Global Proliferation of Weapons of Mass Destruction*, Parts 1, 2 and 3, 104th Congress, first session, 31 October and 1 November 1995, 20 and 27 March 1996.

6. CONGRESSIONAL RESEARCH SERVICE REPORTS FOR CONGRESS

Collins, J.M., Davis, Z.S., and Bowman, S.R., 'Nuclear, Biological and Chemical Weapons Proliferation: Potential Military Countermeasures', CRS 94-528S (5 July 1994)
Davis, Z.S., 'U. S. Counterproliferation Doctrine: Issues for Congress', 94-734 ENR (21 September 1994).
Shuey, R.D., Bowman, S.R., and Davis, Z.S., 'Proliferation Control Regimes: Background and Status', 97-343F (10 March 1997).

7. HOUSE OF COMMONS REPORTS

Defence Committee, Fifth Report, *Implementation of Lessons Learned from Operation Granby*, 43, session 1993–94 (25 May 1994).

8. MISCELLANEOUS REPORTS

Canada, *Novel Toxins and Bioregulators: The Emerging Scientific and Technological Issues Relating to Verification and the Biological and Toxin Weapons Convention* (Ottawa, September 1991).
Krosen, Gen. F.J. et al., *Chemical Warfare Study: Summary Report*, IDA Paper P-1820 (Bethesda, Maryland: Institute for Defense Analyses, February 1985).
National Academy of Sciences, *The Future of U.S. Nuclear Weapons Policy* (Washington, DC: National Academy Press, 1997).
The Canberra Commission on the Elimination of Nuclear Weapons, 'The Nuclear Weapon Debate', Parts 1 and 2 (Canberra: Department of Foreign Affairs and Trade, Australia, 1996).
The H.L. Stimson Center, *An Evolving US Nuclear Posture, Second Report of the Steering Committee Project on Eliminating Weapons of Mass Destruction* (Washington, DC: December 1995).

Books and Monographs

Ali, J., Rodrigues, L., and Moodie, M., *Jane's US Chemical–Biological Defense Guidebook* (Alexandria, VA: Jane's Information Group, 1997).
Alibek, K. with Handelman, S., *Biohazard: The Chilling True Story of the Largest Covert Biological Weapons Program in the World – Told from the Inside by the Man Who Ran It* (London: Hutchinson, 1999).
Arnett, E.H. (ed.), *New Technologies for Security & Arms Control: Threats & Promise* (Washington, DC: American Association for the Advancement of Science, 1989).
Bailey, K.C., *Doomsday Weapons in the Hands of Many: The Arms Control Challenge of the '90s* (Champaign: University of Illinois Press, 1991).
——, *The UN Inspections in Iraq: Lessons for On-Site Inspection* (Boulder, CO: Westview Press, 1995).
—— and Rudney, R. (eds), *Proliferation and Export Controls* (Lanham, MD: University Press of America, 1993).
Baker, J. with Defrank, T.M., *The Politics of Diplomacy* (New York: Putnam's, 1995).
Beaton, L., *Must the Bomb Spread?* (London: Penguin, 1966).

—— and Maddox, J., *The Spread of Nuclear Weapons* (London: Chatto & Windus, 1962).

Billière, General P. de la, *Storm Command: A Personal Account of the Gulf War* (London: HarperCollins, 1992).

Blackwill, R.D. and Carnesale, A. (eds), *New Nuclear Nations: Consequences for U.S. Policy* (New York: Council for Foreign Relations, 1993).

Blair, B.G., *The Logic of Accidental Nuclear War* (Washington, DC: The Brookings Institution, 1993).

Brauch, H.G., van der Graaf, H.J., Grin, J., and Smit, W.A. (eds), *Controlling the Development and Spread of Military Technology: Lessons from the past and challenges for the 1990s* (Amsterdam: VU University Press, 1992).

Brenner, M.J., *Nuclear Power and Non-Proliferation: The Remaking of U.S. Policy* (Cambridge: Cambridge University Press, 1981).

Brown, S.J. and Schraub, K.M. (eds), *Resolving Third World Conflict: Challenges for a New Era* (Washington, DC: Institute of Peace Press, 1992).

Burck, G.M. and Floweree, C.C., *International Handbook on Chemical Weapons Proliferation* (New York: Greenwood Press, 1991).

Burrows, W.E. and Windrem, R., *Critical Mass: the Dangerous Race for Superpowers in a Fragmenting World* (New York: Simon & Schuster, 1994).

Carp, R.C. (ed.), *Security with Nuclear Weapons? Different Perspectives on National Security* (Oxford: OUP, 1991).

Carter, G., *Porton Down 75 Years of Chemical and Biological Research* (London: HMSO, 1992).

Carus, W. Seth, *Ballistic Missiles in Modern Conflict* (New York: Praeger, 1991).

Chemical Disarmament: Basic Facts (The Hague: Organisation for the Prohibition of Chemical Weapons, 1998).

Cordesman, A.H., *Weapons of Mass Destruction in the Middle East* (London: Brassey's, 1991).

Dando, M., *Biological Warfare in the 21st Century: Biotechnology and the Proliferation of Biological Weapons* (London: Brassey's, 1994).

Douglass, J.D. and Livingstone, N.C., *America the Vulnerable: The Threat of Chemical/Biological Warfare* (Lexington, MA: Heath, 1987).

Evron, Y., *Israel's Nuclear Dilemma* (London: Routledge, 1994).

Feldman, S., *Israeli Nuclear Deterrence: A Strategy for the 1980s* (New York: Columbia University Press, 1982).

Findlay, T. (ed.), *Chemical Weapons & Missile Proliferation: With Implications for the Asia/Pacific Region* (Boulder, CO: Lynne Rienner, 1991).

Geissler, E. (ed.), *Biological and Toxin Weapons Today* (Oxford: Oxford University Press, 1986).

Goldblat, J., *Nuclear Non-Proliferation: A Guide to the Debate* (London: Taylor & Francis, 1985).

Harris, R. and Paxman, J., *A Higher Form of Killing: The Secret Story of Gas and Germ Warfare* (London: Chatto & Windus, 1982).

Head, W. and Tilford, E.H. (eds), *The Eagle in The Desert: Looking Back on U.S. Involvement in the Persian Gulf War* (Westport, CT: Praeger, 1996).

Hiro, D., *Desert Shield to Desert Storm* (London: Paladin, 1992).

Howard, L. (ed.), *Terrorism: Roots. Impact. Responses* (New York: Praeger, 1992).

Johnson, S.E. (ed.), *The Niche Threat: Deterring the Use of Chemical and Biological Weapons* (Washington, DC: National Defense University Press, 1997).

Kaplan, D.E. and Marshall, A., *The Cult at the End of the World* (London: Hutchinson, 1996).

Karsh, E., Navias, M.S. and Sabin, P. (eds), *Non-Conventional-Weapons Proliferation in the Middle East: Tackling the Spread of Nuclear, Chemical and Biological Capabilities* (Oxford: Clarendon Press, 1993).

Klare, M., *Rogue States and Nuclear Outlaws [America's Search for a New Foreign Policy]* (New York: Hill & Wang, 1995).

Leventhal, P. and Alexander, Y. (eds), *Preventing Nuclear Terrorism: The Report and Papers of the International Task Force on Prevention of Nuclear Terrorism* (Lexington, MA: Lexington Books, 1987).

Levran, A., *Israeli Strategy After Desert Storm* (London: Frank Cass, 1997).

Lewis, W.H. and Johnson, S.E. (eds), *Weapons of Mass Destruction: New Perspectives on Counterproliferation* (Washington, DC: National Defense University, 1995).

Lundin, S.J. (ed.), *Verification of Dual-use Chemicals under the Chemical Weapons Convention: The Case of Thiodiglycol*, SIPRI Chemical & Biological Warfare Studies, no. 13 (Oxford: Oxford University Press, 1991).

Marks, A.W. (ed.), *NPT: Paradoxes and Problems* (Washington, DC: Arms Control Association, 1975).

Martin, L., *Arms and Strategy* (London: Weidenfeld & Nicolson, 1973).

Mauroni, A.J., *Chemical–Biological Defense U.S. Military Policies and Decisions in the Gulf War* (Westport, CT: Praeger, 1998).

Mazarr, *North Korea and the Bomb: A Case Study in Nonproliferation* (New York: St. Martin's Press, 1995).

McNaught, L.W., *Nuclear Weapons & Their Effects* (London: Brassey's, 1984).

Moodie, M., *Chemical and Biological Weapons: Will Deterrence Work?* (Alexandria, VA: Chemical and Biological Arms Control Institute, 1998).

Murphy, S., Hay, A., and Rose, S., *No Fire No Thunder: The Threat of Chemical and Biological Weapons* (London: Pluto Press, 1984).

Myrdal, A., *The Game of Disarmament: How the United States and Russia Run the Arms Race* (Manchester: Manchester University Press, 1977).

Navias, M.S., *Going Ballistic: The Build-up of Missiles in the Middle East* (London: Brassey's, 1993).

Nolan, J.E., *Trappings of Power: Ballistic Missiles in the Third World* (Washington, DC: Brookings Institution, 1991).

Norris, R.S., Burrows, A.S., and Fieldhouse, R.W., *Nuclear Weapons Databook vol. V: British, French and Chinese Nuclear Weapons* (Boulder, CO: Westview Press, 1994).

Pimlott, J. and Badsey, S. (eds), *The Gulf War Assessed* (London: Arms and Armour Press, 1992).

Purver, R., *Chemical and Biological Terrorism: The Threat According to the Open Literature* (Ottawa: Canadian Security Intelligence Service, June 1995).

Record, J., *Hollow Victory: A Contrary View of the Gulf War* (London: Brassey's, 1993).

Reiss, M., *Bridled Ambition: Why Countries Constrain Their Nuclear Capabilities* (Washington, DC: Woodrow Wilson Center Press, 1995).

——, *Without the Bomb: The Politics of Nuclear Nonproliferation* (New York: Columbia University Press, 1988).

—— and Litwak, R.S. (eds), *Nuclear Proliferation after the Cold War* (Washington, DC: The Woodrow Wilson Center Press, 1994).

Rioux, J.-F. (ed.), *Limiting the Proliferation of Weapons: The Role of Supply Side Strategies* (Ottawa: Carleton University Press, 1992).

Roberts, B. (ed.), *Biological Weapons: Weapons of the Future?* (Washington, DC: Center for Strategic and International Studies, 1993).

—— (ed.), *Terrorism with Chemical and Biological Weapons* (Alexandria, VA: Chemical and Biological Arms Control Institute, 1997).

—— (ed.), *Weapons of Mass Destruction in the 1990s* (Cambridge, MA: MIT Press, 1995).

—— and Moodie, M., *Combating NBC Terrorism: An Agenda for Enhancing International Cooperation* (Livermore, CA: Center for Global Security Research, n.d.).

Royal United Services Institute for Defence Studies, *Nuclear Attack: Civil Defence* (London: Brassey's, 1982).

Sagan, S.D., *The Limits of Safety: Organizations, Accidents, and Nuclear Weapons* (Princeton: Princeton University Press, 1993).

—— and Waltz, K.D., *The Spread of Nuclear Weapons: A Debate* (New York: W.W. Norton, 1995).

Schneider, B.R., *Future War and Counterproliferation: U.S. Military Responses to NBC Proliferation* (Westport, CT: Praeger, 1999).

Schwarzkopf, General H.N. with Petre, P., *The Autobiography: It Doesn't Take a Hero* (New York: Bantam Press, 1992).

Shultz, G.P., *Turmoil and Triumph: My Years as Secretary of State* (New York: Scribner's, 1993).

Simpson, J. and Howlett, D. (eds), *The Future of the Non-Proliferation Treaty* (London: Macmillan, 1995).

Sokolski, H. (ed.), *Fighting Proliferation: New Concerns for the Nineties* (Maxwell Air Force Base, AL: Air University Press, 1996).

Spiers, E.M., *Chemical and Biological Weapons: A Study of Proliferation* (London: Macmillan, 1994).

——, *Chemical Warfare* (London: Macmillan, 1985).

——, *Chemical Weaponry: A Continuing Challenge* (London: Macmillan, 1989).

Stockholm International Peace Research Institute, Fact sheet, *Iraq: The UNSCOM Experience* (Stockholm, October 1998)

Stringer, Col H., *Deterring Chemical Warfare: US Policy Options for the 1990s* (Cambridge, MA: Institute for Foreign Policy Analysis, 1986).

Taylor, P.M., *War and the Media: Propaganda and Persuasion in the Gulf War* (Manchester: Manchester University Press, 1992).

Utgoff, V., *Nuclear Weapons and the Deterrence of Biological and Chemical Warfare* (Washington, DC: Henry L. Stimson Center, Occasional Paper No. 36, 1997).

——, *The Challenge of Chemical Weapons: An American Perspective* (London: Macmillan, 1990).

van Creveld, M., *Nuclear Proliferation and the Future of Conflict* (New York: Free Press, 1993).

Wander, W. Thomas and Arnett, E.H. (eds), *The Proliferation of Advanced Weaponry: Technology, Motivations, and Responses* (Washington, DC: American Association for the Advancement of Science, 1992).

Weaver, G. and Glaes, J. David, *Inviting Disaster: How Weapons of Mass Destruction Undermine U.S. Strategy for Projecting Military Power* (McLean, VA: AMCODA Press, 1997).

Wiegele, T.C., *The Clandestine Building of Libya's Chemical Weapons Factory: A Study in International Collusion* (Carbondale: Southern Illinois University Press, 1992).

Wilkinson, P. (ed.), *Technology and Terrorism* (London: Frank Cass, 1993).

Wright, S. (ed.), *Preventing a Biological Arms Race* (Cambridge, MA: MIT Press, 1990).

Articles

Albright, D., 'How Much Plutonium Does North Korea Have?' *The Bulletin of the Atomic Scientists*, vol. 50, no. 5 (1994).

——, 'Pakistan: The Other Shoe Drops', *The Bulletin of the Atomic Scientists*, vol. 54, no. 4 (1998).

——, 'The Shots Heard Round the World', *The Bulletin of the Atomic Scientists*, vol. 54, no. 4 (1998).

—— and Hibbs, M., 'Iraq's Bomb: Blueprints and Artifacts', *The Bulletin of the Atomic Scientists*, vol. 48, no. 1 (1992).

—— and Kelley, R., 'Has Iraq Come Clean at Last?' *The Bulletin of the Atomic Scientists*, vol. 51, no. 6 (1995).

—— and Zamora, T., 'India, Pakistan's Nuclear Forces: All the Pieces in Place', *The Bulletin of the Atomic Scientists*, vol. 45, no. 5 (1989).

Babievsky, K.K., 'Chemical and Biological Terrorism', *Low Intensity Conflict & Law Enforcement*, vol. 6, no. 2 (1997).

Bailey, K.C., 'Can Missile Proliferation Be Reversed?' *Orbis*, vol. 35, no. 1 (1991).

——, 'Responding to the Threat of Biological Weapons', *Security Dialogue*, vol. 26, no. 4 (1995).

Baker, J.C., 'Non-Proliferation Incentives for Russia and Ukraine', *Adelphi Papers 309* (1997).

Beal, G., 'An Invisible Enemy', *International Defense Review*, vol. 28, no. 3 (1995).

Bermudez, Jr, J.S., 'Inside North Korea's CW Infrastructure', *Jane's Intelligence Review*, vol. 8, no. 8 (1996).

Betts, R.K., 'The New Threat of Mass Destruction', *Foreign Affairs*, vol. 21, no. 1 (1998).

——, 'What Will It Take to Deter the United States?' *Parameters*, vol. 25, no. 4 (1995–96).

Bhimaya, K.M., 'Nuclear Deterrence in South Asia: Civil–Military Relations and Decision-Making', *Asian Survey*, vol. 34, no. 7 (1994).

Blix, H., 'Verification of Nuclear Nonproliferation: The Lesson of Iraq', *The Washington Quarterly*, vol. 15, no. 4 (1992).

Bowen, W. and Koch, A., 'Non-proliferation Is Embraced by Brazil', *Jane's Intelligence Review*, vol. 8, no. 6 (1996).

Bracken, P., 'Nuclear Weapons and State Survival in North Korea', *Survival*, vol. 35, no. 3 (1993).

Buchanan, Captain H. Lee, 'Poor Man's A-Bomb?' *Proceedings of the US Naval Institute*, vol. 123, no. 4 (1997).

Bukharin, O., 'Nuclear Safeguards and Security in the Former Soviet Union', *Survival*, vol. 36, no. 4 (1994–5).

Burns, E.L.M., 'The Nonproliferation Treaty: Its Negotiation and Prospects', *International Organization*, vol. 23, no. 4 (1969).

Carpenter, Lt-Col. G.W. et al., 'Biological Warfare: A Historical Perspective', *JAMA*, vol. 278, no. 5 (1997).

Carter, A.B. and Omand, D., 'Countering the Proliferation Risks: Adapting the Alliance to the New Security Environment', *NATO Review*, vol. 44, no. 5 (1996).

Carter, G., 'Biological Warfare and Biological Defence in the United Kingdom 1940–1979', *RUSI Journal*, vol. 137, no. 6 (1992).

Chellaney, B., 'After the Tests: India's Options', *Survival*, vol. 40, no. 4 (1998/99).

——, 'An Indian Critique of U.S. Export Controls', *Orbis*, vol. 38, no. 3 (1994).

Conadera, A., 'Biological Weapons and Third World Targets', *Science for the People*, vol. 13, no. 4 (1981).

Croddy, E., 'Urban Terrorism: Chemical Warfare in Japan', *Jane's Intelligence Review*, vol. 7, no. 11 (1993).

Dando, M., ' "Discriminating" Bio-weapons Could Target Ethnic Groups', *Jane's International Defense Review*, vol. 30, no. 3 (1997).

Danzig, R. and Berkowsky, P.B., 'Why Should We Be Concerned About Biological Warfare?' *JAMA*, vol. 278, no. 5 (1997).

David, C.-P., 'Who was the Real George Bush? Foreign Policy Decision-Making Under the Bush Administration', *Diplomacy & Statecraft*, vol. 7, no. 1 (1996).

Davis, J.C. and Kay, D.A., 'Iraq's Secret Nuclear Weapons Program', *Physics Today*, vol. 45, no. 7 (1992).

Deutch, J.M., 'The New Nuclear Threat', *Foreign Affairs*, vol. 71, no. 4 (1992).

De Villiers, J.W., Jardine, R., and Reiss, M., 'Why South Africa Gave up the Bomb', *Foreign Affairs*, vol. 72, no. 5 (1993).

Douglass, Jr, J.D., 'The Expanding Threat of Chemical–Biological Warfare: A Case of U.S. Tunnel Vision', *Strategic Review*, vol. 14, no. 4 (1986).

Dunn, L.A., 'Containing Nuclear Proliferation', *Adelphi Papers 263* (1991).

Dunn, P., 'The Chemical War: Journey to Iran', *Nuclear, Biological and Chemical Defense and Technology International*, vol. 1, no. 1 (1986).

Dunn, Vice-Admiral R.F., ' "Gas Attack, This Is No Drill!" ', *Proceedings of the US Naval Institute*, vol. 123, no. 5 (1997).

Erickson, J., 'The Soviet Union's Growing Arsenal of Chemical Warfare', *Strategic Review*, vol. 7, no. 4 (1979).

Falkenrath, R.A., 'Confronting Nuclear, Biological and Chemical Terrorism', *Survival*, vol. 40, no. 3 (1998).

Faulkner, A., 'CTBT: Towards Its Entry into Force', *Disarmament*, vol. 20, no. 1 (1997).

Feaver, P.D., 'Command and Control in Emerging Nuclear Nations', *International Security*, vol. 17, no. 3 (1992/3).

Fetter, S., 'Ballistic Missiles and Weapons of Mass Destruction: What Is the Threat? What Should Be Done?' *International Security*, vol. 16, no. 1 (1991).

Finder, J., 'Biological Warfare, Genetic Engineering, and the Treaty That Failed', *The Washington Quarterly*, vol. 9, no. 2 (1986).

Foxwell, D. and Hewish, M., 'GPS: Is It Lulling the Military into a False Sense of Security?' *Jane's International Defense Review*, vol. 31, no. 9 (1998).

Freedman, L., 'The Gulf War and the New World Order', *Survival*, vol. 33, no. 3 (1991).

Gaddis, J. Lewis, 'The Long Peace: Elements of Stability in the Postwar International System', *International Security*, vol. 10, no. 4 (1986).

Garrity, P.J., 'Implications of the Persian Gulf War for Regional Powers', *The Washington Quarterly*, vol. 16, no. 3 (1993).

Gee, J., 'CBW Terrorism and the Chemical Weapons Convention', *Politics and the Life Sciences*, vol. 15, no. 2 (1996).

——, 'Implementing the CWC: The First Year', *The Arena*, no. 8 (July 1998).

Gerardi, G. and Bermudez, Jr, J.S., 'An Analysis of North Korean Ballistic Missile Testing', *Jane's Intelligence Review*, vol. 7, no. 4 (1995).

Gergen, D., 'America's Missed Opportunities', *Foreign Affairs*, vol. 71, no. 1 (1992).

Gompert, D., Watman, K. and Wilkening, D., 'Nuclear First Use Revisited', *Survival*, vol. 37, no. 3 (1995).

Gourley, S.R., 'Ready or Not: Preparing for the Chemical Onslaught', *Jane's International Defense Review*, vol. 30, no. 3 (1997).

Hagerty, D.T., 'Nuclear Deterrence in South Asia: The 1990 Indo-Pakistani Crisis', *International Security*, vol. 20, no. 3 (1995/96).

Harvey, J.R., 'Missiles and Advanced Strike Aircraft Comparing Military Effectiveness', *International Security*, vol. 17, no. 2 (1992).

Heisbourg, F., 'The Prospects for Nuclear Stability between India and Pakistan', *Survival*, vol. 40, no. 4 (1998/99).

Heller, M.A., 'Coping with Missile Proliferation in the Middle East', *Orbis*, vol. 35, no. 1 (1991).

Hemsley, Brig. J., 'The Soviet Bio-chemical Threat: The Real Issue', *The RUSI Journal*, vol. 133, no. 1 (1988).

Hewish, M., 'On Alert against the Bio Agents: Tactical Biological-agent Detection Approaches Reality', *Jane's International Defense Review*, vol. 31, no. 11 (1998).

——, 'Providing the Umbrella', *International Defense Review*, vol. 28, no. 5 (1995).

——, 'Surviving CBW Detection and Protection: What You Don't Know Can Kill You', *Jane's International Defense Review*, vol. 30, no. 3 (1997).

—— and Janssen Lok, J., 'Air Forces Face up to NBC Reality', *Jane's International Defense Review*, vol. 31, no. 5 (1998).

——, 'Stopping the Scud Threat: Engaging Theater Ballistic Missiles on the Ground', *Jane's International Defense Review*, vol. 30, no. 6 (1997).

Hippel, F. von, 'Russian Whistleblower Faces Jail', *The Bulletin of the Atomic Scientists*, vol. 49, no. 2 (1993).

Hoffman, B. 'Responding to Terrorism across the Technological Spectrum', *Terrorism and Political Violence*, vol. 6 (1993).

——, 'Terrorist Targeting: Tactics, Trends, and Potentialities', *Terrorism and Political Violence*, vol. 5, no. 2 (1993).

Hurwitz, E., 'Terrorists and Chemical/Biological Weapons', *Naval War College Review*, vol. 35, no. 3 (1982).

Huxsoll, D., Parrott, C.D., and Patrick III, W.C., 'Medicine in Defense Against Biological Warfare', *JAMA*, vol. 262, no. 5 (1989).

Isaacs, J., 'Senate: Test Ban Prospects Shaken', *The Bulletin of the Atomic Scientists*, vol. 54, no. 4 (1998).

Jackson, J. Heinz, 'When Terrorists Turn to Chemical Weapons', *Jane's Intelligence Review*, vol. 4, no. 11 (1992).

Jenkins, B.M., 'Will Terrorists Go Nuclear?' *Orbis*, vol. 29, no. 3 (1985).

Johnson, R., 'The In-Comprehensive Test Ban', *The Bulletin of the Atomic Scientists*, vol. 52, no. 6 (1996).

Joseph, R., 'Proliferation, Counter-Proliferation and NATO', *Survival*, vol. 38, no. 1 (1996).

Joseph, R.G. and Reichart, J.F., 'The Case for Nuclear Deterrence Today', *Orbis*, vol. 42, no. 1 (1998).

Kadlec, R.P., Zelicoff, A.P., and Vrtis, A.M., 'Biological Weapons Control Prospects and Implications for the Future', *JAMA*, vol. 278, no. 5 (6 August 1997).

Karl, D.J., 'Proliferation Pessimism and Emerging Nuclear Powers', *International Security*, vol. 21, no. 3 (1996/97).

Kier, E. and Mercer, J., 'Setting Precedents in Anarchy: Military Intervention and Weapons of Mass Destruction', *International Security*, vol. 20, no. 4 (1996).

Knudson, Maj. G.B., 'Operation Desert Shield: Medical Aspects of Weapons of Mass Destruction', *Military Medicine*, vol. 156 (1991).

Krause, J., 'Proliferation Risks and Their Strategic Relevance: What Role for NATO?' *Survival*, vol. 37, no. 2 (1995).

Krauthammer, C., 'The Unipolar Moment', *Foreign Affairs*, vol. 70, no. 1 (1991).

Larsen, Col. R.J. and Kadlec, Lt-Col. R.P., 'Biological Warfare: A Silent Threat to America's Defense Transportation System', *Strategic Review*, vol. 26, no. 2 (1998).

Latter, R., 'Nuclear Weapons in the Twenty-First Century', *Wilton Park Papers 128* (April 1998).

——, 'Preventing the Proliferation of Biological Weapons', *Wilton Park Papers 109* (October 1995).

Leitenberg, M., 'A Return to Sverdlovsk: Allegations of Soviet Activities Related to Biological Weapons', *Arms Control*, vol. 12, no. 2 (1991).

——, 'Biological Weapons Arms Control', *Contemporary Security Policy*, vol. 17, no. 1 (1996).

Lewis, J. Wilson and Di, Hua, 'China's Ballistic Missile Programs: Technologies, Strategies, Goals', *International Security*, vol. 17, no. 2 (1992).

Luttwak, E.N., 'An Emerging Postnuclear Era?' *The Washington Quarterly*, vol. 11, no. 1 (1988).

Mack, A., 'North Korea and the Bomb', *Foreign Policy*, no. 83 (1991).

——, 'The Nuclear Crisis in the Korean Peninsula', *Asian Survey*, vol. 33, no. 4 (1993).

Mandelbaum, M., 'Foreign Policy as Social Work', *Foreign Affairs*, vol. 75, no. 1 (1995).

Mazarr, M.J., 'Going Just a Little Nuclear', *International Security*, vol. 20, no. 2 (1995).

McCain, Senator J., 'Proliferation in the 1990s: Implications for US Policy and Force Planning', *Strategic Review*, vol. 17, no. 3 (1989).

McColl, Lt-Cdr A., 'Is Counterproliferation Compatible with Nonproliferation?' *AIRPOWER Journal*, vol. 9, no. 1 (1997).

McGeorge, H.J., 'Chemical and Biological Terrorism: Analyzing the Problem', *The ASA Newsletter*, no. 42 (16 June 1994).

McNaugher, T.L., 'Ballistic Missiles and Chemical Weapons: The Legacy of the Iran–Iraq War', International Security, vol. 15, no. 2 (1990).

Mearsheimer, J., 'Back to the Future: Instability in Europe After the Cold War', *International Security*, vol. 15, no. 1 (1990).

Miller, S.E., 'The Case against a Ukrainian Nuclear Deterrent', *Foreign Affairs*, vol. 72, no. 3 (1993).

——, 'Western Diplomacy and the Soviet Nuclear Legacy', *Survival*, vol. 34, no. 3 (1992).

Naughton, B., 'The Third Front: Defence Industrialization in the Chinese Interior', *China Quarterly*, no. 115 (1988).

Navias, M. 'Ballistic Missile Proliferation in the Third World', *Adelphi Papers 252* (1990).

'New Foxes enter Service', *International Defense Review*, vol. 26, no. 5 (1993).

Nitze, P.H., 'A Conventional Approach', *Proceedings of the U.S. Naval Institute*, vol. 120, no. 5 (1994).

Nolan, J.E., 'Third World Ballistic Missiles', *Scientific American*, vol. 263 (1990).

Nye, J.S., 'What New World Order?' *Foreign Affairs*, vol. 71, no. 2 (1992).

Omand, D., 'Nuclear Deterrence in a Changing World: The View from a UK Perspective', *RUSI Journal*, vol. 141, no. 3 (1996).

Orton, Maj.-Gen. R.D. and Neumann, Maj. R.C., 'The Impact of Weapons of Mass Destruction on Battlefield Operations', *Military Review*, vol. 73, no. 12 (1993).

Park, M.Y. (Michael), ' "Lure" North Korea', *Foreign Policy*, no. 97 (1994–5).

Patrick III, W., 'Biological Terrorism and Aerosol Dissemination', *Politics and the Life Sciences*, vol. 15, no. 2 (1996).

Payne, K.B., 'Post-Cold War Deterrence and Missile Defense', *Orbis*, vol. 39, no. 2 (1995).

Pearson, G.S., 'Chemical and Biological Defence: An Essential National Security Requirement', *The RUSI Journal*, vol. 140, no. 4 (1995).

——, 'Chemical/Biological Terrorism: How Serious a Risk?' *Politics and the Life Sciences*, vol. 15, no. 2 (1996).

——, 'Forbidden, Not Forgotten', *Jane's International Defense Review*, vol. 30, no. 3 (1997).

——, 'Prospects for Chemical and Biological Arms Control: The Web of Deterrence', *The Washington Quarterly*, vol. 16, no. 2 (1993).

——, 'The Complementary Role of Environmental and Security Biological Control Regimes in the 21st Century', *JAMA*, vol. 278, no. 5 (6 August 1997).

Perkovich, G., 'Nuclear Proliferation', *Foreign Policy*, no. 112 (1998).

Perry, W.J., 'Defense in an Age of Hope', *Foreign Affairs*, vol. 75, no. 6 (1996).

Porteus, H., 'Grappling with the BW Genie', *International Defense Review*, vol. 28, no. 3 (1995).

Posen, B.R., 'The Security Dilemma and Ethnic Conflict', *Survival*, vol. 35, no. 1 (1993).

Postol, T.A., 'Lessons of the Gulf War Experience with Patriot', *International Security*, vol. 16, no. 3 (1991–2).

Ranger, R. (ed.), 'The Devil's Brews 1: Chemical and Biological Weapons and Their Delivery Systems', *Bailrigg Memorandum 16* (Lancaster University, Centre for Defence and International Security Studies, 1996).

Rathmell, A., 'Chemical Weapons in the Middle East: Lessons from Iraq', *Jane's Intelligence Review*, vol. 7, no. 12 (1995).

Redick, J.R., Carasales, J.C., and Wrobel, P.S., 'Nuclear Rapprochement: Argentina, Brazil, and the Nonproliferation Regime', *The Washington Quarterly*, vol. 18, no. 1 (1994).

Roberts, B., 'Arms Control and the End of the Cold War', *The Washington Quarterly*, vol. 15, no. 4 (1992).

——, 'Chemical Disarmament and International Security', *Adelphi Papers 267* (1992).

——, 'From Nonproliferation to Antiproliferation', *International Security*, vol. 18, no. 1 (1993).

—— and Pearson, G.S., 'Bursting the Biological Bubble: How Prepared Are We for Biowar?' *Jane's International Defense Review*, vol. 31, no. 4 (1998).

Rothstein, R.L., 'Democracy, Conflict and Development in the Third World', *The Washington Quarterly*, vol. 14, no. 2 (1991).

Sagan, S.D., 'The Causes of Nuclear Proliferation', *Current History*, vol. 96, no. 609 (1997).

Sawhney, P., 'A Force in Waiting: India's Defense Organization Sets Its Sights on the Future', *Jane's International Defense Review*, vol. 31, no. 6 (1998).

Schulte, G.L., 'Responding to Proliferation: NATO's role', *NATO Review*, vol. 43, no. 4 (1995).

Shelton, Lt-Col R.S., 'No Democracy Can Feel Secure', *Proceedings of US Naval Institute*, vol. 124, no. 8 (1998).

Sidel, V., 'Weapons of Mass Destruction: The Greatest Threat to Public Health', *JAMA*, vol. 262, no. 5 (1989).

Sigal, L.V., 'Jimmy Carter Makes a Deal', *The Bulletin of the Atomic Scientists*, vol. 54, no. 1 (1998).

Simon, J.D., 'Biological Terrorism: Preparing to Meet the Threat', *JAMA*, vol. 278, no. 5 (1997).

Slocombe, W., 'Is There Still a Role for Nuclear Deterrence?' *NATO Review*, vol. 45, no. 6 (1997).

Smithson, A., 'Playing Politics with the Chemical Weapons Convention', *Current History*, vol. 96, no. 609 (1997).

Sokolski, H., 'Fighting Proliferation with Intelligence', *Orbis*, vol. 38, no. 2 (1994).

——, 'Nonapocalyptic Proliferation: A New Strategic Threat?' *The Washington Quarterly*, vol. 17, no. 2 (1994).

Sopko, J.F., 'The Changing Proliferation Threat', *Foreign Policy*, no. 105 (1996/97).

'Soviets Violate Ban on Biological Warfare', *The Army Chemical Journal*, vol. 3, no. 1 (1987).

Sprinzak, E., 'The Great Superterrorism Scare', *Foreign Policy*, no. 112 (1998).

Steinberg, G.M., 'Non-proliferation: Time for Regional Approaches?' *Orbis*, vol. 38, no. 3 (1994).

Stephenson, J., 'Pentagon-Funded Research Takes Aim at Agents of Biological Warfare', *JAMA*, vol. 278, no. 5 (1997).

Stern, J.E., 'Weapons of Mass Impact: A Growing and Worrisome Danger', *Politics and the Life Sciences*, vol. 15, no. 2 (1996).

——, 'Will Terrorists Turn to Poison?' *Orbis*, vol. 37, no. 3 (1993).

Subrahmanyam, K., 'Export Controls and the North–South Controversy', *The Washington Quarterly*, vol. 16, no. 2 (1993).

Sundarji, Gen. K., 'Leashing the Nuclear Menace', *Foreign Service Journal*, vol. 69 (1992).

Talbott, S., 'Post-Victory Blues', *Foreign Affairs*, vol. 71, no. 1 (1992).

——, 'Democracy and the National Interest', *Foreign Affairs*, vol. 75, no. 6 (1996).

Thraenert, O., 'Biological Weapons and the Problems of Nonproliferation', *Aussen Politik*, vol. 48, no. 2 (1997).

——, 'Strengthening the Biological Weapons Convention: An Urgent Task', *Contemporary Security Policy*, vol. 17, no. 3 (1996).

Tucker, J.B., 'Chemical/Biological Terrorism: Coping with a New Threat', *Politics and the Life Sciences*, vol. 15, no. 2 (1996).

——, 'Lessons of Iraq's Biological Warfare Programme', *Arms Control*, vol. 14, no. 3 (1993).

——, 'National Health and Medical Services Response to Incidents of Chemical and Biological Terrorism', *JAMA*, vol. 278, no. 5 (1997).

——, 'The Biological Weapons Threat', *Current History*, vol. 96, no. 609 (1997).

'UK to join European TMD assessment', *Jane's International Defense Review*, vol. 32, no. 2 (1998).

'US Air Force to test anti-CBW warheads', *Jane's International Defense Review*, vol. 28, no. 6 (1995).

Van Evera, S., 'Why Europe Matters. Why the Third World Doesn't: American Grand Strategy After the Cold War', *The Journal of Strategic Studies*, vol. 13, no. 2 (1990).

Venter, A.J., 'Poisoned Chalice Poses Problems: The Terrorist Threat to the World's Water', *Jane's International Defense Review*, vol. 32, no. 1 (1999).

——, 'UNSCOM Odyssey: The Search for Saddam's Biological Arsenal', *Jane's Intelligence Review*, vol. 10, no. 3 (1998).

——, 'The Invisible Threat: What Does Russia Have up Its Biological Warfare Sleeve?' *Jane's International Defense Review*, vol. 31, no. 9 (1998).

Vicary, Col. A.G. and Wilson, Wing Commander J., 'Nuclear, Biological and Chemical Defence', *Journal of the RUSI*, vol. 126, no. 4 (1981).

Wells, M., 'Informed Risk-Taking: the UK's First Line of Defense', *Jane's International Defense Review*, vol. 30, no. 3 (1997).

Weltman, J.J., 'Managing Nuclear Multipolarity', *International Security*, vol. 6, no. 3 (1981/82).

Whitby, S. and Rogers, P., 'Anti-crop Biological Warfare: Implications of the Iraqi and US Programs', *Defense Analysis*, vol. 13, no. 3 (1997).

Whyte, S. 'Military Glasnost and Force Comparisons', *International Defense Review*, vol. 22, no. 5 (1989).

Wooten, Maj.-Gen. R.G., 'Protecting the Force: The 21st-Century Chemical Corps', *Military Review*, vol. 76 (1996).

Zelicoff, A., 'Preparing for Biological Terrorism: First Do No Harm', *Politics and the Life Sciences*, vol. 15, no. 2 (1996).

Zilinskas, R.A., 'Aum Shinrikyo's Chemical/Biological Terrorism as a Paradigm?' *Politics and the Life Sciences*, vol. 15, no. 2 (1996).

——, 'Iraq's Biological Weapons: The Past as Future?' *JAMA*, vol. 278, no. 5 (6 August 1997).

Index